Albert Pike

The Man Beyond The Monument

Photo: Earl McDonald

The Albert Pike Monument
Judiciary Square, Washington, D.C.

The Pike Monument, sculpted by G. Trentanove and erected by The Supreme Council, 33°, A.&A.S.R., S.J., USA, in 1901, bears these inscriptions at the eight corners of its base: AUTHOR, POET, SCHOLAR, SOLDIER, PHILANTHROPIST, PHILOSOPHER, JURIST, ORATOR and, in the front, *VIXIT LABORUM EJUS Super Stites SUNT FRUCTUS; He has lived. The fruits of his labors live after him.*

The Man Beyond The Monument

James T. Tresner II

Scottish Rite Research Society

M. Evans and Company, Inc.
New York

M. Evans and Company, Inc.
216 East 49 Street
New York, NY 10017

Library of Congress Cataloging-in-Publication Data

Tresner, James T. II
Albert Pike : the man beyond the monument / James T. Tresner II
p. cm.
Includes bibliographical references (p.) and index.
ISBN 0-87131-791-5 (cloth)
1. Pike, Albert, 1809–1891. 2.Freemasons—United States—Biography. 3. Authors, American—19th century—Biography.
I. Title.
HS511.P6T74 1995
366'.1'092—dc20
[B] 95-33029
CIP

Editing: John W. Boettjer
Jacket Design: Kevin McGuinness
Book Design: Jason A. Naughton

Manufactured in the United States of America

9 8 7 6 5 4 3 2

For information about or membership in the Scottish Rite Research Society contact:

Plez A. Transou
P.O. Box 1850
Dallas, TX 75221–1850
Fax: (214) 748–5155

Dedication

To my parents and grandparents, all of whom were active in the various branches of the Masonic Family, for giving me a heritage far more wealthy than that of Cyrus; to the Brethren of Garfield Lodge No. 501 of Enid, Oklahoma, and Albert Pike Lodge No. 162 of Guthrie, Oklahoma, for support and patience; and to my friends, for daily showering me with riches which shame the jewels of Ophir.

J. T.

TABLE OF CONTENTS

Foreword

Heroes first make themselves. Then they are made over—again and again—by friend and foe alike. No person of genius, no great leader, no pioneer in any field enters history as he or she actually was. In their times, epic individuals were seen, warts and all. But as the years pass, the vibrant flesh-and-blood individual recedes. Colorful reality fades into yellowed pages of dusty history.

The purpose of this book is to reverse this process for one of America's most interesting and accomplished figures, Albert Pike. He died in 1891. Since then, Pike has become more revered than read, more exalted or reviled than understood.

To know Albert Pike is to respect him. He was a musician and teacher of note, a western frontiersman and pioneer, a journalist and a general, a lawyer, philosopher, and poet. To Freemasons, he is best known for taking the undramatic degrees of the Southern Jurisdiction Scottish Rite in mid-19th-century America and transforming them into the basis of an institution whose main teachings, toleration and personal responsibility, are as vital today as in Pike' s time.

The respect with which Pike is held by Scottish Rite Masons of the Southern Jurisdiction, USA, has had two results—one good, one unfortunate. On the positive side, Scottish Rite esteem for Pike has fueled the careful preservation and explication of his works. In recent years, for instance, Dr. Rex R. Hutchens expanded understanding of Pike through four excellent books: *A Bridge to Light, The Bible in Albert Pike's "Morals and Dogma," A Glossary of "Morals and Dogma,"* and *Pillars of Wisdom: The Writings of Albert Pike.* On the negative side, Pike is more esteemed than understood. A bronze statue has tended to replace the epic character and real contribution of the man himself.

I am very pleased to write the foreword for this latest book, *Albert Pike: The Man Beyond The Monument,* in a growing revival of Pike studies. The book's author, James T. Tresner, has captured the real Albert Pike in all his diversity of thought and activity. You will find Albert Pike the man, fleshed and faulted, yes, but, at the same time, a man whose thoughts can lift one beyond the ordinary and reveal the rich potential of the human spirit.

Finally, a warning. This book is about Pike. It is not about Freemasonry or the Scottish Rite of Freemasonry. What Pike did or said does not define the Masonic Fraternity. Pike is Pike, only. While it is true he shaped and directed the Scottish Rite of Freemasonry, Southern Jurisdiction, USA, for 32 years (1859–1891) as its head, he did not then nor does he now define the Scottish Rite, especially outside the Southern Jurisdiction, USA. In a similar manner, a president of the United States may be a key figure in a specific era of history, but he does not define the nation even in that limited time period, much less in all of American history. The people are America. Whoever the Chief Executive may be, the people, their history and ideals, not the resident in the White House define and compose the nation.

Pike understood this and applied it to the Scottish Rite. Starting in 1871 with the first edition of *Morals and Dogma*, his greatest and longest work, Pike prefaced every edition saying:

> The teachings of these Readings are not sacramental, so far as they go behind the realm of Morality into those of other domains of Thought and Truth. The Ancient and Accepted Scottish Rite uses the word "Dogma" in its true sense, of doctrine, or teaching; and it is not dogmatic in the odious sense of that term. Everyone is entirely free to reject and dissent from whatsoever herein may seem to him to be untrue or unsound. It is only required of him that he shall weigh what is taught, and give it fair hearing and unprejudiced judgment.

Remember that this book describes Pike, the unique individual presented in his own words, and not the Masonic Fraternity. I hope you enjoy, as much as I have, reading these pages and meeting, through them, a man whose life and thought will forever benefit all humankind.

Warren D. Lichty
President, Scottish Rite Research Society

Introduction

Some Music About Words

"Ve can't all be der first violiners," futurist E. E. "Doc" Smith once observed. "Some of us has got to push der vind thru der tuba."

In many ways, pushing wind through the tuba is the purpose of this book. Pike was a first violiner (played the violin quite well, as a matter of fact). His prose soars and sings, it catches an idea and plays with it, tossing it high into the air, turning it inside out and backwards and upside down, making you look at it from new viewpoints, just as Bach does in his *Art of the Fugue*. It's a virtuoso performance.

Nevertheless, there's a use for the tuba as well. It provides context for the flights of the violin, it helps to draw attention to some passages, and even sometimes serves as a counterpoint to highlight a theme.

If you don't have the talents to be a first violiner, there's something to be said for being given a chance to push some "vind."

That "something" is "thanks!"

I greatly appreciate the chance to share Pike with others. One of the highlights of my footlights experience was playing the part of Pike in George Williams's one-man play, "An Evening with General Albert Pike." Pike has been the love of a lifetime for me, and what man doesn't enjoy the chance to pull the pictures of his loved ones from his billfold and show them around!

This book is an unbiased assessment of some of his work—just as unbiased as a man is in showing off pictures of his family. Also, I'll try to be a good tubaist, to provide a little counterpoint and to highlight and to give context to Pike's themes.

But be prepared to be surprised—there's a lot to Pike that doesn't appear on a casual reading. You'll be kicked back listening him play, with lush vibrato, a mid-Victorian song such as "Father, Dear Father, Come Home with Me Now," and suddenly discover he's actually playing one of the more angular passages by Bartók. His barbed sense of humor is a case in point, his dry and devious sense of humor even more so.

The use of musical terminology to open a book on Pike is not quite as idiosyncratic as may first appear. Pike loved music. As we'll see, he was a good enough violinist that the most famous conductor in America at the time enjoyed spending evenings playing duets with him. He sang in a beautiful voice. He wrote the lyrics for many songs, most of them comic, which are included in his collections of poetry. He wrote indications for music throughout the degrees of the Scottish Rite, Southern Jurisdiction, USA. These degrees are full of such notes as, "music plays during the circumambulations," "a wild strain of music is heard," "sad and mournful music accompanies the following," and so forth. He oversaw the printing of four very large volumes of music to be used to accompany the degrees. Pike frequently drew from music in his writing. Only his other great love, nature, served him as a source of imagery more often.

While on the topic of Pike's imagery and symbolism, however, there's a point I should make at once. Some of what we'll look at in this book comes from Pike's *Morals and Dogma.* Next to Milton and, perhaps, the American Constitution, I doubt if there is any work so widely owned and so seldom read. Indeed, it sometimes appears to be read almost exclusively by people who are trying to use it to attack Pike and Freemasonry. It has the reputation for being almost impossible to understand. That is unfortunate, because, while there are some difficult passages, most of it is easy.

But it's very important to understand what Pike was trying to do with *Morals and Dogma.* It is not some kind of "Bible" of Masonry. That thought would have horrified Pike. It was, instead, virtually the first attempt ever made to write a survey text on philosophy and religion.

We're accustomed, now, to college courses, such as "Philosophy 101," which survey a whole field to give a beginning student bits and pieces of the writings of various thinkers. There are many textbooks for such courses. But not at the time Pike was writing. There simply was no one source a person could go to in order to get an overview of the thinking of people across many ages on some topic or other. Pike was writing one of the very first texts in "Philosophy of Religion 101." It was a massive undertaking. Much of the material had never been translated into English. His purpose was simple, and it was the natural impulse of a good teacher—to expose his "students" to as wide a range of thought and information as possible. He made mistakes—today we organize such books differently. Pike had no examples to follow.

Still, this book is not intended as a scholarly treatise to explicate *Morals and Dogma.* There is a place for scholarship, of course, but that place is a classroom, not a conversation between friends. This book is intended as just such a conversation about a fascinating man. Flawed, human, prone to error, and capable of astonishing wisdom, insight, and expression. Pike was not right about everything, although when he found he was wrong, he corrected the error. A case in point is the age of Masonry. At the beginning of his career he thought, like many Masons of his time, that Masonry in its present form started in remote antiquity.

As you'll see in the chapter on Masonry, he corrected that view when he discovered the truth. There are other areas in which Pike was, by the standards of our day if not those of his, wrong. I've generally ignored those for the purposes of this book which is not a psychoanalysis of Pike, nor a narrow analysis of his social opinions. Rather, it's a celebration of his wit, his insight, and his sheer genius with words. I hope you get as big a kick out of reading this as we did out of putting it together.

I say "we" because, as always, there are lots of people who are really essential to a book, and whose names don't appear on the cover. I'll miss some, for which I apologize, but let me make mention of a few.

First and foremost, of course, was my father, Jack N. Tresner. From age 21 until his death, he was very active in Masonry and especially in the Scottish Rite. He gave me a deep love of the Craft and, in particular, Albert Pike. And my mother, Margaret, who has always supported everything I and every member of my family have ever done in Masonry.

And then there's The Group—that's what we usually call it—of Brothers who have for years supported each other in everything: Jimmy Dean Hartzell, Greg Smith, John and Arlett Caton, Clay Comer, Will Hurd (special thanks to Will for permission to include one of his paintings in this book), Tim Heaton, Dana Clark, and Bob Davis. They all suffered patiently while I read passages from the manuscript to them and, less patiently, having me call them in the small hours of the morning to say, "Listen to what I just found!" with no greater a remonstrance than, "Tresner, what time is it on whatever planet you happen to be on?"

More to the point, at those moments known to every writer when the project seems impossible, the world is a gloom-filled place and one wants only to retire to a monastery in Tibet and brew yak-butter tea, they administered the therapeutic kick in the seat of the trousers which got me going again, and without which this book would still be nothing but a memory in a computer.

Bob Davis, General Secretary of the Guthrie, Oklahoma, Scottish Rite Valley, well known to readers of the *Scottish Rite Journal, The Philalethes,* and to anyone involved in Masonic Renewal, read every page of this text and helped me find the blunders (so if you find a mistake, blame him).

Other readers were: W. Gene Sizemore, Grand Executive Director of The Supreme Council, 33°, S.J., USA; Dr. William L. Fox, Grand Historian and Grand Archivist of The Supreme Council, 33°; Warren D. Lichty, President, Scottish Rite Research Society; and Dr. S. Brent Morris, Book Review Editor, *Scottish Rite Journal.* To one and all, thank you!

In addition, thanks to the staff of the *Scottish Rite Journal.* I owe everything regarding this book to the *Journal*'s editor, Dr. John W. Boettjer. He conceived this project, helped find resources in the Library of the House of the Temple, located artwork for illustrations, and supported me at every step of the way—not to mention turning the manuscript into a finished book. Also, Jason Naughton, desktop publishing specialist in the *Journal* office in the House of the Temple, aided with the design and "look" of the book. He is a true "font" of every blessing. "Graphic" thanks as well to Dr. S. Brent Morris for his valuable suggestions regarding typography and book design.

My thanks, also, to Joan Kleinknecht, Librarian of the House of the Temple, for endless photocopying (much of Pike' s work exists only in his manuscript or in fading newspaper clippings), for help with research, and for great patience. In addition, Earl McDonald photographed nearly all of the book's illustrative material.

Special thanks go to Mrs. Pauline Boyer Rodriquez, with the library system of Norman, Oklahoma, who located sources for copies of Pike' s early magazine articles. It turned out that three of them were on microfilm at the Library of the University of Central Oklahoma. And special thanks, also, to a lady whose name I do not know, a research librarian at that University Library, who helped me find the right rolls of microfilm, and who said almost nothing when I put the reel on the reader backward and promptly spooled 1,354 feet of microfilm onto the library floor. She is a mistress of the pitying but non-judgmental glance.

Thanks also to Glenn Dowlen, Professor Emeritus of Voice at Oklahoma State University (to hear him sing is a great experience) who dug out the score to "Benny Havens, Oh!" from music of the last century so that I could include it in the chapter "On Pike Attending His Own Wake." Also, thanks to Robert Shipe for the photographs of the school at which Pike first taught in Arkansas.

Also, thanks to the Brethren of the McAlester, Tulsa, and Guthrie Scottish Rite Bodies in Oklahoma, who made their libraries available to me and helped in many different ways, and very special thanks to Paul T. Million, Jr., Sovereign Grand Inspector General in Oklahoma. His fierce determination to make the Scottish Rite in Oklahoma a real center of excellence in Degree work, education, and scholarship has opened so many possibilities to me that the only difficulty has been in finding time to explore all of them.

I owe a great debt of thanks to the Scottish Rite Research Society, one of the most active associations of Brethren dedicated to enriching awareness of our Masonic heritage and its foundations in a long history.

Finally, of course, thanks must be expressed to C. Fred Kleinknecht, Sovereign Grand Commander, Scottish Rite of Freemasonry, S.J., USA, and the Founding Member of the Scottish Rite Research Society. Anyone who loves the work of Pike must appreciate the Grand Commander's efforts to preserve and strengthen the traditions of the Scottish Rite and to make certain Pike and his work do not slip into obscurity. In recent years, there has been a resurgence in Pike studies and a reawakening to Pike's worth as a philosopher, writer, teacher, reformer, and Mason. This renewed interest in Pike was partially created and has been greatly strengthened by the Grand Commander' s support of the books on Pike by Dr. Rex R. Hutchens. I hope this book may serve in the same cause.

To all these people, and to many others, thank you for letting me take the credit for all you did. We' ve had a lot of fun.

Jim Tresner
Scottish Rite Research Society

I

A Little Less Plaster, A Little More Fire

On Albert Pike The Man

I'd like you to meet a friend. His name was Albert Pike, and he knew how to live!

Generally, people seem to react to Albert Pike in one of three ways. One group (which usually has not read Pike) says "Ah, Pike!" and then assumes a pose of silent rapture, supposedly at Pike's overwhelming greatness but actually so no one can ask them anything about him.

The second, larger group, says, "Uck, Pike!" and then stomps off. They haven't read Pike either, but everyone's told them he's too hard to understand, so why try?

The third group **has** read Pike, and they say, "Wow! What a man!"

Albert Pike suffers from too much plaster. He's been cast as a plaster saint—the unapproachable intellectual giant who created the Scottish Rite of Freemasonry in its present form in the Southern Jurisdiction, USA, the mind so vast as to be incomprehensible. Busts in bronze or marble (as well as plaster) portray him as the patriarch, penetrating of eye and stern of brow whom one cannot understand, but can only admire in awe-struck wonder. Or sneer at in contempt.

Albert Pike, The Patriarch
Bust by U. S. J. Dunbar

There was much of the patriarch in Pike, although less than subsequent generations have invested there. But there was far more than patriarch, far more than marble or bronze or plaster. There was fire.

The Pike we need to know better is not the patriarch but the pioneer, the friend, the crusader for justice for Native Americans (well liked enough that one tribe paid

Albert Pike, the Explorer
Taken from a 1850 daguerreotype, this painting shows Pike in a "great coat," a buffalo or bear skin garment favored by plainsmen and mountain men.

him the almost unheard of honor of making him an honorary Chief), the practical joker, the poet,† the teacher, the cook, the social lion, the reformer, the explorer referred to by the historian Grant Foreman as "one of the most remarkable and interesting characters in the annals of the Southwest"[1]—we need to know the man.

And man he was! He was dashing and handsome, and a genuine heartbreaker in his earlier years.

> *He was a powerful man, six feet and two inches tall, finely formed, with dark eyes and fair skin, fleet of foot and sure of shot, able to endure hardship, greatly admired by the Indians.*[2]

He was known as the best shot in town. His laugh was so famous it was written about in the social columns of the Washington, D.C., news-

† Weber points out *"Pike's contemporaries considered him an outstanding poet and his work appears in several anthologies of the day. Edgar Allan Poe thought highly of Pike's verse, claiming that 'there are few of our native writers to whom we consider him inferior.'"* "Introduction" to David Weber's edition of Pike's *Prose Sketches and Poems Written in the Western Country*, p. xviii.

papers. He always had a new joke or story to tell his friends. He was considered one of the best dancers in the capital, and society hostesses fought to get him as a guest at their parties. If General Pike were there, the party was sure to be a success.

He wore his hair long, when it was not the fashion, and it gave him an extra air of the exotic. He hardly needed it—he was naturally an exotic in almost every sense. He was an accomplished violinist,† and he sang in a beautiful voice[3]—and it's quite possible that not all the songs were for mixed company.

He organized hunting and camping parties lasting many days, and served as the cook for the expeditions (he was famous for his stews of game and vegetables).[4] Indeed, the leaders of Washington fought to be included as guests on those trips.

He made and lost fortunes. The story is told that he literally partied away a large sum of money on a steamer trip up the river from New Orleans to Little Rock.[5] Allsopp suggests that, even if the story is apocryphal, the spirit of it is true.[6]

He had hundreds of devoted friends. Once, while he was away from Washington, an erroneous report of his death reached the city. A great wake had been planned, and, when a very much alive Albert Pike suddenly appeared in Washington, D.C., his friends decided to go ahead with the wake anyhow. Rather like Tom Sawyer and Huck Finn, Pike got a chance not only to observe but to participate in his own obsequies. The event, recorded in the press, nearly turned into a riot. Some of his friends tried to match him drink for drink, and that was a mistake.

But, with all that, he was a student. He loved to learn and loved to share what he had learned. His friend, Thomas Hatch, wrote of Pike shortly after his death:

> *He would spread out the stores of his knowledge with such infinite tact and grace that the ignorant man would not feel oppressed by the contrast between them, and the learned would listen to him, wondering at his wisdom.*[7]

Pike had had to educate himself, and he did a remarkable job of it. He had wanted to enter Harvard and had done all the study, on his own, to "test out" of the first two years so that he could enter with advanced placement. The school was willing to accept his accomplishments, but insisted he pay the full tuition for the first two years, even though he had not taken the courses. Pike couldn't afford it, and

† Walter Lee Brown, in his four-volume biography of Pike, notes that Pike played privately with Ostenelli, the conductor of the Boston Symphony, when the conductor came to Newburyport, Massachusetts, on a concert tour, and that Pike and his father played Sunday mornings with the choir of the Newburyport Episcopal Church.

completed his education on his own. As Hatch remarks:

The action of the authorities of Harvard in, as it always seemed to him, "demanding wages not their due," he looked upon as most outrageous, and I have heard him express his profound contempt for the system which would add anything to the burden of an already overweighted youth struggling for an education. However, when he had made a name for himself, as a poet, a lawyer, and an editor, Harvard, like so many other institutions and so many other men, seeing the opportunity to gain reflected honors, connected his name with her own by conferring, in 1859, an honorary degree upon him—too late to be of any advantage to him, or even to please him by the empty compliment.[8]

Education was, for Pike, a life-long process. He taught himself languages, history, philosophy, theology, and law. His ability in the law was sound enough for him to become one of the best-known lawyers in the South and to serve as a Justice of the Supreme Court of Arkansas during the Confederacy.[9] On March 9, 1849, he was admitted, with Abraham Lincoln and Hannibal Hamlin, to practice before the U.S. Supreme Court.[10] He also was an educator, and in 1853, he was elected President of the Board of Trustees of St. John's College, of Little Rock.[11] Nor did Pike's talents dull with age. As Moore points out:

After he was seventy years of age, he learned the Sanscrit language and translated from it into English the Veda, that source of the "World-Old" Philosophy of the Hindoos [Hindus].[12]

The sheer excitement of information breaks out again and again in Pike's writing.

Albert Pike was a member of the committee to obtain a charter for St. John's College in Little Rock, Arkansas, in 1850, and in 1853, he was elected President of the college's Board of Trustees.

He wrote extremely well indeed. The contemporary Canadian scholar, Wallace McLeod, writes of him:

He had a sound instinct for right and wrong, and (in Coil's words) "a profound belief in an all-wise, moral, and beneficent God." And, oh, he could write! He could recognize essential truths on which all good men agree, and express them clearly in such a way that they sound fresh, compelling, and even inspiring; you find yourself listening, and inwardly nodding your head.[13]

He loved good food, good company, travel, justice, the feel of a quill pen in his hand, and, perhaps above all, his pipe.

Critics who don't know Pike have saddled him with a reputation as an ivory-towered intellect, remote from and indifferent to the "real world." The image fits well with the plaster patriarch, but it doesn't fit reality. There are few ivory towers on the battlefield, and Pike was a general. Ivory towers were even rarer on the frontier where a man ate only if he could hunt his dinner, where he was at constant risk of death from bandits and marauders, where there was often the danger of dying of thirst in the desert or freezing in a blizzard, and where losing one's horse could mean a 500-mile trek to the nearest outpost. All those things happened to Pike. As Admiral Winfield Scott Schley, wrote:

There was little known of the vast regions lying West of the great Mississippi River. They were covered with primeval forests, arid plains and forbidding mountain ranges, over which wild...animals roamed to the menace of life and limb of anyone whose hardihood these venturesome fastnesses [impenetrable wildernesses] *attracted. New Mexico at that period (1831) was far beyond the frontier of our country and between the two lay a veritable "Terra Incognita" into which few ventured with any hope of return.*[16]

Pike's thoughtfulness and introspection did not come from ease and comfort. As he wrote:

I have acquired, by wild and desolate life,† a habit of looking steadily in upon my own mind, and of fathoming its resources; and perhaps solitude has been a creator of egotism.[15]

Not egotism, exactly; but since Pike arrived at a position only after considerable thought, he was not easily swayed. He was always willing to discuss his opinions, however, and could be convinced, with sufficient evidence, when he was in error.

So who was this man?

† Pike was in his early 20s when he wrote this, so he was not quite the aged rip the line would suggest.

As a teacher, he commanded an immense knowledge of both classical literature and history. As a lawyer, he offered such legal expertise and personal honesty that he became one of the most respected counsels of mid-19th-century America. As a pioneer, he traveled extensively and recorded his impressions vividly. As a general, he was a leader. As a writer and poet, he transformed the literature of our Scottish Rite.

Truly, Albert Pike was a multidimensional man. His special genius was the ability to infuse every endeavor with absolute commitment. He had faith in himself and, as importantly, in America. Love of country motivated him and freedom was his unswerving guide.[16]

So wrote C. Fred Kleinknecht, in 1986. Similarly, near the beginning of this century, Fred Allsopp wrote:

When the mass of the output of the brain of this man Pike is considered, is it any wonder that Judge John Hallum exclaimed that his labors equalled Bonaparte's in another field? Think of his activities! He performed as much creative writing as most authors do who devote their lives to literature. Yet he served altogether perhaps three-fourths of the mature years of his life on the editorial tripod, in the field as a soldier, as a lawyer at the bar, and as Grand Commander of the Supreme Council, Southern Jurisdiction, of the Scottish Rite—and excelled in every line of endeavor.[17]

He was all that, and he was more. He was a profound student of philosophy—who loved the sight of a pretty face, a well-prepared meal, and a belly laugh. He was the principal expounder of the Scottish Rite for the Southern Jurisdiction—who got fired from a teaching job for "playing the fiddle on Sunday," ate horse meat when starving in the prairie, wrote satiric verse, and provided the entertainment at his own, premature, wake. He was a great lover of peace and supporter of the Constitution—who was a General for the South in the Civil War and fought in the last duel ever held in Arkansas. He was a lover of nature and beauty and wilderness—who was one of the first, if not the first, to suggest a railroad linking the East and West coasts and who tried to convince the South to industrialize.

He was, in short, a man of great imagination, daring, creativity, and determination who never lost his love of a practical joke. He was, in short, a man.

A Few Words About Writing Styles

Not long ago, at a Scottish Rite meeting, I was standing near Dr. Rex R. Hutchens, when a Brother came up to him and started talking about Pike. "I don't think I would have liked to know him," the Brother remarked. "I think he would have talked way over my head."

"No," Rex replied, "he seems to have been able to talk to anyone in a way they could understand and enjoy."

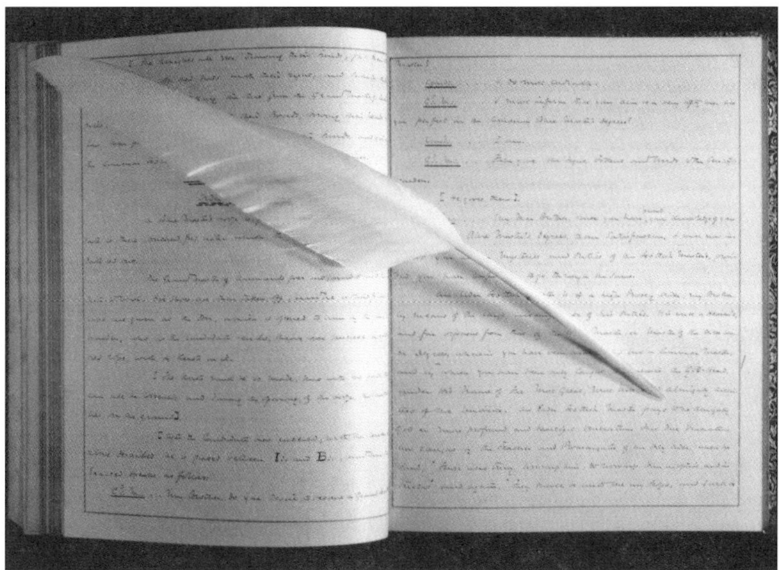

Pike's tiny, neat handwriting is illustrated in the pages of *The Degree of Master Mark Mason, Being the Work of The Gr.·. Council of Princes of Jerusalem of South Carolina* recorded and attested to by Pike on May 8, 1858, from a manuscript in the Archives of The Supreme Council, then at Charleston. Also pictured above is one of the quill pens Pike sometimes used.

True. Pike adjusted his style of writing to the purpose of the words. He was perfectly capable of writing simple, easy-to-understand prose—as he often did in his essays, editorials, and letters. He was a very effective communicator. In some of the materials we'll look at later, Pike wrote beautiful explanations for children of the nature of God's love, and what it means to love your neighbor as yourself—and a child can understand them. In addition, as we'll see, even the majority of *Morals and Dogma* is written in easy-to-understand prose.

But there are a few things we must remember.

First of all, Pike was writing more than a century ago, and people were much more accustomed to reading then. One computer program I have tests the reading level of material. The average newspaper story today is written somewhere between the fifth-grade and the ninth-grade reading level—as we now define those levels. When I measured several newspaper stories from the late 1800s (not written by Pike), I found they averaged the fifteenth-grade level—the level of a Junior in college. And these stories were read and understood by people who, on average, did not go past the third grade. One wonders what has happened to our standards.

And there was another factor at play. Eloquence was especially important in the 1800s. The most popular books printed were collections of sermons and speeches. It was assumed a public speech would last at least two hours—the audience felt cheated if it were shorter—and that the speaker would demonstrate his ability with the clever and exciting use of words. So Pike's audience was not only experienced in listening and reading, but they expected an idea would be "clothed in excellence and imagery." (Remember, that while we now consider Lincoln's Gettysburg Address one of the greatest speeches given, most of the people of the time thought it shoddy and over simplified, and the newspapers of the day pointed out that it was a disgrace that the President of the United States should speak in so plain, simple, and unornamented a style.) Pike's style, far less ornate and elaborate in most places than was the typical sermon or speech of the day, really isn't difficult to follow.

But it isn't intended for scanning or speed reading. Pike is not a fast-food hamburger to be gulped down on the run. He is a feast, prepared by a master chef, to be enjoyed at leisure.

His daughter, Lilian Pike Roome, wrote in the introduction to *General Albert Pike's Poems*, a collection of her father's lyrical works:

Lilian Pike Roome, one of only three of Pike's six children who survived him

Although he never in later years referred to it with any expression of bitterness, he lived constantly in an atmosphere of restraint when a boy; for he was by heredity and by nature a thinker, a student and a poet; large-minded, high-strung, sensitive, chivalrous, munificent, communicative with those he loved, but reserved to strangers and uncongenial persons; ambitious and conscious of his powers, yet diffident and modest, easily depressed by unkind words and sneers, but steadfast in his determination to do something, to be a power in the world. Thrown with rigid Puritans, who had little toleration for sentiment, and scorned poetry and "flowery talk," as they called anything imaginative and ideal, it is not to be wondered at that he longed to breathe a freer air, to lead a wider life than the purely materialistic one of wage-earning and eating and drinking, with no thought of greater things, no interchange of ideas, no aspirations toward intellectual development.[18]

As much as I love Pike's prose and much as I really enjoy reading his light verse and satire, I must admit in some of his "serious" poetry that "sentiment" and "flowery talk" make it all but unreadable for me. Highly regarded as his *Hymns to the Gods* was during his life, I, having read it once from a sense of duty, probably will not read it again unless as an act of penitence. But let him start to have fun in verse, as he does with "One

Spree at Johnny Coyle's," or "The Fine Arkansas Gentleman," or "Oh, Jamie Brewed a Bowl of Punch," or "A Dollar or Two," or, in his "serious stuff," let him forget the conventions of his day and just *write*, and I'm with him to the end, and only wish he had written more.

Pike, incidentally, was aware of his shortcomings as a poet, much as he had once longed to make that his career. In his autobiography, he writes:

> I felt that I was a pretty good lawyer, and could do some things pretty well with a pen; but I did not think I was a very great poet.[19]

Actually, he was a good critic, both of poetry and of drama, with an excellent sense of judgment when it came to the work of others. He said, in one of his essays, that he knew the difference between a good and a bad poem, and knew what made a poem good. He just couldn't do it. His remarks on the lesser-known poets of early England show remarkable insight, taste, and judgment. Even so, one of the things with which he was most impressed when he studied them was the way in which the concerns of the world had changed since they wrote.

> Among these [fragments of poetry which have come down from the past] are the writings of many of the old English poets, forgotten, little more known to us beyond their names, (if even these are known) than the dead of the last generation, in their coffins, under the ground.
>
> I read these, now and then, and it seems strange and a wonder, that the men and things in which they took so living and eager an interest should have been as actual as we and the things of this day are and that they should have passed away, and all the hopes and fears and loves and hates and vanities and ambitions and the questions and interests in which the fate of the world and of coming generations seemed to depend should so utterly have come to naught, and be as though they had never been at all, and no more to us than the story of a dream, which interests only him who tells it, and wearies everyone who hears it.... When I read the political satire of some of these old poets and consider how utterly forgotten are the men and events that aroused their indignation, how totally alien to our sympathies all the feelings are that they express as much as if they had been uttered when the pyramid was building, I feel inclined to burn what I have written and to write no more.[20]

Fortunately for us, that fire was never built.

It is an irony that Pike has become so much discussed and so little read. The irony is even more bitter because the same thing happened to Pike that he described as having happened to George Washington. In the seventh and eighth decades of the nineteenth century, Washington was far less regarded than he is now. Pike pictures Washington's fate in much the same words that one might use in writing of Pike himself, today.

He is mentioned occasionally, because it is the proper thing to do, but he has long ceased to be an idol. Twenty or thirty years ago his Farewell Address was read on solemn occasions, but few boys of this day have even heard of it. His writings, in twelve volumes, are little more regarded than backgammon-boards, lettered on the backs to look like books. The fashion of visiting Mt. Vernon has not entirely died out, but it is in feeble health, and his monument [the Washington Monument obelisk], commenced twenty and more years ago, will be finished when the world is.

Is this wholly a proof of the ingratitude of the people? No: the people never had a familiar affection for Washington. Those who grew up after the Revolution were taught to revere him as the most pure, immaculate, passionless and infallible of all mankind. He was made too god-like a character, having the perfection, with the immobility, the want of human sympathy, of a marble statue, with its snowy luster and its colors. He was made to seem

Photo: Office of the Curator, U.S. Capitol

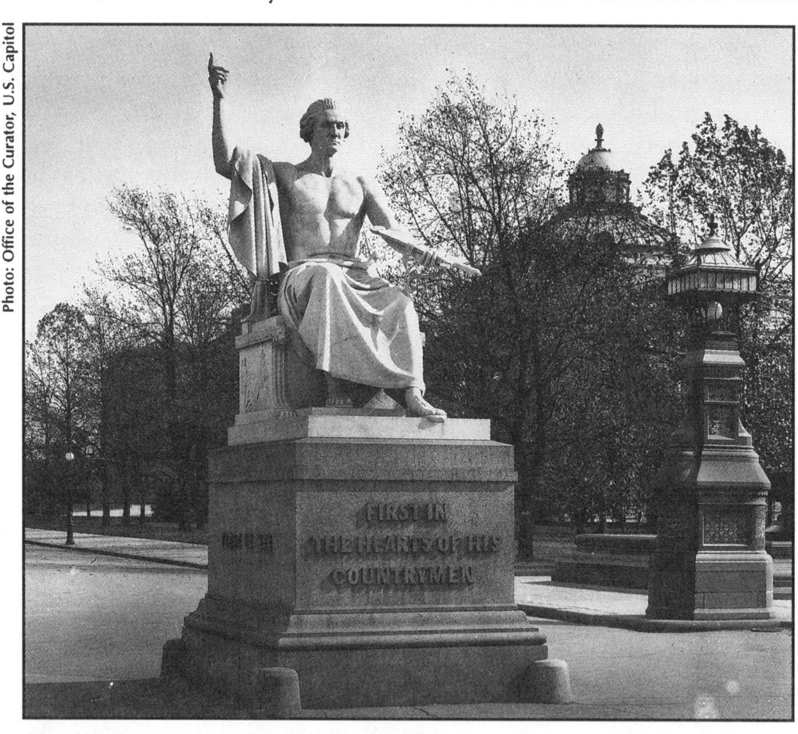

Horatio Greenough's marble statue of George Washington in Roman toga, originally on the lawn of the U.S. Capitol, now in the Smithsonian Institution's National Museum of American History

too rigidly righteous, too dignified, unapproachable, formal, prim and precise, a serene and majestic Jupiter.

As it is, the statue in the Capitol grounds, huge, cold, half naked, half clad in a Roman toga, fitly expresses the people's conception of him; and his memory is as unregarded as the statue.[21]

In the pages that follow, you'll have a chance to meet my friend Albert Pike as he plays and thinks and muses and jokes. You'll have a chance to hear him speculate on Masonry and morality and love and politics. You'll share his comments of backwoodsmen in Arkansas and women's fashions in Washington. And I think you'll find him to be inspiring and provoking and rewarding—and possessed of a really pointed sense of humor. Perhaps you, too, will come to share my "familiar affection" for him.

I'll do my best to stay out of the way, just setting up some of Pike's material with a little background when that seems helpful. To help distinguish who is speaking, Pike's words are in a separate type and look like this. *Other authors are in italics, like this.* My comments are in this type. Chapter endnotes in shortened form are grouped at the end of the book. (Check the bibliography for full citations.) Only in cases where I thought you might want faster access to an explanation did I enter it as an annotation at the bottom of the page.

The reader may justly complain that the book is less than organized—it does not provide a smooth overview of the historic development of Pike's thinking. But then, neither did Pike. The chapters have been arranged topically rather than chronologically. And even then there are overlaps. Religion sneaks into nature, sensuality creeps into education, and humor pokes its head into almost everything. But Pike is perfectly capable of hitting five topics in two sentences and never pausing for breath. It's a large part of his charm that he relates topics not normally related, and makes it work. There is an index to help bring *ordo ab chao* if need be.

Because our language changes and words come into and go out of fashion and common use, I've put some words in [brackets] to explain or define a term Pike uses which is no longer common.

But Pike needs no further explanation. Enjoy!

II

"The Motives That Aggravate Him"

On Pike's Sketches Of Extraordinary People

Albert Pike loved people. All sorts of people. He was a friend of the upper crust in Washington, D.C., Little Rock, and virtually every place he visited. He was perfectly at home in the layers of formal clothing which an evening with the best people demanded. At the same time he was a friend of frontiersmen, hunters and trappers, and loved nothing better than sitting around a campfire at night.

He had hope for humanity—and that is a little surprising in a man who went through so many reverses in fortune. That hope shines out in almost every degree in the Scottish Rite of the Southern Jurisdiction, where Pike makes it clear that the primary duty of every Mason is to make life better for those around him, no matter what it might cost.

Pike was a keen observer of people and excellent at description. We find less of that in his rituals, of course, but in his essays, articles for newspapers and letters, those little descriptions—some painfully funny, some equally painfully biting—are among the best things he did.

So this chapter looks at Pike's people: the people of the frontier, of Arkansas in the very early days, of Washington, D.C., in those same years, and others scattered throughout his travels. It was a time of great characters, and Pike has given us some great characterizations.

MEN OF THE WEST

Pike knew many of the men whose names became famous in the West. Many of them, of course, were Masons. Others he encountered in his travels. He has given us some of the finest portraits of the men in the westward frontier.

Tom Smith, Rhodes, Tom Banks, Jeru

The person who appeared to be the commander of this company, was a middle sized, stout man, with a bold, rather handsome and expressive countenance, and which was more singular [unusual] for one in his manner of life, a wooden leg. He had lost one "pin" some years before, I think, without any possible fault of his own—for a half-breed, I think, shooting at some person against whom he had a grudge, had missed his mark and broke the wrong leg.

If Tom Smith thought that this way of breaking one's leg was unceremonious, he certainly found that the remedy was no less so—for as it was in the mountains, and as trappers are not generally accompanied by a medical staff, the leg was taken off with a handsaw, and seared with an axe. Tom, however, who was a man of the most dauntless bravery, and one of the most generous of human beings, still stuck to the old trade, and stumped about after beaver nearly as well as the best of his trappers.

Near him was another individual, who, if this should ever meet his eye, will excuse me for mentioning his name, which I do with the utmost respect and friendship. Rhodes was and is, the best specimen of the old hunter that I have ever seen. Take him out of the woods, the prairie, and the mountains, and he languishes. He is like a transplanted exotic. He has been in the woods for many years, till that life is his element. He has traversed the country from the heads of the Arkansas and the Columbia to the mouth of the Del Norte, and is still, though old, a hale and hearty hunter. A few years ago, he took a fancy that no teeth were better than loose teeth, so pulled out the seven or eight which he had left, and so remains without a "peg." It is a grievous trouble to him, whenever he is forced to assail a tough piece of buffalo bull or horse—but an antelope and bear he manages very well.

Title page illustration from *Albert Pike: Frontiersman* by William Waldo, Missouri Historical Society, c. 1850

Then there was Tom Banks, an Irishman—and a most tremendous archer at the long bow. Tom was as brave as a lion, too, or said he was, which is the same thing. It is almost always the case, that we have nothing but men's words for such matters. However, he was a merry, good-humored fellow, and like most of the children of St. Patrick, rarely objected to a mug of *posheen.*

Close by was old Jeru—the most comical and quizzical of all old Frenchmen—withered , lean, almost toothless—but with a soul as big as that of many a man of two tons—loquacious and given to sententious discourses.[1]

Bill Irons

I have never seen better order in a court than that which prevailed in the court of Hot Springs County, about the year 1838, when twenty or thirty rifles belonging to the hunters who were in attendance as jurors, witnesses and spectators stood in the corners of the room, leaning against the logs. Bill Irons, an old hunter, living at the sulfur spring, some twenty-five miles distant, which bore his name, was to be tried for murder, and all the county was there to see. I was to defend him, and reached the Hot Springs on Sunday in the fall of the year, the day before the term of the court was to commence.

I was the guest of Samuel P. Carsen, once a Member of Congress from North Carolina, and he told me that he should give me the best fare he could; but, he said, "I am afraid you will have no game. We cannot get wild meat for love or money. The people are too busy with their crops, to hunt now."

"Never mind," I said, "we will have game to-morrow, if there is any in the county to be had"; and we did, for in the morning I went to Irons when [he] had surrendered to the sheriff, and said, "Bill, I am stopping with Carsen, and I want some venison. You must get your horse and gun, and kill me a deer and some turkeys, can you?"

"I wouldn't admire if I could," he said, "but how about the Sheriff? He's got me now, you know." "Well," I said, "I'll be answerable for you. You'll not be wanted today. You go and kill the meat; and I'll make it all right with him."

What a Little Rock Lawyer said was law and gospel, of course; and Bill went without further question, and returned long before sunset with a deer and two turkeys, the Sheriff being content when told that he had gone into the woods to kill me a deer.

But the reader must not be left to suppose that his offense was a murder like those that have now become too common. Summoned by the Sheriff to assist in capturing a thief, and the fellow taking to his heels, and being likely to escape, the Sheriff or someone of the posse cried "Shoot him!" and Bill took a long shot at the game on the wing, and brought it down. To indite [indict] him for murder was absurd, and he was acquitted, of course, and would at anytime afterwards have risked his life for me, nor have thought it much to do, either, for he risked it fifty times a year, in one way or another.[2]

Hedgman C. Triplett

Hedgman C. Triplett was a huge, tall, strong, ungainly, ugly man, who pretended to practice law in the country during the first years of my attendance there. Hedge never had any money. When he traveled on a boat, some victim had to pay his fair, or it was not paid at all. He never bought any wood for his office-fire, but waited in the fall until wood was hauled to the court house, at the expense of the county, and then levied what he considered his share.

I landed at Columbia once, after 10 o'clock of a cold December night, to attend the court, and found the Clerk, Triplett, and one or two others at the Clerk's office. An hour later we were thirsty, but all the places where liquids were dispensed were closed. "Come with me," said Hedge, "I can find liquor." He led the way to the front of the village, stopped at a store, in front of which, against the wall, was a long high pile of wood, seized the end of a stick in the middle of the pile, and working it this way and that, brought tumbling down a cord or so of the wood, with a great noise, and in two minutes the door flew open and the proprietor rushed out with a pistol in each hand, saying, "Hedge Triplett, ... let my wood alone, and be off!" I omit the expletives, which were emphatic.

Hedge was behind him in a moment, pinioned his arms, and invited us in to drink. We were heartily welcomed, found champagne and a barrel of oysters just from New Orleans inside, and made a night of it.[3]

Davy Crockett

Davy Crockett came to Little Rock on his way to Texas, and we gave him a supper. He was a back-woodsman, but could talk well enough on occasion.

Davy Crockett

There was a show here in Washington once, when he was here, and they had a monkey. Davy, standing by in the crowd, said to some one near him, "That monkey looks for all the world like my colleague, Campbell of Tennessee." Someone punched him in the side, and he turned around, and there was Campbell himself who heard the remark. Crockett took off his hat with apparent embarrassment and said: "Campbell, I owe an apology, sir, but whether to you or to the monkey I do not know."[4]

Bill Williams

The reader need not expect much delineation of character. Trappers are like sailors: when you describe one, the portrait answers for the whole genus. As a specimen of the genuine trapper, Bill Williams certainly stands foremost. He is a man about six feet one inch in height, gaunt, and red-headed, with a hard, weather-beaten face, marked deeply with the small pox. He is all muscle and sinew, and the most indefatigable hunter and trapper in the world. He has no glory except in the woods, and his whole ambition is to kill more deer and catch more beaver than any other man about him. Nothing tires him, not even running all day with six traps on his back. His horse fell once, as he was gallopping along the edge of a steep hill, and rolled down the hill with him, while his feet were entangled in the stirrups, and his traps dashing against him at every turn. He was picked up half dead, by his companion, and set upon his horse, and after all he outwitted [his hunting companion], and obtained the best set [placement] for his traps. Neither is he a fool. He is a shrewd, acute, original man, and far from illiterate. He was once a preacher, and afterwards an interpreter in the Osage nation.[5]

Sam Houston

Pike had been pressing the claims of several Indian Tribes against the government, trying to get the money paid to them which was their due. His encounter with Sam Houston took place over this topic.

Sam Houston

[Sam Houston, then U.S. Senator] stopped, and we talked a little, and after a while he said, "Well, Pike, I guess I shall have to vote against your Choctaw claim. I don't think I will vote for it."

Well, I was astonished. I knew that he had expressed himself over and over favorably to it, that it was a just claim and ought to be paid, and that it was a disgrace to the government that it was not paid. I said, "What is the matter now, General? I thought you were strongly in favor of it; I thought you were perfectly satisfied that it ought to be paid, even before I argued it."

"Well," he says, "I was, and I am; but you know this government never made a treaty with the Indians which it kept. Every treaty has been a disgrace to the government, because they have always broken them; and if we make an award giving the

Choctaws the proceeds of their land which they are entitled to, what will be the consequence? The government won't pay them, and we will be doubly disgraced. We had better leave the matter as it is. Why, I tell you, sir, if we make a decision that will give the Choctaws the proceeds of their land, it is doubtful if the government will ever pay a cent; and it will be a scandal and a disgrace to the government. I think I will vote against it, and keep the country from a disgrace."

Well I laughed and he laughed. It showed he was a good prophet.[6]

Elias Rector

Elias Rector had important influences on Pike at several points in his career, but as Walter Duncan points out in *Albert Pike, Reluctant General*, some of the most important were on appearance and life-style. Rector wore his hair long as a young man (although he had had it cut by the time the engraving, see next page, was made) and, after seeing it, Pike wore his hair long for the rest of his life. Rector was a wealthy planter in Arkansas, as well as the Federal Government's Indian Agent for all the lands west of Arkansas. He gave lavish parties, was a brilliant conversationalist, and Pike took him for a role model in many ways.

Pike paid an unusual tribute to Rector in completing a comic song. But let Pike tell us about it in his note to "The Fine Arkansas Gentleman" published in *Lyrics and Love Songs*.

THIS WAS WRITTEN IN THE WINTER OF 1852–3, AT WASHINGTON [D.C.].

The credit of originating it is due to William M. Burwell, then of Liberty, Virginia, now of New Orleans, who was that winter at Washington,—a person of infinite humor, a capital scholar and most original thinker. He composed three or four of the verses and handed them to Albert Pike, who completed the song.

The subject of it, "The Fine Arkansas Gentleman," was Major Elias Rector, of Arkansas, long a resident of that State and living near the border, of the Choctaw and Cherokee lines, but who was that winter at Washington, seeking the position of Marshal of the Arkansas district, which he had before held for several years, but lost upon the accession of President Taylor.

Major Rector was a zealous Democrat, but with many warm friends on the other side. These friendships, which were lasting ones, he owed to his genial nature, his generosity, courage, high sense of honor, and abundant hospitality. He was a person of fine presence, of great intelligence, and of an excellent and most original quaint wit; one of his peculiarities being that he wore his hair long, and put up with a comb, like a woman's. In the earlier days of Arkansas, when the strife of politics was exceedingly bitter, he was a bold, daring partizan [partisan], often

Elias Rector

engaged in personal difficulties and making many enmities, all of which he outlived. No man had a kinder heart, warmer affections, or a more true, generous and loyal nature. Nor was any man more courtly and like an English gentleman in his manners.

The song was sung for the first time when he was present, and at a party given by Robert W. Johnson, then a member of the House of Representatives, and afterwards Senator from Arkansas.

Dr. Wm. P. Reyburn was a physician residing in New Orleans, and at that time in Washington. He had, many years before, lived in Arkansas, and was an intimate friend of Major Rector. The Doctor was immensely corpulent, and brimful of joke, jest and anecdote, a gourmand, easy and indolent, but of vigorous intellect and great shrewdness, jovial, generous, and loyally trustworthy, a better Falstaff, in all the huge Knight's good qualities, including his wit, than Hackett himself. Dear old fellow! He returned to Arkansas in 1861, a Surgeon in the Confederate Army, after an absence of more than twenty years, to die and be buried there.

Prindel, though the keeper of a gaming house on Pennsylvania Avenue, was a good, true, honest, generous man, whose kindness of heart and lavish bounties and his own improvidence at last made him poor. He had often returned to young men the money they had lost to his Bank; and was therefore liked and respected by many who knew him well, and among whom many had National reputation.[7]

Those names will be important in understanding the poem.

A word about the sort of humor here may be in order. Pike makes use of a poetical joke by violating the strict rhyme scheme which he sets up. Remember that this is a song, intended to be sung. The extra words were probably sung on the same pitch, while the singer pantomimed running out of breath, gasping, etc. It is rather as if you were to try to sing "Twinkle Twinkle, Little Star" written like this:

Twinkle, Twinkle little star;
How I wonder what you are?
Up above the world so high
Like a diamond, or, if not a diamond, perhaps an unusually cunningly polished piece of cut glass, or at any rate something of a roughly equal refractive index in the sky.

The Fine Arkansas Gentleman

I.

Now all good fellows, listen, and a story I will tell
Of a mighty clever gentleman who lives extremely well
In the Western part of Arkansas, close to the Indian line,†
Where he gets drunk once a week on whiskey, and immediately
sobers himself completely on the very best of wine;
A fine Arkansas gentlemen,
Close to the Choctaw line!

II.

This fine Arkansas gentleman has a mighty fine estate
Of five or six thousand acres or more of land, that will be worth a
great deal some day or other if he don't kill himself too soon,
and will only condescend to wait;
And four or five dozen servants that would rather work than not,
And such quantities of horses, and cattle, and pigs, and other poultry,
that he never pretends to know how many he has got;
This fine Arkansas gentleman,
Close to the Choctaw line!

III.

This fine Arkansas gentlemen has built a splendid house
On the edge of a big prairie, extremely well populated with deer,
and hares, and grouse;
And when he wants to feast his friends he has nothing more to do
Than to leave the pot-lid off, and the decently-behaved birds fly
straight into the pot, knowing he'll shoot them if they don't; and
he has a splendid stew,
This fine Arkansas gentlemen,
Close to the Choctaw line!

IV.

This fine Arkansas gentleman makes several hundred bales,
Unless from drought or worm, a bad stand, or some other damned
contingency, his crop is short or fails;
And when it's picked, and ginned, and baled, he puts it on a boat,
And gets aboard himself likewise, and charters the bar, and has a devil
of a spree, while down to New Orleans he and his cotton float,
This fine Arkansas gentlemen,
Close to the Choctaw line!

† That is, near the present border of Arkansas and Oklahoma.

V.

And when he gets to New Orleans, he sacks a clothing store,
And puts up at the City Hotel, the St. Louis, the St. Charles, the Veranda, and all the other hotels in the city, if he succeeds in finding any more;
There he draws upon his merchant, and goes about and treats,
Every man from Kentucky, and Arkansas, and Alabama, and Virginia, and the Choctaw nation, and every other damned vagabond he meets!
This fine Arkansas gentleman,
Close to the Choctaw line!

VI.

The last time he was down there, when he thought of going back,
After staying about fifteen days, more or less, he discovered that by lending and by spending, and being a prey in general to gamblers, hackmen, loafers, brokers, hoosiers, tailors,
servants, and many other individuals, white and black,
He distributed his assets, and got rid of all his means,
And had nothing left to show for them, barring two or three headaches, an invincible thirst, and an extremely general and promiscuous acquaintance in the afore-said New Orleans;
This fine Arkansas gentlemen,
Close to the Choctaw line!

VII.

Now, how this gentleman got home is neither here nor there,
But I've been credibly informed that he swore worse than forty-seven pirates, and fiercely combed his hair;
And after he got safely home, they say he took an oath
That he'd never bet a cent again at any game of cards, and moreover, for want of decent advisers, he foreswore whisky and women both;
This fine Arkansas gentlemen,
Close to the Choctaw line!

VIII.

This fine Arkansas gentleman went strong for Pierce and King,†
And so came on to Washington to get a nice fat office, or some other equally comfortable thing;
But like him from Jerusalem that went to Jericho,
He fell among thieves again, and could not win a bet whether he coppered it or not, so his cash was bound to go—
This fine Arkansas gentleman,
Close to the Choctaw line!

---

† Franklin Pierce of New Hampshire was nominated in June 1852 as the presidential candidate of the Democratic National Convention in Baltimore, Maryland. His running mate was William R. King of Alabama. The Convention adopted a platform favoring the Compromise of 1850 as a solution to the slavery problem. Pierce and King won over General Winfield Scott and John P. Hale.

IX.

So when his moneys all were gone, he took unto his bed,
And Dr. Reyburn physicked him, and the chamber-maid, who had a
great affection for him, with her arm held up his head;
And all his friends came weeping round, and bidding him adieu,
And two or three dozens preachers, whom he didn't know at all, and
didn't care a damn if he didn't, came praying for him too;
This fine Arkansas gentlemen,
Close to the Choctaw line!

X.

They closed his eyes and laid him out all ready for the tomb,
And merely to console themselves they opened the biggest kind of a
game of faro right there in his own room;
But when he heard the checks, he flung the linen off his face, and
sung out, just precisely as he used to do when he was alive,
"Prindle, don't turn! hold on! I go twenty on the king and copper
on the ace!"
This fine Arkansas gentlemen,
Close to the Choctaw line![8]

LAWYERS

Pike was a lawyer himself, one of the most successful lawyers in what was then the southwestern United States. Allsopp remarks:

He made rapid progress is the legal profession. The South has produced many great lawyers and orators, and Pike, at thirty years of age, became one of the most prominent of the early days. Indeed, he was often proclaimed the foremost lawyer of the Southwest.

His industriousness was proverbial. He was the first Reporter of the Arkansas Supreme Court, appointed early in 1836, and as such officer administered the oath of office to James S. Conway, the first governor of the state to be elected by the people. When the territorial Legislature passed an act providing for the revision of the Statutes of the State, he was tendered the position to perform the work. He rewrote and codified the Statutes, and at the next session of the Legislature the work was adopted in its entirety.[9]

In his biographical study of Pike, Brown points out that Pike probably had the largest law practice in the state,[10] and that even today legal scholars rank Pike as one of the four top experts in comparative law of the 1800s.[11]

He was self-educated in the law, as he was in everything else. Thomas Lacey, the judge of the Superior Court of Arkansas, who issued him his original license to practice law remarked that, after all, it wasn't as if it were a license to practice medicine—he couldn't kill anybody by doing it badly.[12]

From that kindly, if somewhat less than ringing, endorsement, Pike went on to make many contributions to the study of law. One of the more impressive was his massive study of the Louisiana Civil Code, which, drawing as it does both from Roman Law and from the Code of Napoleon, is distinctive in the United States. Pike's study "required years to complete and reflected more than 20 years of meticulous research."[13]

Pike knew some of the best lawyers, and some of the notably less skilled. And he left us some powerful descriptions.

Three Unidentified Lawyers

He was a tall, lank man, with hair of a dirty red, and repulsive countenance, small and malignant eyes, an unsocial, repellent churl, with not a drop of the milk of human kindness in his whole body, a thoroughly read lawyer, especially in the old books, of which his library chiefly consisted....

He rented a house on the edge of town beyond Judge Field's, where he lived with his wife, having no child (fortunately, as Tristan Burgess said in the Senate to John Randolph, monsters are incapable of propagating their species), in impenetrable seclusion.[14]

A limb of the law once defended a client for assault and battery before a justice. He opened his case by saying, "May it please your honor, I appear before you this day, an humble advocate of the peoples' rights, to redress the peoples' wrongs. Justice, may it please your honor, justice is all we ask: and justice is due, from the tallest and highest *archangel* that sits upon the throne of heaven, to the meanest and most insignificant *demon* that broils upon the coals of hell. If my client, may it please your honor, has been guilty of any offense at all, he has been guilty of the *littlest* and *most insignificant offense* which has ever been committed from *the time when the morning stars sung together with joy—Shout heavenly muse!*"[15]

A story was told of some fellow who went to Texas from Arkansas and got into trouble, and went to employ a lawyer. The lawyer said to him, "Did you tell them your side of the matter?" referring to parties he had met immediately after the occurrence.

"Well," he said, "if I have got to tell you the truth about it, I did."

"Well," said the lawyer, "can they prove it on you?"

"Yes, they can prove it."

"Then," said the lawyer, "my advice to you is to run away, and to lose no time about it."

"But, hell, ain't I in Texas now?"[16]

John J. Crittendon

John J. Crittendon

Many curious anecdotes are told of [John J. Crittendon]. He prosecuted a man for shooting another man's dog. The two men had quarreled. The one who had had his dog shot was in the habit of hunting along a certain road, and the other man cut a lane through the brush, by which he could see one passing along the road within gun shot. Then he squatted down there, and waited for this other man to come along and, as he was passing along, he shot his dog—his favorite dog. For this, Crittendon prosecuted him, and in his speech, he dwelt on how the man had raised and reared his dog in the free air of his native country, and then dwelt on all the details of the other man cutting a lane, a clear way to the road, and then lying down in the way with a gun and, not satisfied with the opportunity of seeing the neighbor go by, instead of shooting the neighbor, had the meanness of shooting the neighbor's dog. He got a verdict for his client of fourteen or fifteen hundred dollars.[17]

Prentiss

I have heard Prentiss talk and make speeches—and he did tell a story before a jury! Anyhow, he never lost a case, I believe. No matter if he had been drinking, when he got into the court house or before the Supreme Court or before a jury either, and had to hold himself up against the railing, he never failed to make a fine argument, I used to see him often in New Orleans. He was a delightful companion—a great conversationalist. He knew a great deal, and could repeat a great deal of what he knew. He talked well on any subject.

Prentiss was by no means an imposing looking man. He was short, with rather a large head, and not by any means a symmetrical face. He was lame of one leg. But when he got up to speak, you never thought anything more of Prentiss at all but only of the oratory. There did not seem to be any mental process going on when he spoke, and nobody ever knew how long he talked. A man would stand up and listen to him three hours, and not think it was half an hour....

Prentiss was always the same—full of fire, beautiful imagery. He had a very fine voice, modulated well. He used perfectly pure English, and he had the great art of making all his figures of speech contain argument. His illustrations on the stump, no matter how poetical, were always to enforce a point.

When I heard him speak in Nashville, he fainted away three times during the delivery of the speech. He was, by all odds, the most extraordinary orator I ever heard.... He delivered a speech in the House of Representatives which was not reported—it was impossible for the reporters to take [it down] because they were so carried away by his eloquence.[18]

John Taylor

[Then there] was John Taylor, who came to Little Rock and then [rode] on the circuit and practiced law for three or four years. It was said that he ran once for the Senate of the United States, in Alabama, against William R. King. I never knew a more fluent speaker, nor one with as great mastery of language. He had the whole dictionary at his tongue's end, and his diatribes were sometimes magnificent.

He was a tall thin man, with reddish hair, the wild eyes of a lunatic, a sneering, sarcastic, malignant face, and in speaking continually put out the end of his tongue and kept it in motion at the corner of his mouth, like a snake.

Unsocial, misanthropic, always armed with pistols, he rode alone to the courts, and seemed to delight in making enemies. Utterly without geniality, kindness, generosity, charity or honor, he observed none of the courtesies of the Bar, and was universally detested, for he was much more like a wolf than a man. Wherever he went, he stirred up litigation, for his greed for money was enormous.

He especially delighted in getting up slander suits; and, in one county, Pope, after bringing half a dozen, he instituted half a dozen more, against his own clients, for those whom he had

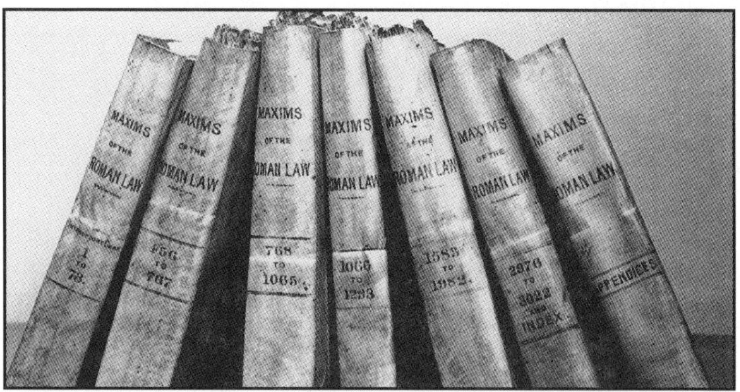

An ardent student of the law, Pike transcribed seven volumes titled *Maxims of the Roman Law* which have been preserved in his original manuscript.

sued for them, and had all them pending and for trial at the same time. One thing must be admitted, that in the trials he was utterly impartial in the distribution of his abuse, for he lavished it equally on both sets of clients.

At last he fancied and believed that the lawyers had poisoned his well, and removed to Texas. I believe he is living there yet.[19]

John W. Cocke

You might have searched the whole world over, without finding a more chivalrous, noble and generous gentleman than John W. Cocke, son-in-law of John Pope, of Kentucky (who was governor of Arkansas when I settled in the territory). A kinder and a truer heart than his never beat. Unostentatious, simple in all his habits, careless as to dress, tall and spare, homely in features, with singularly bright, soft, beautiful eyes, a little ungainly and slovenly, he had rare genius and admirable eloquence, with perfect integrity, no concealments and the nicest possible sense of fairness and honor.

He was a man whom you could not help loving, and in those days of fun and frolic was the most delightful of companions. We were very much together and very intimate for years, without an unkind word, without an unkind thought even for a moment of either, in the mind of the other. He was unfortunate and unhappy in the later years of his life, and the habit of drinking grew upon him, but he was always the same good, true, generous friend and noble gentleman.[20]

POLITICIANS

Pike had a love/hate relationship with politics and politicians for most of his life. He had much to say about them, and little of it was good. Partially that may have been because he was sure until his death that the Civil War could have been avoided if only the politicians had been willing to show some courage and conviction. But politics in Pike's day was a rough business: he lived through the carpet baggers and a great deal of turmoil. And Pike was popular with many of the politicians in Washington, even though it was one of his proudest boasts that he had never held a political office. He truly felt that the desire for political office was ruining the country. In one essay, he suggested that one ought to be able to sue politicians and bureaucrats for malpractice. He remarked:

If the law applied to legislators and Secretaries and heads of bureaus, and damages were recoverable to the full amount of injuries done by their improvidence in making and deciding under laws, and they were able to pay the judgments, the nation might seriously diminish the national debt.[21]

Two Arkansas Politicians

I can tell you a story about that [the political parties in Arkansas]. A county was formed in the northern part of the state called Randolph. They cast about six hundred votes in that county, and I think there were not more than fifteen or twenty Whigs,† so it was never any use for a Whig to run for any office. All the candidates were democratic. It happened one year that two democrats ran against each other for the same office. There was no Whig candidate for that office, and they made an agreement between them that neither of them should get up any story on the other or tell any story against the other, unless they were both together, so that the one the story was told on could defend himself. Pretty soon, one heard that the other had at one time gone to a precinct somewhere in the county, and had told his hearers that about a year before that, or a year and a half, he was out in the woods one day hunting, and came across a man who had just about finished disposing of a hog he had killed. He said that he had cut the ears off‡ and was about to bury them, and it was a hog of this man that was out hunting. And the party who did the killing was the opposing candidate. And so he told the story, and it was understood that it was a penitentiary offense. (They didn't have a penitentiary then, though.)

When the other fellow heard about the story, he was very mad, of course, and they met pretty soon afterward, And he says to him, "Didn't we make an agreement that neither of us would tell anything about the other unless the other was present?"

"Yes, we did."

"Didn't you go down to such a precinct, and say that you had caught me in the woods, and that I killed one of your hogs and had cut the ears off to bury them?"

"Yes."

"What did you go and tell that for, until I met you and had a chance to reply? I kept my part of the bargain, I have not told anything on you."

"Well, it was true, was it not?"

"Yes, of course it was true, but—look here, you go and tell that story again if you dare, and damned if I don't tell them you are a Whig!"[22]

---

† The Whig party (1834-56) was formed from the old Republican party in order to oppose Andrew Jackson and the Democrats. Pike was an active Whig.

‡ Hogs were allowed to run wild and forage for themselves at the time. A man marked his hogs by cutting their ears in a pattern recognized as his own (rather like branding cattle). To cut off the ears and dispose of them, therefore, was a way of hiding the original ownership of the hog.

Old Claraday

There was an old fellow by the name of Claraday, that lived out in the southern part of the state, south of Little Rock.... Claraday was a great democrat and a very ignorant man. He had natural good sense enough, but was as ignorant as a horse. I got very well acquainted with him and stopped with him very frequently too.† He liked me pretty well, however. I went to court regularly twice a year. After I had been travelling three of four or five years, a circumstance happened that I have never forgotten.

There was a little Doctor in Little Rock—and a fine Doctor he was, too. I was down town and met him on the street. He hailed me and said, "Don't be in a hurry; I want to tell you a story.

"You know old Claraday," he continued.

"Of course I know him."

"You know what an awful democrat he is. You know he always wanted to be a candidate for the legislature. He goes before the county convention and tries to get nominated year after year. They would always nominate someone else, and Claraday would get mad.

"Well, they just had a convention and, as usual, Claraday has been defeated. I stopped with him down there, and he was very full of it. I got there about the middle of the afternoon, and I had to sit there and hear him talk. He talked all of dinner time, and then he sat himself down by me outside the house and talked. At last I got tired of his talk, and I went upstairs and laid down in the bed. And, will you believe it, he followed me up there, and sat down by the bed and kept talking until finally I got sleepy and dozing. Suddenly I was waked up by his saying; 'Well, I think the best thing we can do is, to take the best men in the state and put them in the best offices.'

"I was half awake and I was half asleep. I said, 'Yes, I think so to. I think the best thing we can do is to take Pike and put him in the Senate of the United States.'"

"What do you suppose the old fellow said to that? 'Oh, no! I don't know about that. Pike may be a very good lingerest, but he excludes himself too ouxtraordinary to common people ever to be very populist; howsomedever, I am an unlettered man, and don't pretend to cumbert the motives that aggravate him.'"[23] [Translated, this appears to mean: "Pike may be a very good linguist, but he expresses himself too extraordinarily for common people ever to be very popular (Populism was an American political movement);

† This was during the time that Pike, a lawyer in Arkansas, was riding the circuit—a trip through the countryside which often lasted for weeks.

howsoever, I am an unlettered man (Indeed!), and don't pretend to comprehend the motives that activate him."]

Amos Kuykendall

Wolves were a problem in Arkansas, and a bill was introduced into the legislature to offer a bounty on them. It was the occasion for a great deal of humor, and many other predators were added, including opossums and rats, not for serious intent but just to liven things up a bit. One frontier legislator, Amos Kuykendall by name, arose to speak in favor of the bill, and Pike gives us his speech.

"Mr. President—If I'm in order I want to say this and thus on this here subject. I think it is one of the most glorious, one of the most valuable, frontier works that can be.... Now, as to minks, I hadn't no objection. I've seen a mink catch a chicken—I'll catch a chicken too, if my wife tells me to, and treat a gentleman. And as to 'possums, I hadn't no sort of objection.... I don't eat 'possum—I eat hogmeat—that's good—that makes sop. I ask for a wolf first—he's a big fellow—he catches a big hog. Let him that wants a 'possum catch him and eat him. All them things catches chickens. I only ask a liberal price.... Understand me, my Sons! You all know *Uncle Amos*; some of you twenty-five year. Now don't let him be brutified! Don't treat him with contempt!!"[24]

MEN OF INDIAN TERRITORY

Pike spent a great deal of time in Indian Territory, both in his official capacity with the Confederate government and purely for pleasure. He has left us some striking characterizations.

An Ex-Chief of the Comanche

There was among [the Chiefs coming to a meeting to discuss a treaty with Pike] a very old man with emaciated frame, mere skin and bones, apparently having for all clothing only an old dirty blanket, but with a thin, keen face, and evidently intelligent. He had been a great war chief, but becoming too old to lead his people on the war path, he had then been, according to their custom, deposed. The Chiefs and Braves sat on benches, on opposite sides of the passage between two cabins, and on a buffalo robe, spread on the ground in the centre, sat this old ex-chief.

[The Chief and War Captain of the Creeks then addressed the others, explaining the benefits they had found in living a more settled life.]

Then the old war ex-chief, sitting upon his buffalo robe, commenced to speak. He used no gestures and spoke about twenty minutes, earnestly, almost vehemently at times, the language sounding wonderfully like Spanish. I did not understand a word, but I never in all my life heard a speech more fluently and impressively delivered, more musically, with better emphasis and perfect intonation. At times there was a singular pathetic sadness in his voice; and in a sentence or two the words rang out like a trumpet. He spoke of me and of Kekanciwa, as his glances toward us showed, and I thought he was advising rejection of the treaty, accusing me of meaning them harm, and denouncing Kekanciwa for having abandoned the nomad life and living among the trees in a house.

I was mistaken. He was advising his people to come in and settle, telling them that they ought to confide in me, and that Kekanciwa had tried the experiment and found it good. The next day the treaty was signed with great formality and evident satisfaction.[25]

Opothliyahola

Pike had been an attorney for Indian tribes, helping them press their claims in Congress. The money for their lands, promised to them when they were moved, had been delayed for years by a Congress which saw no reason to honor a treaty to Indians, once they were out of the way. He had finally secured the payment, but some Congressmen, annoyed that Pike had pressed the claim, wrote into the provisions that no fees were to be paid to attorneys from the proceeds before they were distributed, contrary to the usual practice. It was the belief, expressed on the floor of the House, that Pike would never get his fee (a percentage from each tribal family) once the money was paid out.

When the payment was about to commence, I stood on the inside of the pay-table. I had looked at the roll, and seen that Opothliyahola's tribe was to be called first, and his name stood first on the roll. He was National Speaker, and deserves especial mention. In the old nation, east of the Mississippi, he had aided to kill William McIntosh, the Chief, for making the Treaty of Indian Springs.... He was a tall, large man, with large head and features, somewhat more heavily moulded than those of Daniel Webster, but resembling them, and strongly indicative of power of will, indomitable firmness, quick decision, self-possession and strong intellect,—the face, in every way, of a man whom one would not seek to have for an enemy.

Quanah
Comanche Indian Chief

He was born, he told me, the year peace was made with Great Britain, after the Revolutionary War. He had been an exceedingly eloquent and powerful speaker; was considered a man of ill temper and vindictive, had some friends and many enemies, especially the two sons of General McIntosh, one of whom became Colonel and the other Major with the Confederate service.

I knew him well, in 1858, and tried to induce him to sit for a photograph, but could not, and when the payment was about to commence he sat in front of and near me, silent, and with the same expression of profound melancholy that was so habitual to Daniel Webster. I could not catch his eye. He would not look at me, and I concluded that he did not intend to permit the clerk to take the per centum [for Pike's fee] out of his money. Of course, I knew that if he set the example it would be followed, perhaps by all.

His tribe was called. And he came and sat on a bench close to the table to identify the persons called to be paid. His name was called and he rose, and stood in front of the table, facing it and me, his arms folded on his chest and still he would not look at me. I could read nothing in his face. It was as inscrutable in its massiveness and melancholy gloom as the face of the Egyptian sphinx.

The amount to be paid him was named, counted in gold and silver, and pushed toward him. He did not stir to touch it. The clerk was afraid to move his hand toward it. Then the old man shot a quick, keen look at me, reached his left hand out as if slowly to take the money, I thought, and pushed it toward the clerk, then folded his arms again, looked full at me, and a smile lighted up his face, full of glee at having deluded and played upon me. I never saw a human face so changed in my life. It lighted up all over.[26] [Pike, it appears, received his fee.]

Jeru Pockmank

Jeru Pockmank was a remarkably good-looking and pleasant person, about thirty years of age, five nine in height, weighing perhaps 150 pounds, muscular, slender, but broad-shouldered and strong, agile as a panther, and rode like a Comanche. I heard a rifle shot ahead one day, as we were moving, and saw Jeru go riding off to the left, among the grass, and on my coming up he brought me a great turkey whose head he had shot off as he ran from him. He was remarkably shrewd and intelligent, and his eyes fine, clear and frank. Always good humored, ready and obliging, he was liked by everyone, and respected too, for his unpretending ways and perfect courage. It is a great charm of these red men that they are always self-possessed, quiet and without the least servility or feeling out of place, or not knowing what to do with their hands or feet.

Pockmank was accompanied by his wife. He always was. She was a pleasant-featured woman, nearly as tall as he, not delicate or slender, but with small hands and feet. She cooked the game he killed, and sewed for him, in camp, and rode with him wherever he went, hunted with him, and had often gone with him on the war-path. They were very fond of each other, and she never spoke to anyone else. She could ride and shoot, he said, as well as he could. He hunted buffalo with a bow and arrow, and had two horses, one of which could run down three buffalo in succession; and her arrows were as fatal as his.[27]

THE SETTLERS OF ARKANSAS

The people of Arkansas, when I first knew them, and long afterwards, were for the most part poor. They had come from other states and remote regions, they and their families, carrying their household-goods and gods, their wives and little ones, all, often, in a single wagon; the father and the half-grown boys striding by its side, a-foot, with rifle on shoulder, and the girls and the old grand-father and grand-mother, perhaps, riding their little ponies, all in search of a place wherein to settle, in the heavy woods or on the unbroken prairie—camping at night by a spring or a rivulet in the woods, and up and away by sunrise—with fewer cares and anxieties, than are found in rich and fashionable households, and more true generosity and hospitality.

And of their households, in their modest and narrow cabins of rough logs, that I have passed many a day and night in…you will find nothing to warrant you in congratulating yourself on your greater good fortune and larger estate of real happiness, but much to make you like and envy them….

Compare the life that these men lived, industrious, active, contented, invigorating, temperate, sober, with its healthy excitements and quiet enjoyments, with those of the great who struggle to rise higher and of the rich, frantic to be richer!

All their ambition was to send the bullets from their rifles straight to the mark, to follow and slay the deer in the woods, and—not without danger—to kill the panther and brown bear. When the country needed their services in the war, they neither sought exemption nor looked about for substitutes, nor asked for bounty. It was such men as these that crowned with historic glory Bunker Hill and King's Mountain, and made Tippecanoe famous, and followed Jackson into Florida and routed the Peninsular veterans at New Orleans. It is one of the compensations of poverty, that its legions may serve the Republic in war, and shed their blood and lay down their lives for her, without the hoped-for reward and the inducement of glory and eternal remembrance of their names, or of fortune in the shape of pay, to lessen the merit of heroic service and disinterested sacrifice.[28]

III

"The Greatest–The Only Safeguard Of Liberty"

On Education

Education was central to Pike's life in every possible way. His first real brush with the frustrations of academic bureaucracy came when he applied to Harvard and found that, even though he had "tested out" of the first two years, he would still be required to pay the tuition for them. He refused. In spite of his lack of formal higher education, he was a school teacher on several occasions. He firmly believed in self-education and continued learning until his death. For instance, when among the Indian tribes, he took the opportunity to make notes on their languages and, in his prairie sketches, showed a remarkable understanding of the various tribal language groups.

He saw Masonry as a lifelong course in education. *Morals and Dogma* was written essentially as a text book in the history of theology and philosophy, one of the very first attempts at such a "survey" text. Pike served as President of the Board of Trustees of St. John's College in Arkansas, a college founded by Masons to meet the educational needs of the young people of the area.

And he readily accepted the fact that education leaves much in doubt or unanswered—a fact which many people before and since have found very hard to swallow. He knew it was essential that men and women learn to doubt and question if they are to learn to think.

Christianity, it is said, begins from the burning of the false gods by the people themselves. Education begins with the burning of our intellectual and moral idols; our prejudices, notions, conceits, our worthless or ignoble purposes.[1]

Doubt, the essential preliminary of all improvement and discovery, must accompany all the stages of man's onward progress. His intellectual life is a perpetual beginning, a preparation for a birth. The faculty of doubting and questioning, without which those of comparison and judgment would be useless, is itself a divine prerogative of the reason. Knowledge is always imperfect, or complete only in a prospectively boundless career, in which discovery multiplies doubt, and doubt leads on to new discovery. The boast of science is not so much its manifested results, as its admitted imperfection and capacity of unlimited progress. The true religious philosophy of an imperfect being is not a system of creed, but, as Socrates thought, an infinite search or approximation.[2]

There is a well-known story of the young man who graduated with his degree. "Here I am, World," quoth he, "I have my B.A.!"

"Sit down, son," said the world, "I'll teach you the rest of the alphabet."

It was even so with Pike when he left New England to make his mark on the world.

I thought that I was finely educated and that, therefore, my opportunities would be greatly improved. When I got out West, I found my education did not amount to much. It was not practical and what a man needed out there more than a school education was practical, common sense.[3]

He traveled around, first looking for a chance to do great and exciting things—then for a chance to earn enough to feed himself, even if it meant teaching again. He ended up in Pope County, Arkansas.

After travelling over a fine, rolling, upland country, I descended into the bottom of a creek called Little Piney, nine miles from the river—and came at once upon a small log house, I stopped to take a survey before entering; for I had been directed to the settler who lived there. It was like most other settlements in this country. A field of about forty acres was under cultivation,—filled with huge blackened trunks, gigantic skeletons of trees, throwing their bare withered sapless branches forth, as though a whirlwind had been among them with its crashing destruction. About the house were a number of peach trees, scattered about with very little regard to regularity. The house itself was roughly built of logs, and in front was a shelter made of poles covered with green branches. The owner of the clearing was sitting in front, dressed throughout in leather, and playing lustily on the fiddle. Hearing that sound, I judged there would be no churlishness in his disposition, and I marched boldly up. He greeted me heartily, and without any attempt at politeness, and in two minutes we were on the best terms in the world.

"Why," said he, "if you would set in, right straight, I reckon thar' might be a right smart chance of scholars got, as we have had no teacher here for the best end of two years. Thar's about fifteen families on the creek, and the whole tote of 'em well fixed

The old schoolhouse where Pike taught, near Van Buren in Crawford County, Arkansas, is preserved as a historical landmark. The dedicatory plaque (pictured on the facing page), includes a Masonic Square and Compasses and is mounted to the right of the schoolhouse door as seen in this photograph.

for children. They want a schoolmaster pretty much, too. We got a teacher about six months ago—a Scotchman, or an Irishman, I think. He took up for six months, and carried his proposals round, and he got twenty scholars directly. It weren't long, though, before he cut up some ferlicues, and got into a priminary; and so one morning he was found among the missing."

"What was the trouble?"

"Oh! he took too much of the essence of corn, and got into a chunk of a fight—no great matter to be sure; but he got whipped and had to leave the diggins."

"And how am I to manage to get a school?"

"I'll tell you. You must make out your proposals to take up school; tell them how much you ask for a month, and what you can teach; and write it out as fine as you can, (I recon you're a pretty good scribe,) and in the morning there's to be a shooting match here for beef; nearly all the settlement," (laying the accent on the last syllable) "will be here, and you'll get signers enough."[4]

Pike got the job. He was paid half in cash and half in hogs.

That experience was to make him a lifelong advocate of public, tax-supported education. As Walter Lee Brown points out in his doctoral dissertation on Pike:

He knew by first-hand experience of the general lack of schools and the appalling condition of those that existed in the territory. He proposed that the legislature provide for an efficient system of free public education. Under his plan each county would be divided into a number of school districts, and each district would have a centrally located schoolhouse to be built at county expense. A permanent school fund could be created from a grant of land to each county by Congress, and the fund would be built up by having fines for certain specified crimes and misdemeanors go into it. Each county should also have a committee to examine the school. Above all, Pike would have the pay of teachers in-

creased to at least forty-five dollars per month. "It is singular," he said, "that men are commonly seen to be perfectly willing to pay more for anything else than the education of their children."[5]

Pike states the case eloquently.

Education is the greatest, yea, the only safeguard of liberty. When was there ever a country where the common people were uniformly uneducated, in which they were not slaves?… A community of ignorant and uneducated men is not capable of self-government….

The schools throughout the country [the "West"], contain from fifteen to twenty-five and in some cases thirty scholars at one dollar per month, out of which the teacher pays his board. Now, who would work for this price at such a business, (for it is work, and that of the hardest, most slavish and thankless kind) when he could obtain any respectable employment? Here and there a good teacher may be met with, but if so, he has been forced into it by misfortune. He is disgusted with the business, and at the earliest opportunity, leaves it. It has been the curse of the western country, that it has been overrun by hordes of lazy and ignorant men, employed in teaching school.

Let, for example, the legislature pass a law at the next session, dividing each county into school districts, each containing at least fifteen families—and let them enact that a school shall be kept in each of those districts for at least four or six months in

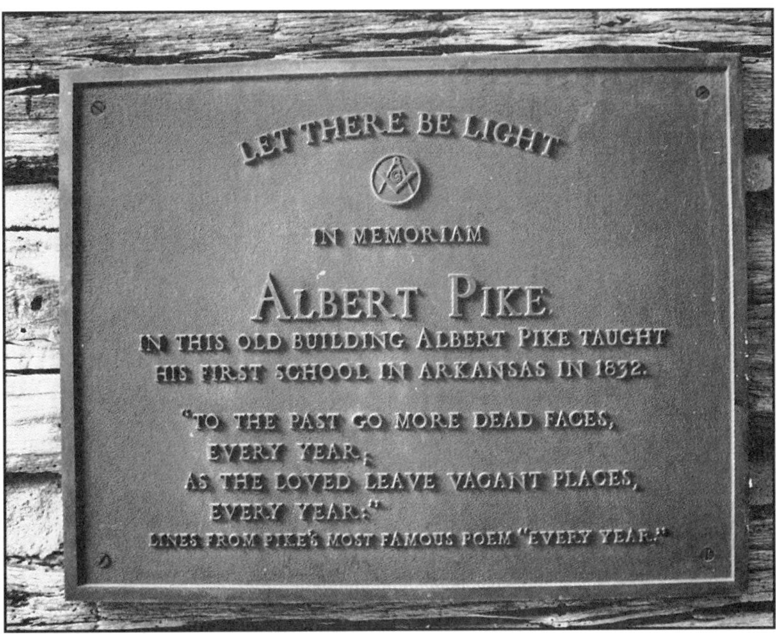

the year, under penalty of a certain sum, to be levied equally on each person over the age of 21 years, in the defaulting district, and paid into the treasury to aid in establishing a school fund.... And then let the legislature petition Congress, and let the people petition Congress...for a grant of land to each county to be applied to establishing a permanent school fund—and, our life upon it, they will get it....

For ourselves, we conceive education to be a matter of common interest, and perfectly subject to legislative interference and supervision—and without pretending to any great patriotism, we say that, feeling our own fortunes identified, in a great measure, with those of Arkansas, we desire to see her use due means to obtain for the coming generation that education without which freedom has been rarely obtained and not long guarded.[6]

Pike returns to that theme in the lecture of the Scottish Rite Ninth Degree, S.J., stressing that education is not a luxury for a state, but a necessity.

It is never safe for a nation to repose on the lap of ignorance; and if there ever was a time when public tranquility was insured by the absence of knowledge, that season is past. Unthinking stupidity cannot sleep, without being appalled by phantoms and shaken by terrors. The improvement of the mass of the people is the grand security for popular liberty; in the neglect of which, the politeness, refinement, and knowledge accumulated in the wealthier classes will some day perish like dry grass in the hot fire of popular fury.[7]

In contemplating rual poverty or the chaos of some inner cities, where high drop-out rates are a chronic problem, one is inclined to agree with Pike that politeness, refinement, and knowledge are early victims.

Pike insisted over and over again that Masonry must be involved with the support of education. He wrote that Masonry's task was to improve the life of the people at large by every available means:

Chiefest of which, within its reach, is to aid in the education of the children of the poor. An intelligent people, informed of its rights, will soon come to know its power, and cannot long be oppressed; but if there be not a sound and virtuous populace, the elaborate ornaments at the top of the pyramid of society will be a wretched compensation for the want of solidity at the base.[8]

Pike expands that idea in the lecture he wrote for the Tenth Degree of the Scottish Rite of Freemasonry, Southern Jurisdiction.

There is no Mason who *cannot* do *some*thing, if not alone, then by combination and association.

If a Lodge cannot aid in founding a school or an academy it can still do something. It can educate one boy or girl, at least, the child of some poor or departed brother. And it should never be forgotten, that in the poorest unregarded child that seems abandoned to ignorance and vice *may* slumber the virtues of a Socrates, the intellect of a Bacon, the genius of a Shakespeare, the capacity to benefit mankind of a Washington; and that in rescuing him from the mire in which he is plunged, and giving him the means of education and development, the Lodge that does it may...perpetuate the liberties of a country and change the destinies of nations, and write a new chapter in the history of the world.[9]

But formal education was not the limit of Pike's concern, nor even where he placed the most emphasis. It was self-education, continuing education, which claimed him as its own. One can only wonder what he would have made of the unlimited educational opportunities for that we have today—or how he would have wept over how much we neglect them.

Perhaps, if we take the word "education" in its narrow and ordinary sense, I may have as good a right as another to speak of *self*-education, and to believe in its value and sufficiency. For all that I have learned since I went to Harvard to be examined for admission to the class of Freshmen at the age of 15, I have acquired without other instruction than that of books, and accumulation by observation and experience. I never attended a law-school, or heard a lecture on law or any other branch of human knowledge. What I have learned, of Greek and mathematics, at school and afterward, I long ago forgot, and had to relearn Latin and French, at the age of forty, in the Pandects of Justinian and French law books.

Pike's love of books is evident in the above photograph from an antique stereoscope picture in the collections of the Library of The Supreme Council, 33°.

I dare say I should have acquired much of the same knowledge more easily and rapidly, if I had had teachers, and perhaps more thoroughly. I do not by any means say that they are unnecessary, or advise anyone to take the more laborious course of self-acquisition. But however many teachers one may have, he must acquire most of his knowledge for himself, or with little aid from them, and must therefore be in large measure self-educated....

When I commenced to read French again, after I had forgotten the grammar, I began with a law-book, and next read a compilation in French from the Talmud. If I met with a word that I could not find in a dictionary, or a phrase whose meanings I could not make out, which occurred oftener than once on every page, I marked it and went on. After a time, I met the same word or phrase in a context in which its meaning was made plain, and upon reading the second time I understood all. So also I relearned Latin, by reading the Pandects, so far as I have relearned it, for I am learning it yet.

But I do not propose to speak, now, of that education as self-education which consists of the acquisition of the knowledge contained in books, for which certainly no teacher is long needed; which education continues all our life, and we learn more in later years than in earlier years, and find, towards the end, that an education has only commenced.

I mean, rather, by "self-education" that process of acquisition of knowledge, discretion, discrimination, discernment, rightwiseness and other wisdom, and other things that go to make up manliness, by which we fit, enable and capacitate ourself, to think and do, profitably and effectively, the right thing, at the right time, and in the right way, in all the concerns and emergencies of life.

The other education only furnishes us with the means of acquiring this, and this each must acquire for himself. We cannot have it by instruction of any teacher.[10]

It was the sheer joy of learning, of knowing something today that he did not know yesterday, which was to motivate Pike all his life.

Nothing in life, I think, gives so profound a pleasure as the solitary and silent acquisition of knowledge: and if the Deity could envy the creatures to whom He has given intellect, it would be because omniscience has no knowledge to acquire, and they have much to learn.[11]

This self-education was an essential part of gaining insight into one's own nature.

We come to know ourself, only by self-education, and chiefly by our failures and reverses.[12]

What is commonly called "education," it cannot be too often repeated nor too continually remembered, is but the acquisition of the means by which to educate oneself.[13]

The greatest value of this self-education is to produce a sense of perspective and, therewith, a toleration—a willingness to accept others as they are.

> While to be lenient or indifferent to the vices, faults, absurdities and follies of others, so that they shall no longer annoy us, is the fruit of self-education, so also is it not to be ignorant of our own, and to place a just estimate on our demerits and deserts. To know one's self is the rarest, the most hardly obtained, and the most profitable of all knowledge. Our eyes are always keen enough to discern the faults and deficits of others.[14]

Because of his love of learning, books were precious to Pike. He accumulated one of the largest libraries in the state. When he moved into an apartment in the House of the Temple in Washington, D.C., he gave his books to the Scottish Rite, S.J. Difficult as it is to imagine, there was no public library in Washington at the time, and so Pike directed that the Library of the House of the Temple was to be open to the public. It still is, and the thousands of volumes he donated form the nucleus of what is today a truly outstanding collection of 175,000 volumes. The following passage from one of his essays clearly reflects Pike's love of books.

The Library at the Scottish Rite House of the Temple in Pike's time

The Library in the current House of the Temple includes Pike's collection

I never hear, without a feeling of sadness, and almost as if some evil had happened to myself, of the sale at auction of the library of one, the pride and joy of whose life it had been to collect it. I resented the sale of the library of Edward Everett. I have few books among mine, purchased at such auctions. I have a superstition that the first owner might claim them as still his, especially if I had purchased them for a tithe of their real value or what they cost him. No doubt the sadness comes chiefly from the admonition, which every such sale gives me, that someday the same fate must befall my own books. But it is not all that. I should not like to see the bones of the dead sold at auction, though I might know that mine would never become articles of commerce. I have a Moliere that belonged to Pompadour, with her arms stamped in gold on the covers, and her autograph on the title page of each volume; and a little book that belonged to Horace Walpole. I do not suppose that the Marchioness would care to claim hers. Walpole's, I hold as a depositor. Why should one want the bones, more than the clothes, of dead men?

Who that loves his books does not sympathize with witty, genial, quaint Charles Lamb, in his half-comical anathema pronounced against borrowers, especially of books? Who, that has books at all, has not had his equanimity of mind disturbed by "those mutilators of collections, spoilers of the symmetry of shelves, and creators of odd volumes"? In the South Western States, laws for many years prescribed hanging, as a preventative, for horse-stealing. A like enactment [in regard to books] would be useful.[15]

IV

"This World, Also, Is Among The Stars"

On Morality

Pike belonged to the school of moral and practical philosophers, and it was his theory that history, science, and art, as well as religion, mean the moral uplift of humanity and that the logical result of true wisdom is to bring about the doing of all things, under all circumstances, that we should do and the abstention, under all circumstances, from doing anything that we should not do....

This conclusion he reached from the deep-seated and unalterable conviction he entertained, that the Divine and Human are intermingled in man. That truest honor and most real success are won in that battle in which intellect, reason, moral sense, and spiritual nature fight against sensual appetites, evil passions, and the earthly and material or animal nature. That the human in man is to be subjugated by the Divine; the appetites and passions conquered by reason, and the moral sense through the continual effort, struggle and warfare against the material and sensual by the spiritual.[1]

"Morality" has become an estranged word in our time. What with certain aspects of the sexual revolution, the "if-it-feels-good-do-it" philosophy, and the other changes we have been through, it seems to belong to another time, another generation.

The term "morality" makes us so uncomfortable today that we have started using "ethics" to cover situations which are essentially moral in nature.

Above all, we have become almost paranoid about any suggestion that we are commenting on anyone else's morality. Where our parents would have referred to someone as "having the morals of a mink," we refer to them as "liberated." This has, at least, the advantage of not casting aspersions on the mink.

To the degree that the change represents genuine toleration, of course, it's all to the good. The problem comes not when we find excuses for others, but when we find excuses for ourselves. Pike says several places in the ritual of the Scottish Rite: Our task is not to be better than our neighbors, but better than ourselves. And he heaps the rich scorn of his contempt on those who feel entitled to comment in the press on the morality of others.

Very often the censure bestowed upon men's acts, by those who have elected and commissioned themselves keepers of the Public Morals, is undeserved. Often, it is not only undeserved; but praise is due instead of censure; and when deserved, it is always extravagant and therefore unjust,

Even the man who does wrong and commits errors, often has a quiet home, a peaceful fireside, a gentle, loving wife and innocent children, who do not know of his misdeeds, past and long repented of, or present and hereafter to be atoned for by sincere penitence and mighty agonies and bitter remorse; or, if they do, do love him all the better, because being mortal he hath erred, and being in the image of God he hath repented, or will, persuaded by their soft and gentle influences, repent and make atonement, if no uninvited censor thrusts himself between him and them. That every blow aimed at this husband and father, strikes brutally at the bosoms of the wife and daughters, and makes them, though innocent, to partake of the same which falls on him, does not stay the hand of the modern guardian of public morals; but, brave as Caesar, he strikes and slays, and then calls on those to whose vicious appetites he had pandered, to admire and praise him for the generous and manly act.[2]

Pike was clear on the question of morality. It was a matter of trying to do what was right. That different people would see right somewhat differently was understandable and acceptable. The point was, were they trying? Were they trying to be better, more self-controlled, more spiritual and less physical today than yesterday, or were they just drifting where the animal took them?

Freemasonry is the subjugation of the Human that is in man by the Divine; the Conquest of the Appetites and Passions by the Moral Sense and the Reason; a continual effort, struggle, and warfare of the Spiritual against the Material and Sensual.[3]

Not that the struggle is ever easy. Pike knew how difficult it could be; and he knew that the Masonic Lodge was helpful in that battle, if for no other reason than that it gave a place where temptation was diminished. The real battles come when the Mason leaves the Lodge and goes out into the world. And we don't always win those.

Here, in the Lodge, virtue and vice are matters of reflection and feeling only. There is little opportunity, here, for the practice of either; and Masons yield to the argument here, with facility and readiness; because nothing is to follow. It is easy, and safe, here, to *feel* upon these matters. But to-morrow, when they breathe the atmosphere of worldly gains and competitions, and the passions are again stirred at the opportunities of unlawful pleasure, all their fine emotions about virtue, all their generous abhorrence of selfishness and sensuality, melt away like a morning cloud.

For the time, their emotions and sentiments are sincere and real. Men may be really, in a certain way, interested in Masonry, while fatally deficit in virtue. It is not always hypocrisy. Men pray most fervently and sincerely, and yet are constantly guilty of acts so bad and base, so ungenerous and unrighteous, that the crimes that crowd the dockets of our courts are scarcely worse.

A man may be a good sort of man in general, and yet a very bad man in particular; good in the Lodge and bad in the world; good in public, and bad in his family; good at home, and bad on a journey or in a strange city. Many a man earnestly desires to be a good Mason. He says so, and is sincere. But if you require him to resist a certain passion, to sacrifice a certain indulgence, to control his appetite at a particular feast, or to keep his temper in a dispute, you will find that he does not wish to be a good Mason *in that particular case;* or, wishing, is not able to resist his worse impulses.[4]

It is a battle, a struggle. And that, in Pike's mind, is one of the things which makes it worthwhile.

Times change, and circumstances; but Virtue and Duty remain the same. The Evils to be warred against but take another shape, and are developed in a different form.

There is the same need now of truth and loyalty as in the days of Frederic Barbarossa.[5]

And, in a biting commentary on the local scene, which strongly reminds one of Twain's remarks on the Gilded Age, Pike wrote:

This is the age of sham and imitation, of brown-stone veneering, stucco, galvanic plating, and mansard roofs on houses of three stories and nine inch walls, of false hair, teeth, and bosoms,—the paper-collar age; and men are veneered with a sanctimony as thinly as cheap furniture is with mahogany… .

Let the lash fall on the knave's back and the hypocrite's, on the loins of the charlatan and the pettifogger, of the coiner and utterer of lies, the corrupter of the public morals, the compounder with villainy and the fingerer of bribes. Mercy to them is injustice to their victims and to the defrauded State: and, as has been said, "Indignation against villainy is a feeling wonderfully strong in wise men, and wonderfully weak in fools."[6]

For that reason, to sell out was a very serious matter. Not only did the person damage himself but those around him. Pike expresses this in some very direct language on those who sell out their own ethics or morality.

To be the pimp of the Great is one of the saddest sights in the world: to be the pimp of the Small is an unspeakable abasement.[7]

Or, in one his essays:

To be the sycophant of the great is bad enough and common enough: to be the sycophant of the small is beneath the dignity of an ape.[8]

But Pike never held the passions or the animal nature of man in contempt; he celebrated humanity and insisted that, if one is to be truly happy, the duality of man must be given full consideration while keeping the spiritual nature dominant. In this he was swimming against a popular idea of his time which filled the pulpits. It was the custom to insist the world and all its ways were evil, and that the spiritual person should have nothing to do with it. Pike found that idea both ridiculous and insulting.

Masonry does not occupy itself with crying down this world, with its splendid beauty, its thrilling interests, its glorious works, its noble and holy affections; nor exhort us to detach our hearts from this earthly life, as empty, fleeting, and unworthy, and fix them upon Heaven, as the only sphere deserving the love of the loving or the meditation of the wise. It teaches that man has high duties to perform, and a high destiny to fulfill, on this earth; that this world is not merely the portal to another; and that this life,

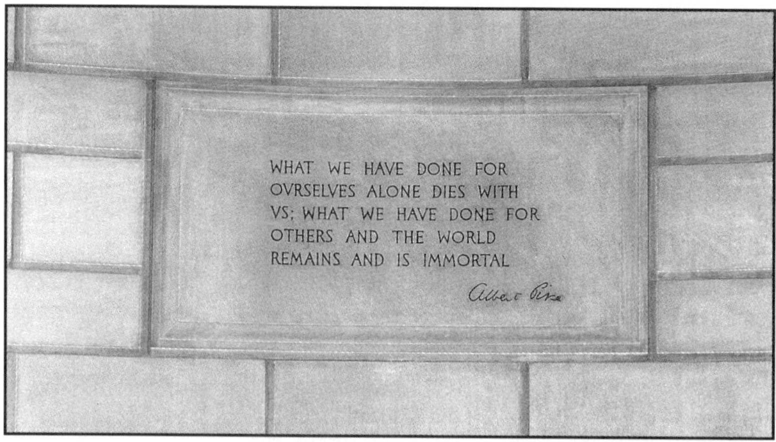

An inscription (85" x 45") on the granite wall of the Grand Staircase in the House of the Temple in Washington, D. C., records Albert Pike's most famous words and includes his signature. Photo: M. Russell Stogsdill

though not our only one, is an integral one, and the particular one with which we are here meant to be concerned; that the Present is our scene of action, and the Future for speculation and for trust; that man was sent upon the earth to live in it, to enjoy it, to study it, to love it, to embellish it, to make the most of it. It is his country, on which he should lavish his affections and his efforts. It is here his influences are to operate. It is his house, and not a tent; his home, and not *merely* a school. He is sent into this world, not to be constantly hankering after, dream of, preparing for another; but to do his duty and fulfill his destiny on this earth; to do all that lies in his power to improve it, to render it a scene of elevated happiness to himself, to those around him, to those who are to come after him. His life here is *part* of his immortality; and this world, also, is among the stars.[9]

It is a serious thing to defame and belie a whole world; to speak of it as the abode of a poor, toiling, drudging, ignorant, contemptible race. You would not so discredit your family, your friendly circle, your village, your city, your country. The world is not a wretched and worthless one; nor is it a misfortune, but a thing to be thankful for, to be a man. If life is worthless, so also is immortality.[10]

Morality is a difficult topic to discuss. Yet one of Pike's most beautiful passages is in the ritual for the Reception of a Louveteau—a young man for whom a Lodge is accepting a special responsibility.

So far as I know, the ceremony has rarely if ever been performed—which seems a pity, because it is one of great beauty.

In this passage, Pike is explaining the concept of morality to the young man—usually about 12 years of age. And he explains it all so clearly, so simply, and with such natural ease.

You are fond of enjoying yourselves. You like to play, and you do not like to study. This is very natural. It is not wrong, but right. Why should you not like pleasure better than work? But when there is anything you *ought* to do, anything that your parents wish you to do, anything that you can do to help a friend or even an enemy, you *know* that you ought to do it, although it will interfere with your amusements, and cause you labor and trouble. It is reflection and reason that tell you this, and when these and your sense of what is right get the better of your fondness for amusement and inclination to be idle, you are satisfied with yourself, because you know you have done your duty. You have conquered. You have acted bravely, and you have a right to be proud of it, and everybody ought to think better of you for it, for you have been resolute and brave, and done your duty.

That is what we are all put here to do—our Duty. If we do it,

Photo: Earl McDonald

W. A. Sharp's 1909 bronze bas relief tablet (39″ x 20″) shows Albert Pike in a Masonic Lodge delivering a lecture from *Morals and Dogma.*

we are good and brave. But if we let indolence and selfishness become our masters, and keep us from doing our duty, then we are very weak and contemptible persons, and shall never do anything worth anybody's recollecting when we are dead.

Now this is what is meant when you are told that you ought to love others as you love yourself. You do not think that you can do that. You do not feel that you *can* love a schoolfellow, and much less one who has wronged you, as you do yourself. You think it does not stand to reason that you should. You cannot help thinking so, and therefore it is not wrong to think so.

You know what is meant by loving your father, mother, sisters, and those who are always kind to you; and you know that you do *not* have the same feeling toward those who hate and wrong you. You know that you *cannot.* No one does or can. But you can forgive an enemy, and be kind to him, as you can to all your companions. You can feel disposed to do them favors. You can get the better of any desire to harm them. That is what is meant by *loving* them.

But what perplexes you is that you are to love them as you love yourself. It is of no use, you think, to try to do that, for you cannot do it. Let us see. You can forgive them, instead of taking revenge, as you are prompted to do by passion. Is that not loving them *better* than you love revenge? You can give up some pleasure to benefit or gratify them. That is to love them better than you love pleasure. You can do a great many things for them because you *ought,* though it costs you trouble and labor, and deprives you of pleasures and indulgence; and when you do so, you love them better than you love yourself.

This is what all good Masons try to do, and we hope you will try to do it. You will not always do it, because no one *always* does what he ought. Sometimes we must punish those who do us injury, that they may not be encouraged to continue doing so, and go from bad to worse, and that others, seeing they escape and have the profits of the wrong they do, may not be tempted to do the same. But we must not punish because we hate them, or for revenge, or for satisfaction.

If you see a boy who is crippled or deformed, you do not *hate* him for it, and it is very wrong and cruel to make fun of him for it. It is a misfortune to be crippled and deformed. It makes him unhappy, and you ought to be kind to him. For you would think it very hard if we should hate or despise you for something you could not help. If you think it hard and cruel and wrong for us to do that, you must not yourself do it. This is the meaning of the saying, "Do unto others that only, and all that, which you would have them do unto you."

Now, a bad, cruel, malicious, revengeful disposition, and evil heart, a lying tongue, a depraved mind, are greater deformities than a crooked body or a hump on the back. They are much sorer misfortunes, and make those afflicted with them more miserable; and we ought the more to pity them.

I think you understand all this. If you do, you understand what your duties to yourself and others are.[11]

The concept of values was closely allied with morality in Pike's thinking. He saw the ability to set the right value on things as an essential part of man's moral development. In his essay "Of Values," he provides some powerful images,

Lift off the city's roof, Asmodeus![†] In one ill-furnished squalid room we see a man of repulsive aspect, with unkempt hair and haggard features, and hungry, cruel eyes, industriously filing, at midnight, upon a rude key,—its money value could be but a few pence. In the next house, another, with a face cheerful, though pale and thin, is filing a thin strip of steel; and in a narrow cell, with a little barred aperture to admit the air, and walls of naked stone, a third is with a like instrument filing the mainspring of a watch into a saw. It is the same dull, tiresome, monotonous labour to each, but is it of the same value to each? With the saw he is making, the convict will cut asunder the bars of his grate; and the value of his labour to him is liberty, and

† An allusion to an old Spanish story, referenced in Washington Irving's *Tales of the Alhambra,* in which a student has a demon, Asmodeus, remove the roofs of the city so that he can see the activities of the occupants.

that liberty to him is life; for by the stern sentence of the law, death awaits him, if the cell holds him until morning.

The little strip of steel on which the honest artizan works, is to be the spring of a chronometer, by means of which determining his longitude, the Master of some ship, sailing from the Indian Sea and daring the stormy antarctic cape, will reach into quiet latitudes, bring the good vessel safely into port, clasp his loved wife to his bosom, and feel his children's arms around his neck. The value of that little strip of steel and of the work upon it, is to be like that of the needle of the compass, incalculable. With the rude key, fashioned after an impression stealthily taken in wax, the burglar will enter an old man's house, and with soft steps glide to his chamber, to rob him of his gold. The miser wakes, clings to the robber and cries for help, and the burglary becomes murder. The price of this man's work is his life; and it is paid him when he swings, strangled, from that instrument of civilization which everywhere stretches its arm over the pulpit while its black shadow falls upon the palace.[12]

And consider this passage on moral values, as Pike reflects over his life.

What a conclusive proof of the abundant and inexhaustible benefice of God it is, that even in the autumn of life we are capable of loving, and that it is still possible for us to be beloved! What a boon, at any time of our life, to have friends and need not be without someone by whom to be loved! And yet how ready men are to put friendship and love in hazard, in the reckless pursuit of place, titles or wealth; to stake the soul, even, and lose it, to win a pitiful counter that is not even a representative of value!

We are too commonly as ignorant of the true values of life as the statesmen are; and we reap misery as the consequence, as the nations reap ruin. It is much if we come at last, when the winter of life is near, to know those values. The beauties of nature, the enjoyment of a contented life in the society of nature, content itself, peace of mind, social intercourse, the approval of our conscience, the genial affections, freedom from greed and ambition, the possession of friendship and love,—all these…are the true wealth of the spiritual Indies, within the reach of everyone who has a heart and a soul to enjoy them. We are commonly too prone to value the dust in the balance, …to clutch its worthless pebbles, and to grovel on the earth, when we might have lived among the stars.[13]

V

Devotee Of The Goddess Nicotine

On Pike And His Pipes

In 1919, a committee was appointed to make suggestions for and to oversee the design of the Scottish Rite Temple in Guthrie, Oklahoma. They designed a space outside the first balcony of the auditorium and opening into the Atrium which they designated the Social Promenade. Their notes read, "Here the devotees of the goddess Nicotine may stroll, take their leisure, and with pipe and cigar send aloft those clouds of incense which their rites make obligatory."

Pike could have been elected Hierophant of those devotees, on the first ballot and without opposition. And if the writings of his friends are correct and he not only loved but frequently committed abominable puns, Pike would have heartily seconded the line of Charles Lamb, English writer, wit, and one of Pike's favorite authors: "May my last breath be inhaled through a pipe and exhaled in a pun!"

Pipes and tobacco crop up with some frequency (and always with a sense of sincere reverence) in Pike's work. In his later years, he wrote he had:

> ...one habit, that many will term a vice,—that of smoking to excess. I have an affection for my pipes.[†] They are indispensable to my well-being. Except when sleeping or eating, or in places where it would be improper, I smoke them all the time. I smoke walking, sitting or reclining, while I talk and while I write. And yet one hardly knows in what the charm of smoking exists.
>
> The act itself is but drawing smoke into the mouth, and permitting it to escape from it; and yet what a pleasure it is idly to lie and watch the blue rings of the smoke revolve, recede and disappear. It soothes and quiets and consoles us, this seemingly useless habit.[1]

[†] It should be noted, perhaps, that the Surgeon General of the United States does not necessarily share Pike's appreciation of tobacco.

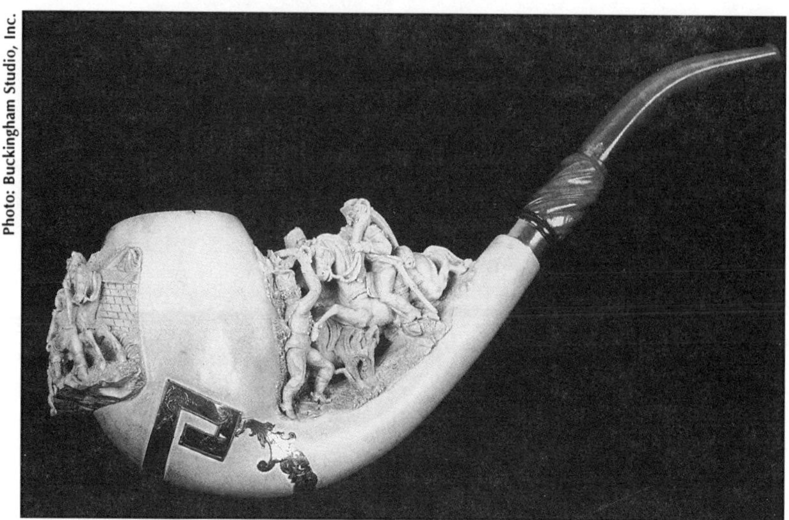

Photo: Buckingham Studio, Inc.

Pike was serious about his smoking. A regular pipe is to his favorite, big, and well-smoked one (pictured above), as a glass of champagne is to a magnum. This pipe was made of meerschaum, a claylike, heat-resistant mineral found primarily in Turkey. Meerschaum slowly colors from its natural pure white through a beautiful golden color to a rich autumn brown. To smoke and color a meerschaum pipe properly is the ultimate test of the art of pipe smoking, and Pike's pipe is perfectly colored. Had we no other evidence of the excellence of his temperament and the quality of his spirit, that pipe alone would bear adequate testimony. To color even a small meerschaum well is painstaking work. To color one the size of Pike's pipe well bespeaks a patience and nobility granted to few mortals.

It was a joy of his life, the solace of his soul-trying hours. And some subhuman abomination purloined it!

I regard my pipes, chiefly the gifts of friends, some of whom are dead, with a true affection. When, lately, one carved of meerschaum, with most elaborate and delicate tracing given to me by a friend who died soon afterwards, was stolen by a Bohemian vagabond, I pursued him unrelentingly, and with a savage pleasure heard him sentenced to a year's confinement in the penitentiary.[†]

I could have forgiven the theft more easily than his selling the pipe for the miserable sum of two dollars and a half, as if it had not cost a thousand franks and won the large gold medal at the

---

[†] Alas, even recovered pipes do not remain forever. In the mid-1980s before the present security system was in place, Pike's favorite pipe was kidnapped again, this time from the Pike Room in the House of the Temple in Washington, D.C. All we have left is the photograph.

Paris Exposition. One could forgive a thief who knew the value of what he stole, and valuing it accordingly, kept it.

Why should I have been so relentless toward the unfortunate knave who stole my pipe? Chiefly, I think, because he did not steal it through a love for the artistic and beautiful, or as a pipe, to smoke which would be more pleasantly soothing because "stolen pleasures are sweetest,"† but as something to be sold, and out of a sordid desire for currency.[2]

Pike was not a late convert to the joys of the pipe. Near the beginning of his life, when he was on his famous explorations outside the then boundaries of the United States across what would become Oklahoma and New Mexico, his party had been without food for some days when they encountered an Indian encampment.

We went into the tent. It was a little cool. I took out a pipe and filled it with tobacco and took a couple of puffs and handed the pipe to the chief and he took a couple of puffs, and then we knew we were safe....

Well, we ran out of tobacco, and that was awful. I remember, I made a pipe out of a piece of oak, and killed a crane and took the leg bone for a stem. When we got out of tobacco we came across a Delaware Indian and his wife.... He gave us some tobacco and he gave us a coon to eat. They were very generous; we have nothing to give him in return. We did give him some little thing or other, but we did not have much to give.[3]

And of a later encounter with an encampment of Osage, he wrote:

After the conference was over, I produced my pipe and began to fill it. A half dozen pipes were immediately shown, and requests were made for tobacco, to which I was, of course, bound to respond, and we had a general smoke. We passed the remainder of this day and the next with them, and were called upon, every hour in the day, to go to some lodge and eat.[4]

And even later:

The contents of the brass kettle were then emptied into a wooden bowl, and placed before us. It was the boiled flesh of a fat buffalo cow, perfectly fresh—and a most delicious meal it was to eat. Kettle after

Pike with one of his favorite pipes

† Speaking of puns!

kettle was filled and emptied, between us and the family of the chief; for it takes but five minutes to boil this meat. A man never knows how much meat he can eat, until he has tried the prairie, but I assure the reader that four pounds at a meal is no great allowance, especially to a hungry man. On ending supper, we paid them with tobacco and a knife or two, and returned to our camp—not, however, without that indispensable ceremony, a general smoke, in which my pipe went once or twice around the whole party, women and all.[5]

In Pike's last years, the pipe remained a primary source of pleasure. In his essay "Of My Books and Studies," Pike describes the pleasure of study in his library in winter. The whole passage is included in Chapter XVI, "Images," but one part fits too well here not to include it.

But I like my library best during the winter, and on the long evenings when the wind, whistling shrilly in the chimney, rattles the loose windows, and I close the shutters and let the curtain fall, and with the coal fire glowing and the lamp softly burning, I lounge and smoke my pipe—indispensable and most faithful companion of all but my eating and sleeping hours—or read or write or muse in the great leather-cushioned chairs.[6]

That passage was written in Pike's last years. It's interesting to compare it to one of the first things he wrote, an article published when he was 21. The article was printed in the *American Monthly Magazine,* an extremely popular periodical in the 1800s. Clearly, this is an early work. The humor is sometimes cumbersome, but, withal, it's a pleasure. "The Philosophy of a Cigar" was published in July, 1830.

I am an inveterate smoker—and therefore I see no reason why I should not descant upon that delight and luxury, as well as other men upon reading, music, poetry and painting. I admire to sit down in the cool of the morning, with some grammar of some language, or some book of a strange tongue before me, and smoke myself into forgetfulness. It is then that I see an Italian sunrise—a Grecian noon or sunset; it is then that maidens come dancing before me, as I am reading and learning expressions of endearment and love, in some soft language—Spanish maids, with the black eyes, and noble features, and beautiful forms—the merry girls of France, with what Hunt would call their laughingness and chattiness—and those of Italy and Greece, the most superb and magnificent of heaven's creatures. Then it is that I lie under orange trees, or in ruined temples, and hear soft music. Oh! there is nothing like a cigar and the study of a modern language in the morning.

Pike's Pipes

One of the highlights of the Pike Room in the House of the Temple is Albert Pike's personal collection of pipes. Pike was an inveterate smoker and collected pipes throughout his life, smoking them with relish until his last days in Washington, D.C.

Pictured in the center of the photo to the right is the longest, a 4 1/2 foot meerschaum pipe which overshadows its companions that range from an Indian red-stone peace pipe (far right) to a pioneer corncob pipe (below, lower right). Also, pictured to the right to indicate scale, is one of Pike's writing quills.

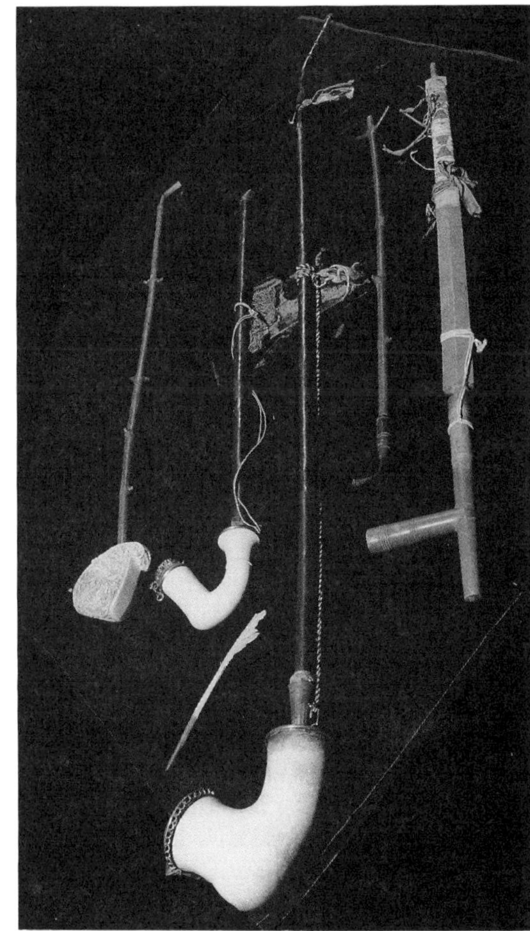

Photos: M. Russell Stogsdill

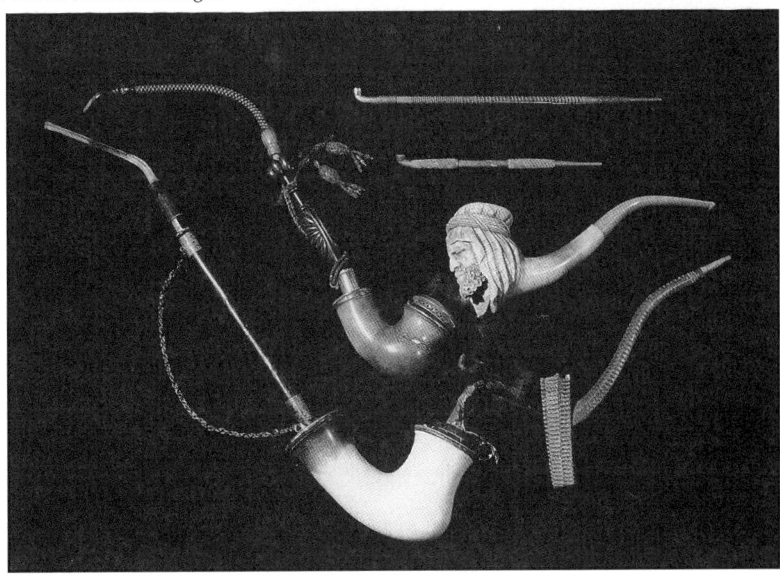

Albert Pike

At night, just after sunset, when the sky is all covered with streamers and banners of gold and jewelry, as if it were unrolling and showing the heavens above it, when I have left my slavery—for I confess in sorrow, but not in shame, that I am a pedagogue—then to sit down, open all the windows, and bury yourself in some fine poem or novel—to be on the silent seas with Coleridge, or under the ruined tower with Genevieve—to be with Shelley away among the clouds of Caucasus, or with his lark, in the sun-light, to range the bottom of the sea with Keats, or sleep with him, with our eyes wide open, in the moon-light, or to walk in the spirit above the earth with Byron; to revel in the pages of Scott or Bulwer; or, more delicious still, to get among the writers of olden days—Oh! there is nothing like this—with your cigar half neglected between your lips—with a kind of half conscious, half positive, idle delight—the most delicious thing in the world—there is nothing like it, indeed—I don't know anything which can be compared to it—it is the most perfect species of Epicurism, joined, as it is, to the mental pleasures.[†]

I hold that it requires a man of good mind to enjoy a cigar. It requires a man who relishes those little nice pleasures, which the *world* never enjoys—such a man as would like the beautiful little jewels of Keats, and the burning flashes of Shelley—such a man as would relish, ay, start to his feet and tingle all over at hearing some of the high notes of Ostinelli's violin[‡]—a man of beautiful, nice and discriminating mind. I think I am far

[†] This is a good example of a style which Pike was to perfect in his later life. This entire paragraph is one sentence, containing 218 words. Near the end it begins to falter a little, to move less than smoothly, and yet, in all those words it is never hard to follow the idea. You don't lose the train in spite of all the cars, parallel tracks and switch-backs. Readers who wish mentally to insert here a phrase in the railroad jargon of "following one's conductor without fear" are at liberty to do so.

[‡] The reader may recall that Pike played violin to accompany Ostinelli.

enough from it yet, but I do hope someday or other to think myself worthy of a cigar. I have a friend, however, of this stamp. I have walked with him, and ridden by his side, when he has been silent for a half hour, and at last has broken the stillness by whispering some line or two of one or the other of his favorite poets—and I believe that I may thank him for all the love I bear to poetry. His taste is exquisite; and he is the only man that I know who enjoys a cigar—that is, as a cigar ought to be enjoyed....

There are men who should never be allowed to smoke a cigar. I have one in my mind's eye, now, who read the Anciente Marinere and told me *it was pretty!* That man would as soon devour a 'long nine'† as revel upon a true luxury from l'Habana. There is another too, who has told me that he would not give a farthing to hear the beautiful sweetnesses of Ostinelli.... *He* would go to sleep with one of my best cigars in his mouth. Then there is one who tells me that Coleridge and Byron are unnatural; and that they are too violent; professing at the same time to know a hawk from a handsaw. He would put a lump of sugar in the best yellow cigar that ever came up by Cape Hatteras, to sweeten the flavor....

People talk of the pleasure of following out a geometrical theorem; or of working a difficult equation in algebra—pooh! much more delightful is it to choose a cigar, and find yourself right—to examine the light and almost imperceptible down on the clear, bright, unspecked surface of a cigar—(yellow if you please, though I like the perfectly black—they are not so common, but I get them sometimes—a beautiful mild cigar, with a perfume sweeter than the gales of Araby). Then to introduce it between your lips—to find no difficulty in smoking, and to see the smoke rolling out and up, and hear the tobacco crackle a little as the fire devours it—Oh, it is glorious![7]

†A large but very cheap (as well as inexpensive) cigar of the time.

VI

The Craft He Loved And Served

On Masonry

It will come as no surprise that a great deal of Albert Pike's writing is concerned with Masonry. When, in 1850, he received the three degrees of Blue Lodge Masonry at Western Star Lodge No. 2, in Little Rock, he knew he had found a home. The more he reflected upon the degrees, the more excited he became.

[Masonry] began to shape itself to my intellectual vision into something imposing and majestic, solemnly mysterious and grand. It seemed to me like the Pyramids in grandeur and loneliness, in whose yet undiscovered chambers may be hidden, for the enlightenment of the coming generations, the sacred books of the Egyptians, so long lost to the world; like the Sphinx half-buried in the sand.... So I came at last to see that [Masonry's] symbolism is its soul.[1]

VIEWED FROM THE OUTSIDE

Pike was fully aware that Masonry, viewed from the outside by those who have never taken the trouble to understand it, can seem rather pointless and strange. In *The Meaning of Masonry,* Pike looks with dispassion at some of those outside opinions, but he then explains just why Masonry is valuable to the man and to the world, and Pike's statement makes a good starting point for our look at the Craft.

It is indeed true that the world at large, the statesmen and the men of business, are not in the habit of attaching much importance to the peaceful operations, the active efforts and silent influences of Masonry. Some even think evil of the order; to others its pretensions are the subject of mirth and food for ridicule; while probably the general impression is that it is a harmless and inoffensive association, rather laudable for its benevolent propensities, its charities, and the assistance its members mutually lend each other; but one in which the world at large is in no wise interested, one whose ceremonies are frivolous, its secrets mere pretense, its titles and dignities absurd, and its dissensions mere childish disputes for barren honors and an empty precedency, fit only to excite the pitying smiles of the grave and the sarcastic laughter of the ill-natured....

Is *society* really interested in the peace and progress of Masonry? Has the world a moral right to demand that harmony shall govern in our Temples? Is that a matter which at all concerns the community? *How* grave and important are the interests that by our mad dissensions we recklessly put at hazard?

Such are the questions which it is demanded of me to consider. To do so, it is evidently necessary first to settle what Masonry *is*, and what its *objects* are, and by what *means* and appliances it proposes to effect those objects.

The well-being of every nation, like that of every individual, is threefold,—*physical, moral,* and *intellectual.* Neither physically, morally, or intellectually is a people ever *stationary*. Always it either advances or retrogrades; and, as when one climbs a hill of ice, to *advance* demands continual effort and exertion, while to slide *downward* one needs but to halt.

The happiness and prosperity of a people consist in advancing on each of the three lines, physical, moral, and intellectual, at once; for the day of its downfall draws nearer, even when its intellect is more developed and the works of its genius are more illustrious, and while its physical comforts increase, if its moral progress does not keep pace with its physical and intellectual,[†] and yet without the last, the two first do not make the loftiest condition of a great people.

That institution deserves the title of "public benefactor," which by a system of judicious charities and mutual assistance diminishes the sum total of haggard want and destitution, and relieves the public of a portion of the burden which the necessities of the poor and shelterless impose upon it: for it thus aids the *physical* advancement of the people.

It still more deserves the title, if in addition, it imperatively requires of its members the strict and faithful performance of all those duties towards their fellow-men as individuals, which the loftiest and purest morality enjoins; and so is the potent auxiliary of the laws, and the enforcer of the moral precepts of the *Great Teacher* who preached the Sermon on the Mount: for it thus labors for the moral elevation of the people.

[†] Pike was remarkably right on this one. How many serious commentators in the fields of medicine, genetics, communications, and other sciences have commented in the last few years that our technology has outstripped our ethics in those areas? And how many of us have wondered why, with increased education, increased opportunities and increased wealth, we also find more poverty, more street crime, and less feeling of security in our daily lives?

And still *more*, if its initiates are also, and of necessity, devoted to the true interests of the people; if they are the soldiery of Liberty, Equality and Brotherhood, and at the same time of good government, of good order, and of the laws, that made by the representatives of all, for the general good of all, must be implicitly obeyed by all: for thus again it aids in elevating still higher the *moral* character of the people.

And *most of all*, if in addition to all this, it strives to elevate the people *intellectually*, by teaching those who enter its portals the profoundest truths of Philosophy, and the wisdom of the Sages of every age; a rational conception of the Deity; of the universe that He has made, and of the laws that govern it; a true estimate of Man himself, of his freedom to act, of his dignity and his destiny.[2]

With that as an overview, how does Masonry go about it?

THE SEARCH FOR LIGHT

The primary symbol of Masonry is, of course, Light. The search for Light is a symbol of education, of knowledge, of enlightenment. *Lux*, meaning light, for instance, is in the mottoes of Yale University and the University of North Carolina. The movement from Darkness to Light, consequently, has played a part in the initiatory rites of all ages and all cultures, as the late Joseph Campbell, noted lecturer and author of *The Hero with a Thousand Faces*, so often demonstrated. Pike remarks:

To the ancients, this [Light] was an outflowing from the Deity. To us, as to them, it is the apt symbol of truth and knowledge.[3]

Masonry is a march and a struggle toward the Light. For the individual as well as the nation, Light is Virtue, Manliness, Intelligence, Liberty. Tyranny over the soul or body, is darkness.[4]

Masonry to the Masonic Brethren is a search after, and a journeying toward Light. The Masonic Light is Truth. It is the inculcation of truth by means of symbols and instructions. Teaching a pure morality by its lessons and lectures, it is also a great system of philosophy and of political and of religious truth concealed by symbols.[5]

THE STRUGGLE TO BE SOMETHING MORE THAN ANIMAL

Closely bound with the search for Light is the struggle to overcome and subordinate the Dark, the passions of the body. Chapter XI, "The Pleasures of the Flesh, the Balance of the Spirit," will explore that question more fully, but a few brief comments by Pike make the Masonic position clear.

Masonry is the struggle of the Divine in us to overcome the human. This is our march towards the Light.[6]

Freemasonry is, or ought to be, a constant endeavor to subordinate that which in us is material, sensual, and human to that which is spiritual, rational, and Divine.[7]

Its charitable nature comes from the fact that Masonry cuts across the artificial barriers which separate men.

[Masonry] is philanthropic; for it recognizes the great truth that all men are of the same origin, have common interests, and should co-operate together to the same end.[8]

THE SECRETS OF MASONRY

The "secrets" in Masonry are personal insights. They are secret not because we are pledged to conceal them, but because they cannot be truly communicated from one person to another.

It is for each individual Mason to discover the secret of Masonry, by reflection upon its symbols and a wise consideration and analysis of what is said and done in the work. Masonry does not *inculcate* [impress upon the mind by frequent repetition] her truths. She *states* them, once and briefly; or hints them, perhaps, darkly; or interposes a cloud between them and eyes that would be dazzled by them. "*Seek*, and ye shall find," knowledge and the truth.[9]

THE ANTIQUITY OF THE FRATERNITY

Few questions have led to so much confusion, not to mention so much spilled ink, as the question of the antiquity of the fraternity. The only answer is, of course, we just don't know how old Freemasonry is. Masonic writers have placed the origin (mythically) at the Garden of Eden, the building of Solomon's Temple, or the continuance of the Knights Templar. Allen E. Roberts, in *Masonic Trivia and Facts* (1994), states that at least 24 theories regarding Masonry's origins have held credence at some time.

Pike in 32nd Degree regalia

Pike, it must be admitted, added fuel to the fire, not by what he wrote so much as by the fact that people did not take the time to understand what he wrote. Pike uses the word "Masonry" to mean two different things. One is an attitude, a view of the world. The other is the fraternity itself. It really isn't hard to figure out in any given case which he means—Pike is too good a writer not to make his meanings clear. But he assumed that someone who read *Morals and Dogma* would come to it with a fair background knowledge in Masonry itself. And he assumed that one would read the book from start to finish—not dip into it here and there looking for a sentence of phrase which could be made to mean something he never intended.

Thus, when he speaks of Masonry as being the successor to the Mysteries, he does not mean that we have somehow kept the ancient rites of Adonis or Osiris going through the centuries. He means that Masonry, like the Mysteries, teaches by means of initiation and through the use of symbols.

And he is equally clear when he is talking about the Freemasonic fraternity itself.

It is of greater antiquity than other orders and associations; but is not so old as to give it the superiority once supposed; for it is now certain that there were no Degrees in Masonry two hundred years ago; and that the Master's Degree is not more than one hundred and sixty years of age.[10]

But those who framed its Degrees adopted the most sacred and significant symbols of a very remote antiquity, used, many centuries before the Temple of the King, Solomon, was built, to express to those who understood them, while concealing from the profane, the most recondite and mysterious doctrines in regard to God, the universe, and man.[11]

MASONRY AND RELIGION

This brings us to another unnecessary confusion, a confusion between Freemasonry and Religion. Anti-Masons are always trying to claim that Masonry is a religion, and they are perfectly willing to invent a doctrine, a theology, and a plan of salvation which they claim Freemasonry teaches. They would *have* to invent it for us, because we certainly don't have one of our own.

And again, poor old Albert gets blamed for most of it. In his writing, he uses the word "religion" to mean two things as well. And again, one of them is an attitude—the sort of thing we might call "spiritual awareness" a conscious or unconscious awareness of the Deity and a desire to do what is pleasing to Him. Pike insists this attitude permeates all human life.

An example is his oft-misquoted line, "Every Masonic Lodge is a temple of religion."[12] Pike has, of course, just spent the two and a half pages before that line explaining what he means by *religion*. He

Pike's 33rd Degree Scottish Rite eagle pendant

points out that there is a religion of work, which is to work honestly and fairly, giving full value for the wages received. He points out that there is a religion to law, when the law is used with justice and equity and mercy to improve the lives of people. He gives several other examples. And then, just in case the reader has missed it up to this point, Pike clearly explains what he means when he says a Lodge is a temple of religion. One just has to read the next few sentences.

Every Masonic Lodge is a temple of religion; and its teachings are instruction in religion. For here are inculcated disinterestedness [unselfishness], affection, toleration, devotedness, patriotism, truth, a generous sympathy with those who suffer and mourn, pity for the fallen, mercy for the erring, relief for those in want, Faith, Hope, Charity. Here we meet as brethren, to learn to know and love each other.[13]

But Masonry is not a religion in the sense that the term is generally used, the sense in which we would speak of Christianity or Islam or Judaism as a religion. And Pike makes that perfectly clear.

Masonry is as little a religious sect as it is a political party. As it embraces all parties, so it embraces all sects, to form from among them all a vast fraternal association. The morals of antiquity, of the law of Moses, and of Christianity, are ours. We recognize every teacher of Morality, every Reformer, as a Brother. No one Mason has the right to measure for another, within the walls of a Masonic Temple, the degree of veneration which he shall feel for any Reformer, or the Founder of any Religion. We teach a belief in no particular creed, as we teach *un*-belief in none. In all religions there is a basis of Truth in all there are *fragments* at least of pure Morality. All that teach the cardinal tenets of Masonry, we respect; all teachers and reformers of mankind, we admire and revere.

We do not undervalue the importance of any Truth. We utter no word that can be deemed irreverent by any one of any faith. ... Masonry, of no one age, belongs to all time; of no one religion, it finds its great truths in all.

It is not disbelief nor skepticism. It has its own creed, simple and sublime, to which every good man of every religion can assent. It expounds all the old philosophies, and modestly and not oracularly utters its own.

To every Mason, there is a God—One, Supreme, Infinite in Goodness, in Wisdom, Foresight, Justice and Benevolence; Creator, Disposer and Preserver of all things. How, or by what Intermediates, Powers or Emanations He creates and acts, and in what way He unfolds and manifests Himself, Masonry leaves to Creeds and Religions to inquire.[14]

[Masonry] teaches what it deems to be the truth in respect to the nature and attributes of God, as the loving and beneficent Father of all mankind, as a Supreme and Perfect Intelligence, as not in anywise the gigantic and distorted image of a man reflected upon the clouds. It no more tolerates false *ideas* of the Deity and accepts *them* as God, than *images* of Him carved of wood or stone. To believe and teach the immortality of the soul, it must of necessity have some not *wholly* erroneous idea of the *nature* of the soul, or else its belief is but an idle formula of empty words.[15]

Following the success of his Civil War photographs, Matthew B. Brady founded a company which specialized in portraits of prominent Americans. Among Brady's subjects, as seen above, was Albert Pike photographed in the regalia of the Thirty-third Degree of the Scottish Rite of Freemasonry, S.J., USA.

The best gift we can bestow on man is manhood. It is that which Masonry is ordained of God to bestow on its votaries: not sectarianism and religious dogma; not a rudimental morality, that may be found in the writings of Confucius, Zoroaster, Seneca and the Rabbis, in the Proverbs and Ecclesiastes; not a little and cheap common-school knowledge; but manhood and science and philosophy.

Not that Philosophy or Science is in opposition to Religion. For Philosophy is but that knowledge of God and the Soul, which is derived from observation of the manifested action of God and the Soul, and from a wise analogy. It is the intellectual guide which the religious sentiment needs....

As to Science, it could not walk alone, while religion was stationary. It consists of those matured inferences from experience which all other experience confirms....

The purpose, therefore, of education and science is to make a man wise. If knowledge does not make him so, it is wasted, like water poured on the sands. To know the *formulas* of Masonry [the words of the ritual] is of as little value, by itself, as to know so many words and sentences in some barbarous African or Australian dialect. To know even the *meaning* of the symbols, is but little, unless that adds to our wisdom, and also to our charity....

Do not lose sight, then, of the true object of your studies in Masonry. It is to add to your estate of wisdom, and not merely to your knowledge.... It is the great truths as to all that most concerns a man, as to his rights, interests, and duties, that Masonry tries to teach her Initiates.[16]

THE ATTITUDE AND ACTIONS OF A MASON

So what is the effect? How is a Mason supposed to act and think and feel? What are we supposed to do? Pike sets a pretty high standard. His friend George Moore summed up Pike's position in a few words:

For him the true Mason is he who each day strives to make some other man wiser and better, and who, for that purpose, constantly strives to become wiser and better.[17]

Pike expends some of his best writing on the question of just who a Mason is supposed to be and what he is to do.

To be trustful, to be hopeful, to be indulgent; these, in an age of selfishness, of ill opinion of human nature, of harsh and bitter judgment, are the most important Masonic virtues, and the true supports of every Masonic Temple.[18]

To sleep little, and to study much; to say little, and to hear and think much; to learn, that we may be able to do, and then to do, earnestly and vigorously, whatever may be required of us by duty, and by the good of our fellows, our country, and mankind,—these are the duties of every Mason who desires to imitate the Master Khūrūm [Hiram].[19]

To make honor and duty the steady beacon-lights that shall guide your life-vessel over the stormy seas of time; to do that which is right to do, not because it will insure you success, or bring with it a reward, or gain the applause of men, or be "the best policy," more prudent or more advisable; but because it *is* right and therefore *ought* to be done; to war incessantly against error, intolerance, ignorance, and vice, and yet to pity those who err, to be tolerant, even of intolerance, to teach the ignorant, and to labor to reclaim the vicious, are some of the duties of a Mason.[20]

The true Mason is a practical Philosopher, who, under religious emblems, in all ages adopted by wisdom, builds upon plans traced by nature and reason the moral edifice of knowledge. He ought to find, in the symmetrical relations of all the parts of this rational edifice, the principle and rule of all his duties, the source of all his pleasures. He improves his moral nature, becomes a better man, and finds in the reunion of virtuous men, assembled with pure views, the means of multiplying his acts of beneficence. Masonry and Philosophy, without being one and the same thing, have the same object and propose to themselves the same end, the worship of the Grand Architect of the Universe, acquaintance and familiarity with the wonders of nature, and the happiness of humanity attained by the constant practice of all the virtues.[21]

There can be no genuine Brotherhood without mutual regard, good opinion and esteem, mutual charity, and mutual allowance for faults and failings. It is those only who learn habitually to think better of each other, to look habitually for the good that is in each other, and expect, allow for, and overlook, the evil, who can be Brethren one of the other, in any true sense of the word. Those who gloat over the failings of one another, who think each other to be naturally base and low, of a nature in which the Evil predominates and excellence is not to be looked for, cannot be even friends, and much less Brethren.[22]

Then he wrote this. It is, to my own personal tastes, probably the single most beautiful statement of Masons and Masonry I have ever read. And the astonishing, the wonderful, thing is there are hundreds of Masons I *know* who fit this description.

The good Mason does the good thing which comes in his way, and because it comes in his way; for a love of duty, and not merely because a law, enacted by man or God, commands his will to do it. He is true to his mind, his conscience, heart, and soul, and feels small temptation to do to others what he would not wish to receive from them. He will deny himself for the sake of his brother near at hand. His *desire* attracts in the line of his duty, both being in conjunction. Not in vain does the poor or the oppressed look up to him. You find such men in all Christian sects, Protestant and Catholic, in all the great religious parties of the civilized world, among Buddhists, Mahometans, and Jews. They are kind fathers, generous citizens, unimpeachable in their business, beautiful in their daily lives. You see their Masonry in their work and in their play. It appears in all the forms of their activity, individual, domestic, social, ecclesiastical, or political. True Masonry within must be morality without. It must become *eminent* morality, which is philanthropy. The true Mason loves not only his kindred and his country, but all mankind; not only the good, but also the evil, among his brethren. He has more goodness than the channels of his daily life will hold. It runs over the banks, to water and to feed a thousand thirsty plants. Not content with the duty that lies along his track, he goes out to seek it; not only *willing*, he has a salient *longing* to do good, to spread his truth, his justice, his generosity, his Masonry over all the world. His daily life is a profession of his Masonry, published in perpetual good-will to men. He *can*not be a persecutor.

Not more naturally does the beaver build or the mocking-bird sing his own wild, gushing melody, than the true Mason lives this beautiful outward life. So from the perennial spring swells forth the stream, to quicken the meadow with new access of green, and perfect beauty bursting into bloom. Thus Masonry does the work it was meant to do. The Mason does not sigh and weep, and make grimaces. He lives right on. If his life is, as whose is not, marked with errors, and with sins, he ploughs [plows] over the barren spot with his remorse, sows with new seed, and the old desert blossoms like a rose. He is not confined to set forms of thought, or

Pike's 33rd Degree jewel

action, or of feeling. He accepts what his mind regards as true, which his conscience decides is right, what his heart deems generous and noble; and all else he puts far from him. Though the ancient and the honorable of the Earth bid him bow down to them, his stubborn knees bend only at the bidding of his manly soul. His Masonry is his freedom before God, not his bondage unto men. His mind acts after the universal law of the intellect, his conscience according to the universal moral law, his affections and his soul after the universal law of each, and so he is strong with the strength of God, in this four-fold way communicating with Him.[23]

Pike could describe the ideal as well as anyone alive. But he was wise enough to realize that an ideal is just that. Reality will often fall short of it. That was all right as long as it was merely a matter of being human. It was as the sound of fingernails on a blackboard to Pike when people not only were prone to human error but also were stubborn about it.

It is the motionless and stationary that most frets and impedes the current of progress; the solid rock or stupid tree, rested firmly on the bottom, and around which the river whirls and eddies: the Masons that doubt and hesitate and are discouraged; that disbelieve in the capacity of man to improve; that are not disposed to toil and labor for the interest and well-being of general humanity; that expect others to do all, even of that which they do not oppose or ridicule; while they sit, applauding and doing nothing, or perhaps prognosticating [predicting] failure.[24]

Albert Pike in 33rd Degree collar

Men will be men, and human nature will be human nature. I suppose, in a way, it's comforting to know that the buzzard's roost, which one finds in some Lodges, composed of those determined to fight any idea they didn't think of themselves fifty years ago, isn't a recent development. But, buzzards and all, Pike still held high hopes and a high vision for Masonry.

The Moral Code of Masonry is still more extensive than that developed by philosophy. To the requirements of the law of Nature and the law of God, it adds the imperative obligation of a contract. Upcn entering the Order, the Initiate binds to himself every Mason in the world. Once enrolled among the children of Light, every Mason on earth becomes his brother, and owes him the duties, the kindnesses, and the sympathies of a brother. On every one he may call for assistance in need, protection against danger, sympathy in sorrow, attention in sickness, and decent burial after death. There is not a Mason in the world who is not bound to go to his relief, when he is in danger, if there be a greater probability of saving his life than of losing his own. No Mason can wrong him to the value of anything, knowingly, himself, nor suffer it to be done by others, if it be in his power to prevent it. No Mason can speak evil of him, to his face or behind his back. Every Mason must keep his lawful secrets, and defend his character when unjustly assailed, and protect, counsel, and assist his widow and his orphans. What so many thousands owe to him, he owes to each of them. He has solemnly bound himself to be ever ready to discharge this sacred debt. If he fails to do it he is dishonest, and forsworn; and it is an unparalleled meanness in him to obtain good offices [kindnesses] by false pretenses, to receive kindness and service, rendered him under the confident expectation that he will in his turn render the same, and then to disappoint, without ample reason, that just expectation.

Masonry holds him also, by his solemn promise, to a purer life, a nobler generosity, catholic [universal] in his love for his race [the human race], ardent in his zeal for the interest of mankind, the advancement and progress of humanity.

Such are, we think, the Philosophy and the Morality, such the True Word of a Master Mason.[25]

VII

All Were Precious In His Sight

On Brotherhood And Social Relations

It is sad, but, perhaps, inevitable that a man who so loved life and his fellowmen, and who constantly taught Brotherhood and Toleration, should be branded a bigot by those who would harm both his reputation and his fraternity. It is self-commenting that the loudest of these few contemporary attackers, Lyndon LaRouche, should be a convicted felon with political ambitions. Frorn that position of dubious integrity and moral worth, he denounces Pike as not only a racist but a plotter against the Constitution—the same Constitution which Pike defended so strongly that he became unpopular in the South before the Civil War.

Pike's position was simple, straightforward, and frequently stated. He believed in, and used Masonry to teach, three great virtues: *Liberty, Fraternity, Equality*.

And he believed in all three. In equality, he went considerably further, as we will see, than most of the thinkers of his time. And since, for some reason which is a little hard to understand, women are now commonly classified as a minority (although in the majority), we'll take a look at some of his writings about women as well.

Writing about this area today does present a dilemma which Pike did not face. The "politically correct" terms to use for various minorities changes so rapidly that one writing today cannot be certain the words will not offend tomorrow. (Anyone who remembers that "Republican" historically used to mean "Democrat" can understand the problems with words changing meanings and "political" correctness.) So, if offense is given, it is not intended—either by Pike or this author.

As a starting point, then, what does Pike have to say about Liberty, Fraternity, and Equality.

LIBERTY, FRATERNITY, EQUALITY

From the political point of view there is but a single principle,—the sovereignty of man over himself. The sovereignty of one's self over one's self is called LIBERTY. Where two or several of these sovereignties associate, the State begins. But in this association there is no abdication. Each sovereignty parts with a certain portion of itself to form the common right. That portion is the same for all. There is equal contribution by all to the joint sovereignty. This identity of concession which each makes to all, is EQUALITY. The common right is nothing more or less than the protection of all, pouring its rays on each. This protection of each by all, is FRATERNITY. Liberty is the summit, Equality the base. Equality is not all vegetation on a level, a society of big spears of grass and stunted oaks, a neighborhood of jealousies, emasculating each other. It is, civilly, all aptitudes having equal opportunity; politically, all votes having equal weight; religiously, all consciences having equal rights.[1]

Pike saw Masonry as the natural supporter of the rights of all men and women.

The great distinguishing characteristic of a Mason is sympathy with his kind. He recognizes in the human race one great family, all connected with himself by those invisible links, and the mighty net-work of circumstance, forged and woven by God.[2]

And he warned against the easy non-thinking of bigotry and pointed out that the Mason must do more than "not harm"; he must make a positive difference.

Custom and Prejudice are the blind guides of the blind.[3]

Masonry endeavors, by its charities, to relieve want and distress, comfort the afflicted and heal the wounds of the broken-hearted. But it aims at more than this; it is the Apostle of Liberty, Equality and Fraternity, and requires of its initiates devotedness and patriotism. These duties of life are more than life.[4]

Masonry is a march and a struggle toward the Light. For the individual as well as the nation, Light is Virtue, Manliness, Intelligence, Liberty. Tyranny over the soul or body, is darkness.[5]

SLAVERY

That conviction that "Tyranny over the soul or body is darkness" was to cost Pike dearly. He lived, after all, in Arkansas at the time, and Arkansas was a slave state. As we'll see in the section on the Civil War, Pike was a firm believer in the Union and in the Constitution—beliefs which he wrote again and again[†] into the ritual of the Scottish Rite—and, unlike many Southerners at the time, Pike did not deceive himself about the evils of slavery.

[†] For examples, see *Morals and Dogma*, pages 26, 36, 178, and 211.

Harriet Tubman
This effective abolitionist speaker became one of the shrewdest conductors of the Underground Railroad which annually led scores of fugitive slaves into the free states and Canada. John Brown, who used her assistance, called her "General Tubman."

[Slavery is] a disease, whose spectral shadow lies always upon America's threshold, originating in the avarice and cruelty of the slave trade....[6]

I am not one of those who believe slavery a blessing. I know it is an evil, as great cities are an evil; as the concentration of capital in a few hands, oppressing labor, is an evil; as the utter annihilation of free-will and individuality in the army and navy, is an evil; as in the world everything is mixed of evil and good. Such is the rule of God's providence, and the mode by which He has chosen so to arrange the affairs of the world. Nor do I deny the abuses of slavery.... Necessarily it gives power that may be abused. Nor will I underrate its abuses. It involves frequent separation of families.... It gives occasion to prostitution. The slave toils all his life for mere clothing, shelter, and food; and lash is heard sometime upon the plantations, and in rare cases, cruelties punishable by the law are practiced.[7]

Nor did Pike deceive himself as to the motives behind slavery.

Commercial greed values the life of men no more than it values the lives of ants. The slave-trade is as acceptable to a people enthralled by that greed, as the trade in ivory or spices, if the profits are as large.[8]

Pike paid for his anti-slavery principles. He was deeply committed to the economic growth of the South; he thought that only by growth could the South break its complete dependence on agriculture and, thus, on slavery. As a result he worked hard politically and in editorials to bring about a sort of economic summit of the South, at which plans could be made for regional development. But the meeting soon turned away from its original purpose and, instead, started agitation to extend the slave trade. That was too much for Pike.

At the latter meeting [a Convention of Southern states, held at Savannah] I opposed a resolution offered in favor of the renewal of the slave trade, and afterwards declined to attend the meeting at Knoxville, because that subject had been agitated and the resolution was likely to be offered again.[9]

For Pike, the considerations of the brotherhood of man were more important than the interests of any region. He truly believed in the great principles of Liberty, Equality and Fraternity. As Walter Lee Brown points out:

In the fact that he openly admitted and impugned the harshness of slavery and hoped to see the amelioration of its abuses, he was extremely liberal for his time and section.[10]

And, years after the Civil War, Pike wrote:

The horrors and atrocities, the grievous losses and calamitous consequences of a great civil war have proven to us that the wrongs done to the negro race by the slave-trade were to bear their inevitable fruit of death, disaster and distress, in our homes and households, when the perpetrators of the wrongs had long since gone to their last account.

All wrongs and cruelties, of individuals or nations, must bear their accursed fruit of evil consequences, simply because God is just; and if the consequences fall upon those who had no part in the wrongs, then the guilt of their doer is double, for he does a double wrong; and if upon his children, it is increased many fold; because his highest duty is to see to it that no harm should come to them through his misdeeds.[11]

THE STRENGTH AND EQUALITY OF WOMEN

Pike's view of women was remarkable for his time. That time is hard for us to recapture now, even though it was not that long ago. It was still a common belief at the time that woman could not be educated; their brains literally would not take in and process the information. (It had been less than a lifetime since Dr. Samuel Johnson had remarked that a woman speaking in public was like a dog walking on its hind legs—you were so surprised it was being done at all that it didn't occur to you to wonder how well it was being done.) The suggestion that a woman could be the equal of a man was, to most of Pike's contemporaries, utter nonsense.

Pike saw it differently. He insisted that, even at the dawn of civilization, women had played a critical role.

Women were their counsellors and companions, honored and beloved, especially among the Irano-Aryans [Indo-Europeans].[12]

He created a ritual for a branch of Masonry to include both men and women, and the emphasis was clearly upon the women. His ritual never became popular—the Order of the Eastern Star took its place. But it's easy to see how Pike felt about the equality of women.

The progress of society and civilization being perhaps more certainly indicated by the ascent of woman in the social scale, than by any other one circumstance or symptom, the coöperation of your sex is indispensable to Freemasonry in carrying into execution its plans, and aiding the onward progress of the human race.[13]

In seeking to infuse new life into the Ancient and Accepted Scottish Rite of Freemasonry, we could not but feel how important it was to have the coöperation of women. Not only have Grace Darling, risking her life again and again amid the hungry breakers, to rescue the crew of a wrecked vessel, and Florence Nightingale and her Sister Angels of Mercy and Beneficence, nursing the sick and wounded in Crimean hospitals, shown us to what sublime heights of heroism and devotedness woman can ascend, strong in Love and Faith; but we have such examples round us everywhere, to-day, among the matrons and the daughters of our own land.

Superior to us in this field of glorious and sublime exertion, your sex have not proved less clearly their equality in the domains of intellect and science. With all the modest dignity of a true woman, Elizabeth Barret Browning stands by the side of the chief masters of song. To women we owe many of those most powerful fictions, creations of intellect and the imagination, which are but the drama of life and character and events in another form. In the sciences, there are female names that stand among the highest. A woman ranks as a geologist with Mantell and Miller and Murchison. A woman is the efficient co-laborer of Herschel in astronomy .

Maria Mitchell
The woman astronomer to whom Pike refers in the text to the right was the first woman elected to the American Academy of Arts and Sciences.

A woman teaches political economy to men; and everywhere it is found that the keen, clear, quick intellect of woman wins unexpected triumphs.[14]

Progress in arts, sciences, morals and religion! In all these, what help cannot woman give; what help is she not now giving! Reason and Conscience are the old sure guides; Conscience, in its last and highest form, is the voice of God, His Will, as expressed in the Reason He has created in us; and who can teach the Reason and the Conscience like the Sister, the beloved One, the Mother? The voice of Conscience is more unerringly in the souls of women than in those of men. You hear the voice of God more clearly and distinctly than we do; and even by us, it is ever heard more distinctly at home, than in the camp, the mart or the forum.[15]

And Pike makes it clear that women's Masonry is not intended to be a sort of auxiliary order. It is full-fledged and equal: anything less, he says, would be an insult.

Sarah Andrews
The wife of Benjamin Pike gave birth to Albert Pike on December 29, 1809, in Byfield–Rowley, Massachusetts.

The first condition of any institution intended for your sex, and bearing the name of Masonry, is, in order for it not to be a fraud upon you, that it should offer you the opportunity of working with Freemasonry toward a common end.... It is only by becoming one of our co-workers, and by meeting in your Lodges for the same purposes for which we meet in ours, by encouraging, cheering, inciting, and if need be shaming us, you can feel that you are not mocked with an unreality, when what is conferred upon you is called Masonry.[16]

THE RIGHTS OF INDIANS

As with women, it is difficult today to understand how far in advance of his time Pike was in his attitude toward the American Indian.[†]

It was not uncommon at the time for the government to adopt policies and actions which amounted to sheer genocide. The phrase, "The only good Indian is a dead Indian" is not just a line sometimes heard in an old Western; it was, often, the policy of the army. And sympathetic writers were few and far between. As Pike remarked of the Creeks:

They have no Froissart to chronicle their deeds of chivalry, and to recount their unnumbered wrongs. Over the graves of their forefathers the white man builds, and plants and runs his plough; it is fortunate for our national reputation that their history cannot be written in full; it would be fortunate for that

---

[†] I am going to rely on my own preference and my Creek heritage as well as the agreement of my Indian friends and use the terms "Indian" and "American Indian" rather than "Native American." The proper term is "The People," but that would only lead to confusion.

reputation, if even what had been allowed upon our records was obliterated.[17]

And of the tribes in general, he wrote:

God would not be just, if the manifold injustices of crimes of the great American republic toward the Indian tribes, to say nothing of other wrongs, did not make inevitable the swift and complete ruin of the commonwealth.[18]

Pike had long association with the Indian tribes of the West. During the Confederacy, he was sent as representative to the several tribes west of Arkansas and dealt extensively with them, especially with the Cherokee. The treaties he negotiated for the Confederacy with the tribes are remarkable documents.

They granted economic rights, political rights, and autonomy which far exceeded anything the Union have been willing to concede.

The points included the right to determine tribal membership, the right to expel unwanted whites from their lands, the legal standing to sue and to be witnesses, a delegate to the Confederate House of Representatives, and the right to control their own trade.[19]

He was fascinated by the Indian culture, and had been for many years. In the early part of his life he had several encounters with the tribes during his explorations through what would become the states of Oklahoma and New Mexico. Told with a touch of the typical Pike humor, he wrote accounts of those encounters.

Photo: Western History Collections, Univ. of Oklahoma

Chief John Ross
Pike spent many hours negotiating treaties between the Cherokee and the Confederacy with this canny and distinguished leader of the Cherokee Nation.

It was past noon when we reached [the Indian village], for it was at least thirteen miles from the river. As we approached, the inhabitants of the village, who had been warned of our approach, not only by various strange shouts, but also by messengers, came out to meet us in great numbers; and after crossing a branch of the river, we entered the camp with our arms nearly shaken off at the elbows, by the rough, but friendly greetings of our new friends. Entering the village, which consisted of about thirty lodges, we were conducted to the chief's tent, where we found a young Frenchman, who could speak very good English. He informed us that this was the tent of the principal chief, and that our property would be very safe in it. We entered and shook hands with the chief and his subordinates, who occupied the interior. We bestowed ourselves in various positions upon the buffalo robes which were laid about the fire, and maintained a true Indian gravity, until they should see fit to address us. The young Frenchman then asked us where we were from. We told him, and he interpreted it to our hosts.... We gave them some details of our route, to which they listened with surprise, and perhaps with incredulity. If so, they were too polite to show it.... After the conference was over, I produced my pipe and began to fill it. A half dozen pipes were immediately shown, and requests were made for tobacco, to which I was, of course, bound to respond, and we had a general smoke. We passed the remainder of this day and the next with them, and were called upon, every hour in the day, to go to some lodge and eat. In the course of the second day and evening, we ate fifteen times, and were obliged to do so, or affront them.

The Osages are generally fine, large, noble-looking men... and fed us bountifully on the meat of the buffalo, bear, deer and pole-cat; of the latter of which, however, we partook merely out of compliment.[20]

He formed relationships with the tribes which were to last the rest of his life. He became an advocate for them (today we would call him a *lobbyist*) before Congress, trying to help settle the claims the Indians had and to enforce the treaty provisions which the government generally forgot before the ink of the signatures had dried. Throughout his life, until advancing age made it impossible, he would leave Arkansas or Washington for weeks at a time and go camping and buffalo hunting with his Indian friends.

He would sometimes join an Indian hunting party and spend weeks in search of game, when his legal practice would admit of his absence. It was in this way that he formed lasting friendships with the Indians, who finally employed him as counsel to represent their interest at the National Capital. His legal work of this character assumed huge proportions. He took a genuine interest in trying to right the wrongs which he said the Red man has suffered at the hands of the White race. He learned to talk to some of the tribes in their own language, and it is stated on good authority that he had actually been recognized as a chief by one tribe of Indians, which is somewhat remarkable.[21]

He became especially irate with the typical habit, both in and out of Congress, of referring to the Indians as "savages." In a biting satire, which reminds the reader strongly of Swift's "A Modest Proposal," Pike attacked the critics of the Indians, pointing out that it was just possible that Indians, too, were human and had souls, and suggesting that, when it came to savagery, the "civilized" would do well to look to their own glass house before throwing too many stones.

I do not know what these red men might have become in war. But knowing what savages war makes of men of our own kith and kin, what horrors followed the taking of San Sebastian, what devilish deeds were done on both sides in our late horrible civil war; and that if Indians scalp even the living and torture and burn their prisoners, there have been the Inquisition and the *auto-de-fay* [auto-da-fé], and ten thousand murders of Christians of one sect by Christians of another, roastings of Jews in England and of the feet of women in our civil war to force disclosure of the hiding places of money and valuables, and a thousand cruel crimes, done where the shadows of Christian churches reached, when law and religions were supposed to reign hand in hand over all the country, I can pity rather than hate the "wild red Indian," and hope that Christ died for him also, as well as for us; and that even in him human nature is not all evil, and can remember with grateful affection my Indian friends.[22]

And so, in the end, Pike was an optimist as he viewed the future of humanity and the relations between the races. That optimism is remarkable for one who fought in the Civil War and was so badly scarred, emotionally and financially, by Reconstruction. But his faith was stronger than his fear, and determination triumphed over despair.

He summed up his faith in the future in the ritual of the Thirty-third Degree, the culmination of the Ancient and Accepted Scottish Rite of Freemasonry, Southern Jurisdiction:

But still, the world does move, and we must not despair, though little come of our labours in our own time. Surely the Earth will at last become God's true Temple, the habitation of Truth and Love, when all men will constitute one people, living as the children of a common Father should, in obedience to His eternal laws of Equity and Charity.

When, all over the world, Truth shall have taken the place of Error, Liberty of Despotism, Justice of Inequity, and Toleration of Persecution, the Holy Empire of Scottish Masonry will be established…and the Holy House of the Temple rebuilt.[23]

VIII

"On Either Side, A Little In Advance, Bigotry Rode, And Harsh Intolerance"

On Toleration And Religious Freedom

The title of this chapter comes from a stanza in Pike's poem "Ariel." He has been describing the evils which come, riding like horsemen, upon the earth.

Next, dark Fanaticism, his haggard face
  Flushing with holy anger, down the track
Went, loud bewailing that the good old days
  Of fire and faggot[†] had not yet come back.
When Error was a crime, and to the ways
  Of Truth men were persuaded by the rack;—
On either side, a little in advance,
  Bigotry rode, and harsh Intolerance.[1]

Photo: Guthrie, Okla., Scottish Rite Temple

Allegorical painting of Intolerance

Pike feared intolerance more than nearly any other social evil. He saw clearly the pain it had caused to so many millions for so many centuries. And he knew that, even in America, the monster was sleeping, not dead. There are still many people who are so convinced that their narrow view of "the truth" is right and that all other views are not only wrong but damnable—you can hear many of them preach or pontificate on television—that they would be perfectly happy to use any means to force others (out of love and for their own good, of course) to worship or believe as

---

[†] A bundle of sticks used for starting a fire, including, on occasion, under a heretic

they do. The utter horror of this impressed itself firmly on Pike's mind, and he was determined to resist it at all costs.

As George Moore wrote:

Freemasonry taught him that we are all children of a common father; that man-made distinctions in His presence are worthless; that God has never given any man or any body of men the right to burn their Brethren at the stake because they did not or could not believe as they were commanded to do. He often spoke of the "excellencies of perfect Brotherhood," and hoped for the new age in which real Brotherhood would be true in practice as well as in theory.[2]

Pike saw toleration as the first essential of civilization, the only hope of any society. And he saw the teaching of toleration as one of the great goods and primary tasks of Masonry. It is hard for us, today, to imagine the scenes he described as ever having taken place, until we reflect on Northern Ireland, Eastern Europe, or the Middle East where the battles between Christian, Jew, and Muslim still rage in spilled blood and shattered, hate-destroyed lives as they have for hundreds of years.

Masonry has ever the most vivid remembrance of the terrible and artificial torments that were used to put down new forms of religion or extinguish the old. It sees with the eye of memory the ruthless extermination of all the people of all sexes and ages, because it was their misfortune not to know the God of the Hebrews, or to worship Him under the wrong name, by the savage troops of Moses and Joshua. It sees the thumb-screws and the racks, the whip, the gallows, and the stake, the victims

From *De Ieone Belgico* by Michael Aitsinger

The Duke of Alva's soldiers torture the inhabitants of the Netherlands.

of Diocletian† and Alva, the miserable Covenanters, the Non-Conformists, Servetus burned, and the unoffending Quaker hung. It sees Cranmer hold his arm, now no longer erring, in the flame until the hand drops off in the consuming heat. It sees the persecutions of Peter and Paul, the martyrdom of Stephen, the trials of Ignatius, Polycarp, Justin, and Irenaeus; and then in turn the sufferings of the wretched Pagans under the Christian emperors, as of the Papists in Ireland under Elizabeth and the bloated Henry. The Roman Virgin naked before the hungry lions; young Margaret Graham tied to a stake at low-water mark, and there left to drown, singing hymns to God until the savage waters broke over her head; and all that in all ages have suffered by hunger and nakedness, peril and prison, the rack, the stake, and the sword,—it sees them all, and shudders at the long roll of human atrocities. And it sees also the oppression still practiced in the name of religion—men shot in a Christian jail in Christian Italy for reading the Christian Bible; in almost every Christian State, laws forbidding freedom of speech on matters relating to Christianity; and the gallows reaching its arm over the pulpit.

The fires of Moloch in Syria, the harsh mutilations in the name of Astarte; the barbarities of imperial Pagan Torturers; the still grosser torments which Roman-Gothic Christians in Italy and Spain heaped on their brother-men; the fiendish cruelties to which Switzerland, France, the Netherlands, England, Scotland, Ireland, America, have been witnesses, are not too powerful to warn man of the unspeakable evils which follow from mistakes and errors in the matter of religion, and especially the investing of the God of Love with the cruel and vindictive passions of erring humanity, and making blood to have a sweet savor in his nostrils, and groans of agony to be delicious to his ears.[3]

---

† This seems a good point to insert a recommendation for *A Glossary to Morals and Dogma* by Dr. Rex R. Hutchens. In it, he lists all the people and events Pike references. The examples were well known in Pike's day (people read a lot more then) but have largely dropped out of our awareness. It's a first-rate book, and a very handy companion when reading Pike. The *Glossary* tells us that Diocletian was the last Roman Emperor to persecute Christians; the Duke of Alva was responsible for mass religious butchery in the Netherlands; Covenanters were a persecuted group of Scottish Presbyterians; Servetus was a Spanish theologian, killed for his anti-Trinitarian (unitarian) teachings; Cranmer was Archbishop of Canterbury, martyred under Queen "Bloody" Mary of England; St. Ignatius was martyred by being devoured by wild animals; Polycarp was another early Christian martyr; Justin Martyr was an outstanding early Christian philosopher and martyr; Irenaeus was another early martyr.

It was that last which so amazed Pike—that men could assume a kind and loving God would approve of or require the death and torture of others, no matter what their opinion. And even more amazing to him was the fact that, considering how very limited any human understanding of God must be, we have still been willing to kill people because their limited understanding and our limited understanding weren't the same.

No true Mason scoffs at honest convictions, and an ardent zeal in the cause of Truth and Justice. But he absolutely denies the right of any man to assume the prerogative of Deity, and condemn his Brother's faith and opinions as heretical and deserving to be punished.... For he knows that Intolerance and Bigotry have been infinitely greater curses to mankind than Ignorance and Error. He does not forget that Galileo was denied the free enjoyment of light and air because he averred that the earth moved.... Better any error than persecution! Better any belief or opinion, however irrational and absurd, than the thumbscrew and the auto de fe! And he knows also how unspeakably absurd it is for a creature, to whom himself and everything within and around him are mysteries, to torture and even slay others, because they do not think as he does in regard to the profoundest of all these mysteries, the least of which is utterly beyond the comprehension of either to understand.[4]

From *Inquisition* by Edward Peters

The *auto de fé* was a sort of public entertainment spectacle in which heretics were "saved up" for mass burning and executions.

A primary hope, as Pike saw it, was education. In education and in a determination to give to others the same right to their religious beliefs that we demanded for ourselves, there was a means of fighting against intolerance. People had to be taught the value of toleration.

Toleration, holding that every other man has the same right to his opinion and faith that we have to ours; and liberality, holding that as no human being can with certainty say, in the clash and conflict of hostile faiths and creeds, what is truth, or that he is surely in possession of it, so every one should feel that it is quite possible that another equally honest and sincere with himself, and yet holding the contrary opinion, may himself be possessed of the truth, and that whatever one firmly and conscientiously believes, is truth, to him—these are the mortal enemies of that fanaticism which persecutes for opinion's sake, and initiates crusades against whatever it, in its imaginary holiness, deems to be contrary to the law of God or verity of dogma. And education, instruction, and enlightenment are the most certain means by which fanaticism and intolerance can be rendered powerless.[5]

Pike stresses again and again that we can only *believe* something to be true—we cannot *know* it in the same sense that we can know the temperature at which water freezes.

What is truth to me is not truth to another. The same arguments and evidences that convince one mind make no impression on another. This difference is in men at their birth. No man is entitled positively to assert that he is right, when other men, equally intelligent and equally well-informed, hold directly opposite opinion.[6]

I was once, many years ago, at an Indian village called Jémés, some distance west of Santa Fe in New Mexico, and being alone with no companion but a servant, the house of the Priest was made available to me. "Do you know," he [the Priest] said, "some years ago, a Navajo Chief was captured and taken to Santa Fe, and in the jail a Padre endeavoured to convert him. He heard the good man patiently, and when he had ended, rose and walked to the window and looked out on the plaza, and called the Padre to him. Pointing to an animal in the plaza, he asked the Padre what he called it. "A horse," the Padre said. "And that?" he asked, pointing to another. "A burro," the Padre replied. Then the Chief said, "God made that animal a horse, and that one He made a burro. Me, He made a Navajo; and you He made a Christian."[7]

If for no other reason, Pike believed that man, with his limited, finite mind, was bound to be in error to some degree when he tried to comprehend the Infinite.

The true religious philosophy of an imperfect being is not a system of creed, but, as Socrates thought, an infinite search or approximation.[8]

But Pike also points out that, while every human conception of God must be limited, and thus imperfect and in error, some of the errors did no harm, while others, especially those which made God into some sort of less-than-human monster, could do great damage.

All errors are not equally innocuous. That which is most injurious is to entertain unworthy conceptions of the nature and attributes of God; and it is this that Masonry symbolizes by ignorance of the True Word. The true word of a Mason is, not the entire, perfect, absolute truth in regard to God; but the highest and noblest conception of Him that our minds are capable of forming; and this word is Ineffable, because one man cannot communicate to another his own conception of Deity; since every man's conception of God must be proportioned to his mental cultivation, and intellectual powers, and moral excellence. God is, as man conceives Him, the reflected image of himself.[9]

Of all the groups of church, state, and social organization, Pike rightly saw that Masonry was the foremost organization teaching the importance of this willingness to let others have their own beliefs. In our day, of course, there are numerous activist groups who fight any attempt to enforce a given creed or dogma on those who are not followers of that creed. But at the time Pike was writing, Freemasonry was a rather lone voice.

Masonry alone teaches Toleration, the right of man to abide by his own faith, the right of all States to govern themselves. It rebukes alike the monarch who seeks to extend his dominions by conquest, the Church that claims the right to repress heresy by fire and steel, and the confederation of States that insist on maintaining a union by force and restoring brotherhood by slaughter and subjugation.[10]

Toleration is deserved not just for the religions and religious opinions of today, but also for those of the past. Pike realized that the view many people have of pre-Christian religions is the result of literalism. We assume that the ancients were literal in their faith, rather than using the stories of the gods as allegories to teach truths. There may well have been literalists among the ancient Greeks, there are among us today, but Pike insisted that to assume a literal interpretation of the antique religions was to do them a disservice and to denigrate the people who believed in them.

Literally taken and materially understood, [religious symbolism] would be but an inconceivable tissue of absurdities and scandals.

The same is the case with all the ancient dogmas, with their brilliant theogonies [the origins and genealogies of the gods as related in myths] and poetic legends. To say that the ancients believed, in Greece, in the amours of Jupiter, or worshipped, in Egypt, the ape and hawk as living and real gods, is to be as ignorant or act in as bad faith as if one were to assert that the Christians adore a triple God, composed of an old man, a person crucified and a pigeon. The non-understanding of symbols is always slanderous. And for this reason we should be careful not to scoff at first at things which we do not know when the enunciation of them seems to suppose an absurdity or even only some singularity, for this is quite as senseless as to admit them without discussion and examination.[11]

Pike was always serious about the problem of intolerance, but he also warned against the trap of becoming intolerant of the intolerant. In the essay "Of Habits and Their Slaves" he takes a passing swing at those who insist on their own rightness—moral, religious, or intellectual.

I leave the topic of such habits as that of gambling, that of drinking and that of other evil and vicious and animal indulgences to the professed moralists, only reminding them of the wise advice given by some one "Not to hate sin so much as to come to love men too little." Intemperate Apostles of temperance, intolerant haters of intolerance and bigoted enemies of superstition, are not at all uncommon.[12]

As a Pike biographer, Fred W. Allsopp, points out, Pike not only supported that toleration in theory, but when the Constitution for the State of Arkansas was being drafted, Pike was a strong supporter of making such toleration a matter of law for the state.

He was equally outspoken in endorsing a section of the Bill of Rights, saying, "Above all, infinitely above all, we admire that clause in the Bill of Rights which provides that the rights, privileges and capacities of no man shall be enlarged or diminished on account of his religion."[13]

And when he was called upon to write the *Objects and Principles of the Democratic American Party* as the official statement of purpose of the new political group, Pike wrote:

To protect the civil and religious rights and privileges of all; to maintain the right of every man to the full, unrestrained and peaceful enjoyment of his religious opinions and mode of worship; and to oppose any attempt by any sect, denomination or church, to obtain an ascendancy over any other in the State, by special privilege or exemption, by any political combination of its members, or by a divided civil allegiance.[14]

Pike deeply feared sectarianism and denominationalism. Although he was strongly opposed to any sort of religious control over the citizens of a state or used in the affairs of the state, he was far from indifferent to religion. He knew that no people could be truly great unless they had within them a deep awareness of religion.

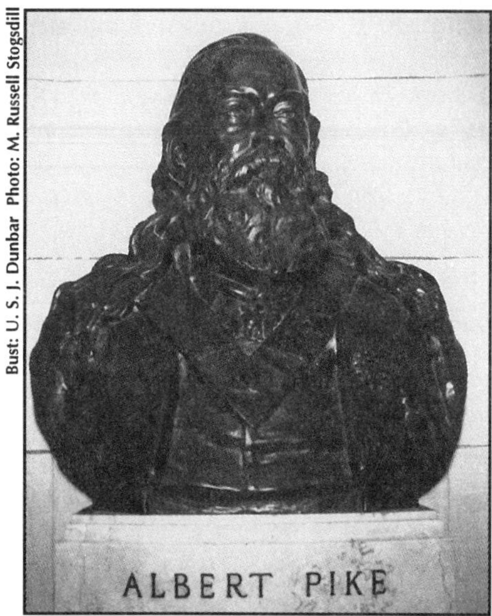

Bust: U. S. J. Dunbar Photo: M. Russell Stogsdill

Life-size bronze bust, Grand Staircase, House of the Temple, Washington, D. C.

> A free people, forgetting that it has a soul to be cared for, devotes all its energies to its material advancement.... The citizens copy after the State, and regard wealth, pomp, and luxury as the great goods of life. Such a nation creates wealth rapidly and distributes it badly. Thence the two extremes, of monstrous opulence and monstrous misery; all the enjoyment to a few, all the privations to the rest.[15]
>
> A religion of craven fear and abortive hopes, without love, as without light and liberty, ends, like the enchantments of Circe,† in transforming men into brutes. A sound and healthy and vigorous morality depends upon a healthy religious faith.[16]

Maintaining that healthy religious faith was not always easy. Pike understood that most religions, historically, have contained the seeds of their own destruction, not in the teachings of the faith but in its practice. Faith, which begins as an intensely personal experience, is easily converted, over generations, into mere spectacle rather than true, individual worship. Dying organizations love both rules and ceremonies—since both limit the amount of thinking permitted or even possible.

> The tendency always is, in every religion, to exaggerate the value and efficacy of public worship, prayer and ceremonial as a means of intercession with the Divine Grace, and in the same proportion to belittle the pious and devotional spirit that either prays in secret or does not utter aloud the petitions that the soul prefers to God.[17]

† Sorceress in Greek mythology who turned men into swine

Masonry takes full account of humanity's religious nature and recognizes that a person cannot be complete without faith. It strives always to strengthen the faith of the individual Mason. In this sense, we sometimes say that Masonry is religious. But it is not, as our critics sometimes fail to understand, a religion. It is true in the same way that one can say he believes in democracy but is not a Democrat. The one is a philosophy of man and the way in which man is best governed—the other is a political party. As the unknown author of the "Introductory" to Pike's *The Meaning of Masonry* points out:

Masonry, as Pike saw it, is morality founded in faith and taught by symbols. It is not a religion, but a worship in which all good men can unite, its purpose being to benefit mankind physically, socially, and spiritually, by helping men to cultivate freedom, friendship, and character. To that end, beyond the facts of faith—the reality of God, the moral law, and the hope of immortality—it does not go.[18]

And, as Pike, himself, wrote:

Masonry does not pretend to be a religion; but it is not *ir*religious or irreverent. It does not assume to take the place of any religion, or claim to make religion unnecessary. To charge it with this is to libel it. It requires its initiates to believe in one God and a Divine Providence, and that the soul survives the dissolution of the body. Thus it teaches those great primary truths on which all religion must repose; and it inculcates those principles of pure morality which have commended themselves to the good and wise of all ages.[19]

Masonry teaches that God is a Paternal Being, and has an interest in his creatures, such as is expressed in the title Father; an interest unknown to all the systems of Paganism, untaught in all the theories of philosophy; an interest not only in the glorious beings of other spheres, the Sons of Light, the dwellers in Heavenly world, but in us, poor, ignorant, and unworthy; that He has pity for the erring, pardon for the guilty, love for the pure, knowledge for the humble, and promises of immortal life for those who trust in and obey Him.[20]

To every Mason, the Infinite Justice and Benevolence of God give ample assurance that Evil will ultimately be dethroned, and the Good, the True, and the Beautiful reign triumphant and eternal. It teaches, as it feels and knows, that Evil, and Pain, and Sorrow exist as part of a wise and beneficent plan, all the parts of which work together under God's eye to a result which shall be perfection.[21]

To understand Pike's views of religion, it's critical to remember two of his basic beliefs—one of which was commonplace in his time, and one of which was rather advanced. (And it should probably be stressed again that we're speaking of Pike's views of religion, not some sort of "official" Masonic position. There is, of course, no such thing as an official Masonic position on religion.)

The first belief was that the natural world revealed something of the nature of God because it was the creation of God. This view ran through most of Christianity and was certainly found in his own denomination (Pike was an Episcopalian). The current *Book of Common Prayer* puts it this way in the Anglican Catechism:

Q: How did God first help us?

A: God first helped us by revealing himself and his will, through nature and history, through many seers and saints, and especially through the prophets of Israel.

Chapter IX, "Step Where We Will, We Tread Upon Wonders," (page 112) is devoted to Pike's writings about nature and filled with his references to the Divine observable in the natural world. He also wrote:

> The first Scriptures for the human race were written by God on the Earth and Heavens. The reading of these Scriptures is Science. Familiarity with the grass and trees, the insects and the infusoria [microscopic organisms], teaches us deeper lessons of love and faith, than we can glean from the writings of Fénélon and Augustine. The great Bible of God is ever open before mankind.[22]

And the same quotation hints at the second great basis of Pike's beliefs: Faith and reason must go together. They are not adversaries but partners. In the liturgy of the Thirty-third Degree, Pike wrote:

> True religion consists in the equilibrium of the two greatest gifts of God to man—faith and reason.

Pike saw science and the advancement of knowledge of the physical world as a strengthener of faith, not a risk to faith.

> Nature is the primitive revelation. Science enlarges our knowledge of God, because it translates for us more of His language, and translates it more truly. Philosophy is the Interpreter of Nature, the Revealer; and Masonry consists in Morality, Science, Philosophy, and Political and Religious Truth.[23]

> Science gratifies the religious feeling without arresting it, and opens out the unfathomable mystery of the One Supreme into more explicit and manageable Forms, which express not indeed His Essence, which is wholly beyond our reach and higher than our faculties can climb, but His Will, and so feeds an endless enthusiasm by accumulating forever new objects of pursuit.[24]

Truth dreads nothing, and he who does not exercise his Reason, even in matters of faith, remains a child, a blind traveller, all his life. To forbid one the use of his reason, and to require him to accept his faith at the dictates of another, is an absurdity; since, if faith be unreasoning, no man can show in what respect his faith deserves the preference over that of any other.[25]

Some of Pike's critics have accused him of being an atheist, or even a satanist. But Pike's writings clearly show a strong faith in God. One of the more beautiful passages in his works is a letter, written when he was an old man, to Dr. Thurston, a friend of many years and one of the men who had accompanied Pike at his duel (see Chapter X, "Bad Day at Fort Smith," page 118). Pike had just learned that Thurston was dying and, indeed, he died the day after Pike's letter reached him.

WASHINGTON, [D.C.,] SEPTEMBER 3, 1885

My Dearest and Best and Truest Old Friend,

I have just received your loving message sent to me by Mr. Sandles. I had already two days ago learned from our old friend Cush, who had the information from James Stewart, that you were about to go away from us. In a little while I shall follow you; and it will be well for me if I can look forward to the departure, inevitable for all, with the same patience and equanimity with which you are waiting for it.

I do not believe that our intellect and individuality cease to be when the vitality of the body ends. I have a profound conviction, the only real revelation, which to me makes absolute certainty, that there is a Supreme Deity, the Intelligence and Soul of the Universe, to whom it is not folly to pray; that our convictions come from Him, and in them He does not lie to or deceive us: and that there is to be for my very self another, a continual life, in which this life will not be as if it had never been, but I shall see and know again those whom I have loved and lost here.

You have led an upright, harmless, and blameless life, always doing good, and not wrong and evil. You have enjoyed the harmless pleasures of life, and have never wearied of it nor thought it had not been a life worth living. Therefore you need not fear to meet whatever lies beyond the veil.

Either there is no God, or there is a just and merciful God, who will deal gently and tenderly with the human creatures whom He has made so weak and so imperfect.

There is nothing in the future for you to fear, as there is nothing in the past for you to be ashamed of. Since I have been compelled by the lengthening shadows to look forward to my own nearly approaching departure, I do not feel that I lose the friends that go away before me. It is as if they had set sail across the Atlantic Sea to land in an unknown country beyond, whither I shall soon follow to meet them again.

But, dear old friend, I shall feel very lonely after you are gone. We have been friends so long, without a moment's intermission, without even one little cloud or shadow of unkindness or suspicion coming between us, that I shall miss you terribly. . . . As long as I live I shall remember with loving affection your ways and looks and words, our glad days passed together in the woods, your many acts of kindness, the old home and the shade of the mulberries, and our intimate communion. . . during more than forty-five years.

The old friends are nearly all gone; you are going sooner than I to meet them. I shall live a little longer, with little left to live for, loving your memory, and loving the wife and daughter who have been so dear to you. Dear, dear old friend, good-bye! May our Father Who is in Heaven, have you in His Holy Keeping and give you eternal rest![26]

Devotedly your friend,

Albert Pike

How did Pike himself conceive of the Deity? He has left us some beautiful passages.

God is the author of everything that existeth; the Eternal, the Supreme, the Living, and Awful Being; from Whom nothing in the Universe is hidden. Make of Him no idols and visible images; but rather worship Him in the deep solitudes of sequestered forests; for He is invisible, and fills the Universe as its soul, and liveth not in any Temple!

Light and Darkness are the World's Eternal ways. God is the principle of everything that exists, and the Father of all Beings. He is eternal, immovable, and Self-Existent. There are no bounds to His power. At one glance He sees the Past, the Present, and the Future; and the procession of the builders of the Pyramids, with us and our remotest Descendants, is now passing before Him. He reads our thoughts before they are known to ourselves. He rules the movements of the Universe, and all events and revolutions are the creatures of His will. For He is the Infinite Mind and Supreme Intelligence.[27]

Among the primary ideas of consciousness, that are inseparable from it, the atoms of self-consciousness, we find the

Creation with Compasses of Light
William Blake (1757–1827) English artist, poet, and mystic

idea of God. Carefully examined by the scrutinizing intellect, it is the idea of God as infinite, perfectly powerful, wise, just, loving, holy; absolute being with no limitation. This made us, made all, sustains us, sustains all; made our body, not by a single act, but by a series of acts extending over a vast succession of years,—for man's body is the resultant of all created things,— made our spirit, our mind, our conscience, affections, soul, will, appointed for each its natural mode of action, set each at its several [individual] aims. Thus self-consciousness leads us to consciousness of God, and at last to consciousness of an infinite God. That is the highest evidence of our own existence, and it is the highest evidence of His.[28]

God and truth are inseparable; a knowledge of God is possession of the saving oracles of truth.[29]

But for sheer elegance in writing, few things equal the passage in Pike's ritual for the reception of a Louveteau (a young son of a Mason for whom the Lodge assumes a special responsibility). Pike is explaining the nature of God to a child.

If you have a friend who is generous, you love him for that. If he is pitiful and sympathizes with you when you are grieved or hurt, and has compassion even upon innocent creatures that the bad like to injure and torment, you love him for that. If he forgives you when you do him a wrong, if he loves you in spite of your ill-nature and perverseness, if he is always just and true to you, never deceiving or wronging you, you love him for all that. It is not his *face* that you love. If it is pleasant to you, it is because it tells you how good and kind his *heart* is. If you love to look into his eyes, it is not because they are bright, but because a good true soul looks at you through them. It is his kindness, generosity, truth, justice, frankness, and affection that you love. That is, you love his soul, himself, and not his body. God is infinitely more loving and kind and just and true, than your friend is, and you owe Him a million times more than you owe your friend. And whenever you love these qualities and virtues in a friend, you love them in God also, who has given them to him; and thus you love God Himself.

Prove that you love Him, by loving these qualities and by obeying His laws. Obey these, not because you *fear* Him, but because you *love* Him, He has written these laws in your heart. Be good and just and generous, be frank and true and manly, be kind and forgiving and gentle and pitiful and merciful, because God wishes you to be so, and His voice within you is always telling you that you ought to be so.[30]

We do not tell you to be good and upright *in order* to get to heaven, or *because* you will go there if you are so, any more than we should try to persuade you to be good by offering to pay you money for it. We do not tell you not to be bad and wicked because if you are you will go to the bottomless pit and be burned with fire and brimstone, any more than we should try to keep you from doing wrong by threatening to starve you or whip you. Do what is right, as nearly as you can, because you know it is right, and that you ought to do it, and will *deserve* to be rewarded for it, whether you are or not. You will soon find that the greatest pleasure in the world is to do what is generous and noble, when you are not compelled to do it by force or fear, or persuaded by the hope of reward.[31]

Pike did his very best to keep his Masonic writing nonsectarian and to keep his own Episcopal background and faith out of it. He generally succeeds, although there's little doubt about the nature of his faith to anyone who reads his work closely. There are several passages in *Morals and Dogma* however, where it becomes clear past any doubt. Consider this passage:

Speak kindly to your erring brother! God pities him; Christ has died for him; Providence waits for him; Heaven's mercy yearns toward him; and Heaven's spirits are ready to welcome him back with joy. Let your voice be in unison with all those powers that God is using for his recovery![32]

But Pike saved some of his best devotional writing for passages in which he was discussing Jesus of Nazareth. When he is discussing the life and work and suffering of Jesus, a love and admiration shines through the words clearly announcing his personal faith.

He commands us to love one another, to love our neighbor as ourself; and we dispute and wrangle, and hate and slay each other, because we cannot be of one opinion as to the Essence of His Nature, as to His Attributes; whether He became man born of a woman, and was crucified; whether the Holy Ghost is of the same substance with the Father, or only of a similar substance; whether a feeble old man is God's Viceregent: whether some are elected from all eternity to be saved, and others to be condemned and punished; whether punishment or the wicked after death is to be eternal; whether this doctrine of the other be heresy or truth;—drenching the world with blood, depopulating realms, and turning fertile lands into deserts; until, for religious war, persecution and bloodshed, the Earth for many a century has rolled around the Sun, a charnel-house, steaming and reeking with human gore, the blood of brothers slain by brother for opinion's sake, that has soaked into and polluted all her veins, and made her a horror to her sisters of the Universe.[33]

Whatever higher attributes the Founder of the Christian Faith may, in our belief, have had or not have had, none can deny that He taught and practiced a pure and elevated morality, even at the risk and to the ultimate loss of His life. He was not only the benefactor of a disinherited people, but a model for mankind. Devotedly He loved the children of Israel. To them He came, and to them alone He preached that Gospel which His disciples afterward carried among foreigners. He would fain have freed the chosen People from their spiritual bondage of ignorance and degradation. As a lover of all mankind, laying down His life for the emancipation of His Brethren, He should be to all, to Christian, to Jew, and to Mahometan, an object of gratitude and veneration.

The Roman world felt the pangs of approaching dissolution. Paganism, its Temples shattered by Socrates and Cicero, had spoken its last word. The God of the Hebrews was unknown beyond the limits of Palestine. The old religions had failed to give happiness and peace to the world. The babbling and wrangling philosophers had confounded all men's ideas, until

Scenic drops of the Crucifixion scenery used in the Scottish Rite Temple in Guthrie, Oklahoma, in staging the Eighteenth Degree, Knight of the Rose Croix

they doubted of everything and had faith in nothing: neither in God nor in His goodness and mercy, nor in the virtue of man, nor in themselves. Mankind was divided into two great classes,—the master and the slave; the powerful and the abject, the high and the low, the tyrants and the mob; and even the former were satiated with the servility of the latter, sunken by lassitude and despair to the lowest depths of degradation.

When, lo, a voice, in the inconsiderable Roman Province of Judea proclaims a new Gospel—a new "God's Word," to crushed, suffering bleeding humanity. Liberty of Thought, Equality of all men in the eye of God, universal Fraternity! a new doctrine, a new religion; the old, Primitive Truth uttered once again!

Man is once more taught to look upward to his God. No longer to a God hid in impenetrable mystery, and infinitely remote from human sympathy, emerging only at intervals from the darkness to smite and crush humanity; but a God, good, kind, beneficent, and merciful: a Father, loving the creatures He has made, with a love immeasurable and exhaustless; Who feels for us, and sympathizes with us, and sends us pain and want and disaster only that they may serve to develop in us the virtues and excellences that befit us to live with Him hereafter.

Jesus of Nazareth, the "Son of man," is the expounder of the new Law of Love. He calls to Him the humble, the poor, the Pariahs of the world. The first sentence that He pronounces blesses the world, and announces the new gospel: "Blessed are they that mourn for they shall be comforted." He pours the oil of consolation and peace upon every crushed and bleeding heart. Every sufferer is His proselyte. He shares their sorrows, and sympathizes with all their afflictions.

He raises up the sinner and the Samaritan woman, and teaches them to hope for forgiveness. He pardons the woman taken in adultery. He selects his disciples not among the Pharisees or the Philosophers, but among the low and humble, even of the fishermen of Galilee. He heals the sick and feeds the poor. He lives among the destitute and the friendless. "Suffer little children," He said, "to come unto me: for of such is the kingdom of Heaven! Blessed are the humble-minded, for theirs is the kingdom of Heaven: the meek, for they shall inherit the Earth: the merciful, for they shall obtain mercy: the pure in heart, for they shall see God: the peacemakers, for they shall be called the children of God! First be reconciled to thy brother, and then come and offer thy gift at the altar. Give to him that asketh thee, and from him that would borrow of thee turn not away! Love your enemies; bless them that curse you; do good to them that hate you; and pray for them which despitefully use you and persecute you! All things whatsoever ye would that men should do to you, do ye also unto them; for this is the law and the Prophets! He that taketh not his cross, and followeth after Me, is not worthy of Me. A new commandment I give unto you, that ye love one another: as I have loved you, that ye also love one another: by this shall all know that ye are My disciples. Greater love hath no man than this, that a man lay down his life for his friend."

The Gospel of Love He sealed with His life. The cruelty of the Jewish Priesthood, the ignorant ferocity of the mob, and the Roman indifference to barbarian blood, nailed Him to the cross, and He expired uttering blessings upon humanity.

Dying thus, He bequeathed His teachings to man as an inestimable inheritance. Perverted and corrupted, they have served as a basis for many creeds, and been even made the warrant for intolerance and persecution. We here teach them in their purity. They are Masonry; for to them good men of all creeds can subscribe.[34]

IX

"Step Where We Will, We Tread Upon Wonders"

On Nature

The humblest object beneath our eye as completely defies our scrutiny as the economy of the most distant star. Every leaf and blade of grass holds within itself secrets which no human penetration will ever fathom.... Wherever we place our hand we lay it on the locked bosom of mystery. Step where we will, we tread upon wonders. The sea-side, the clods of the field, the water-worn pebbles on the hills, the rude masses of rock, are traced over and over, in every direction, with a hand-writing older and more significant and sublime than all the ancient ruins, and all the overthrown and buried cities that past generations have left upon the earth; for it is the handwriting of the Almighty.[1]

It's hardly surprising that a 19th-century Romantic (and Pike was certainly a Romantic) would be in love with nature. What is unusual is that he actually liked it as well. The stereotypical Romantic liked to spend a day in the mountains, communing with nature, or on a rocky sea coast, finding an echo of the crashing waves (distant storm optional but preferable) in the turmoil of his own soul. The day typically ended, however, with a return to a large house, a gracious dinner, servants to apply hot water bottles to chilled feet, a noble cheese, a crusty bottle of port, and a toasty bed.

Pike liked camping out, actually living for weeks at a time in a tent, hunting his own food, and sleeping under the stars. I must confess that for one to whom "roughing it" means the garbage disposer isn't working, this is a little difficult to understand. Although, as we'll see, Pike did himself well on those trips (probably including the noble cheese and crusty port). Walter Lee Brown comments on Pike's love of camping:

The pastime that most delighted Pike and which most occupied him, was hunting and fishing. Frequently, when he grew weary after a heavy stint of work at his law desk, he would close his office, load his gun, fishing rod, tent and camp equipment into his buggy, and drive off to the prairie east of Little Rock to relax for a week or two.[2]

Pike himself wrote:

I have no more pleasant recollections than those of my many happy days of that life, passed by me for weeks at a time, during twenty years, in the intervals of study and professional labors, and which for five years I altogether lived.

Surely my happiest hours, and by far the freest from care, have been passed in the great western woods and on the vast silent plains, amid the mountains and by lakes and rivers, sleeping much in the open air, with not even the murmuring leaves between my eyes and the starry hosts of heaven, or in the hospitable tent, when the rain beat angrily upon it, or the winter cold made its friendly warmth acceptable, or in my hammock, slung with long ropes between two great trees, while the rain poured as it did when it caused the Deluge, upon the double fly stretched above me; and lightning, darting incessantly from cloud to earth, was answered instantly by the quick sharp rattlings of the thunder, each like the report of a rifled cannon.[3]

Now it is all very well to rough it, but Pike believed in roughing it in a civilized manner, whenever possible. Remembering those early days of starving in the prairie, reduced to eating horse and trying to get relief from thirst by chewing on a bullet, Pike was determined not to go through that again. He designed and had built a special camping chest. It was so unusual that a guest on one of Pike's camping trips wrote to the newspaper about it.

It is a curiosity—a living practical demonstration, of what may be achieved in the way of economy of space. It is made of substantial English oak, is 2 feet and scant three inches long-and 1 foot 4 1/2 inches deep, and is wide as it is deep–contains decanters, 12 ivory handle knives, 6 steel forks with ivory handles, 6 ditto of silver, 6 tumblers, 6 wine glasses, 6 coffee cups, 6 egg cups, 6 big spoons and 6 small ones, 6 plates, dishes, coffee pot, sugar dishes, all kinds of contraptions for carrying sugar, tea, coffee, salt, pepper, etc.

There is also outside and separate from it, a circular bucket, 1 foot in depth, and 2 1/2 in circumference, containing tea kettles, tea pots, stew pans, frying pans, chafing dish, with the most complete spirit lamp we have ever seen, together with vessels to hold the spirits of wine. The whole affair can go in an ordinary buggy, and with it in the woods, there is everything that is necessary, to set a table for six persons in the very best style.[4]

All his life, Pike loved nature, especially flowers and birds. Some of his most beautiful imagery in the Scottish Rite degrees uses birds as a

The mountain cabin of Albert Pike in Arkansas

symbol of freedom. From the time he had a permanent home of his own, he kept birds with him, sometimes as many as fifty caged birds at once. He reflected that love in one of his best-known poems, "Ode to the Mockingbird," one stanza of which reads:

> I cannot love the man who doth not love,
> As men love light, the songs of happy birds;
> For the first visions that my boy-heart wove,
> To fill its sleep with, were that I did rove
> Through the fresh woods, what time the snowy herds
> Of morning clouds shrunk from the advancing sun,
> Into the depths of Heaven's blue heart, as words
> From the Poet's lips float gently, one by one,
> And vanish in the human heart; and then
> I revelled in such songs, and sorrowed, when
> With noon-heat overwrought, the music-gush was done.[5]

But nature was more than a background to Pike, it was a revelation of God Himself. One could come to know the Creator by His Creation. Some critics, equipped with dull axes and determined to grind them upon Pike, have insisted that he taught the worship of nature. Which is very much like confusing a painting with the painter. Pike simply believed that the contemplation of nature led the mind to a contemplation of and appreciation of God. Anyone who has had the experience of seeing some natural vista of such beauty that the heart actually seems to hurt will know what Pike meant. But he also meant more. Not only the beauty but the study of nature led the mind to God, for one could not contemplate the intricacies of the created world without honoring the Creator.

The Scriptures for the human race are writ in earth and Heaven. No organ or miserere[†] touches the heart like the sonorous swell

[†] A musical setting of the 51st Psalm

of the sea or the ocean-waves immeasurable laugh. Every year the old world puts on new bridal beauty, and celebrates its Whit-Sunday, when in the sweet Spring each bush and tree dons reverently its new glories. Autumn is a long All-Saint's day; and the harvest is Hallowmass to Mankind. Before the human race marched down from the slopes of the Himalayas to take possession of Asia, Chaldea, and Egypt, men marked each annual crisis, the solstices and the equinoxes, and celebrated religious festivals therein; and even then, and ever since, the material was and has been the element of communion between man and God.[6]

Nature is the great Teacher of man; for it is the Revelation of God. It neither dogmatizes nor attempts to tyrannize by compelling to a particular creed or special interpretation. It presents its symbols to us, and adds nothing by way of explanation. It is the text without the commentary; and, as we well know, it is chiefly the commentary and gloss that lead to error and heresy and persecution. The earliest instructors of mankind not only adopted the lessons of Nature, but as far as possible adhered to her method of imparting them.[7]

The evidence of God has been ploughed into Nature so deeply, and so deeply woven into the texture of the human soul, that Atheism has never become a faith, though it has sometimes assumed the shape of theory. Religion is natural to man. Instinctively he turns to God and reverences and relies on Him. In the Mathematics of the Heavens, written in gorgeous diagrams of fire, he sees law, order, beauty, harmony without end: in the ethics of the little nations that inhabit the ant-hills, he sees the same; in all Nature, animate and inanimate, he sees the evidence of a Design, a Will, an Intelligence, and a God,—of a God beneficent and loving as well as wise, and merciful and indulgent as well as powerful.[8]

It was the mystery, the sheer, glorious wonder of the earth which so impressed Pike and set him in resonance with the divine. Science has answered some of the questions Pike asks in the passage below, but unless we still retain the awe and wonder, we are the poorer.

Here are two minute seeds, not much unlike in appearance, and two of larger size. Hand them to the learned Pundit, Chemistry, who tells us how combustion [oxidation] goes on in the lungs, and plants are fed with phosphorus and carbon, and the alkalies and silex. Let her decompose them, analyze them, torture then in all the ways she knows. The net result of each is a little sugar, a little fibrin, a little water-carbon, potassium, sodium, and the like—one cares not to know what.

We hide them in the ground: and the slight rains moisten them, and the Sun shines upon them, and little slender shoots spring up and grow;—and what a miracle is the mere growth!—the force, the power, the *capacity* by which the little feeble shoot, that a small worm can nip off with a single snap of its mandibles, extracts from the earth and air and water and the different elements, so learnedly catalogued, with which it increases in stature, and rises imperceptibly toward the sky.

One grows to be a slender, fragile, feeble stalk, soft of texture, like an ordinary weed; another a strong bush, of woody fibre, armed with thorns, and sturdy enough to bid defiance to the winds: the third a tender tree, subject to be blighted by the frost, and looked down upon by all the forest; while another spreads its rugged arms abroad, and cares for neither frost nor ice, nor the snows that for months lie around its roots.

But lo! out of the brown foul earth, and colorless invisible air, and limpid rain-water, the chemistry of the seeds has extracted *colors*—four different shades of green, that paint the leaves which put forth in the spring upon our plants, our shrubs, and our trees. Later still come the flowers—the vivid colors of the rose,

In the 1920s, the writer's Great Aunt Myrtle Tresner went with a group of friends on an informal "Pike Pilgrimage" through the Arkansan country familiar to Pike. She made sketches along the way and produced this painting on her return. The writer's Grandmother once remarked that, as best she could remember, they had seen all the elements of the painting in Pike's country—they just didn't all happen to be in the same place. *Sic transit gloria Myrtle.*

the beautiful brilliance of the carnation, the modest blush of the apple, and the splendid white of the orange. Whence come the *colors* of the leaves and flowers? By what process of chemistry are *they* extracted from the carbon, the phosphorus, and the lime? Is it any greater miracle to make something out of nothing?

Pluck the flowers. Inhale the delicious *perfumes;* each perfect, and all delicious. Whence have *they* come? By what combination of acids and alkalies could the chemist's laboratory produce *them*?

And now on two comes the fruit—the ruddy apple and the golden orange. Pluck them—open them! The texture and fabric how totally different! The *taste* how entirely dissimilar—the *perfume* of each distinct from its flower and from the other. Whence the taste and this new perfume? The same earth and air and water have been made to furnish a different taste to each fruit, a different perfume not only to each fruit, but to each fruit and its own flower.

Is it any more a problem whence come thought and will and perception and all the phenomena of the mind, than this, whence come the colors, the perfumes, the taste, of the fruit and flower?

And lo! in each fruit new seeds, each gifted with the same wondrous power of reproduction—each with the same wondrous *forces* wrapped up in it to be again in turn evolved. Forces that had lived three thousand years in the grain of wheat found in the wrappings of an Egyptian mummy; forces of which learning and science and wisdom know no more than they do of the nature and laws of action of God. What can *we* know of the nature, and how can *we* understand the powers and mode of operation of the human soul, when the glossy leaves, the pearl-white flower, and the golden fruit of the orange are miracles wholly beyond our comprehension?[9]

And Pike summed it all up, very simply, with these words:

Everything within us and without us ought to stir our minds to admiration and wonder. We are a mystery encompassed with mysteries.[10]

X

Bad Day At Fort Smith

On Pike's Infamous Duel

In 1846 [Pike] raised a squadron of cavalry which he commanded with the rank of captain, and served in Mexico with distinction, having received special mention from Generals [Zachary] *Taylor and* [John Ellis] *Wool. Here he met Major Robert E. Lee, afterwards Commanding General of the Confederate Army, with whom he corresponded for a while after the Mexican War.*

Shortly after the close of that war there appeared in the columns of a Little Rock newspaper an article written by him, severely criticizing the conduct of a part of the Arkansas regiment at the battle of Buena Vista, of which regiment John Selden Roane was Lieutenant–Colonel. The latter considered these criticisms as reflecting upon him personally, and immediately sent a challenge to Captain Pike. This was promptly accepted, and the meeting took place on the sandbar opposite Fort Smith, in the Indian Territory.

In the Arkansas Gazette *of April 2, 1893, appeared a very interesting article from the pen of Dr. James A. Dibrell Sr., of Van Buren, giving the particulars of the aforesaid duel. Dr. Dibrell wrote:*

> On the bar opposite Fort Smith, Albert Pike as principal, with Luther Chase and John Drennon as seconds, and the writer as surgeon, accompanied by Pat. Farrelly and Wm. H. Cousin and Dr. H. Thurston as friends on one side, and John S. Roane as principal, with Henry M. Rector and R.W. Johnson as seconds, and Dr. Philip Burton as surgeon, met in mortal combat to decide a controversy by the *code d'honneur*, so falsely called. Pike, to the best of my recollection, was the challenging party, at least was so considered on my side of the ground. At call, both parties promptly stepped forward, distance ten paces, when duelling pistols were loaded and placed in their hands. Both stood firm and determined, neither displaying the least agitation. Pike was enjoying a cigar during the firing. At the word, both parties fired, but neither was wounded. A second fire was had, with the same result. Some one has said that Pike's beard was touched; if so, I have no recollection of it. After the second fire, Pike and myself were sitting on a cottonwood log on the edge of the forest that fringed the bar, when Dr.

Burton was seen approaching us, with his usual slow and dignified step, and when within a few paces of us, beckoned to me to meet him. I did so. He remarked; "Dibrell, it's a d—d shame that these men should stand here and shoot at each other until one or the other is killed or wounded. They have shown themselves to be brave men and would fire all day unless prevented. The seconds on neither side can interfere, because it would be considered a great disparagement for either to make a proposition for cessation of hostilities. So, let us, as surgeons, assume the responsibility and say they shall not fire another time; that unless they do as we desire we will leave the field to them helpless, however cruel it might seem."

I replied that I knew nothing about the code, but would consult my principal. I stated Dr. Burton's proposition word for word as made to me. Pike remarked, "I want one more fire at him and will not hit him in a vital part; I believe he has tried to kill me; I have not tried to hit him."

After reflection, he said, "Do as you think proper about it, but do not by anything compromise my honor."

The good offices of Drs. Dibrell and Burton in the interest of peace and humanity were so effective that the matter ended honorably to both parties.[1]

Thus reads the account written by Albert Pike's daughter, Lilian Pike Roome, in her introduction to Pike's collected poems.

It is hard to write about the duel today, harder to wrap one's mind into a world view in which such a thing is possible. Viewed in cold blood, it's remarkable to think of two men, calmly standing there waiting to kill or be killed. What must Pike have been thinking? We know he had already decided to miss Roane, but he had no way of knowing that Roane had made the same decision. So, known only to themselves, both men faced the prospect of being killed, without attempting to harm the other. And the risk was real. Both men were outstanding shots. There was nothing funny about it.

And yet, it has an element of the comic. Even Allsopp, great admirer of Pike though he was, couldn't keep an element of the ridiculous out of his account. Consider these passages.

Mr. Roane was accompanied by Henry M. Rector (afterward Governor of the state, 1861–62) and Congressman Robt. W. Johnson (afterward U.S. Senator) as seconds; with Dr. Phillip Burton as surgeon. All of the party arrived on horseback. Roane, Johnson, Burton and Rector accepted the hospitality of Major Elias Rector [the man Pike immortalized in the poem "A Fine Arkansas Gentleman"], *at whose house they rested for two days before the meeting and where Roane practiced shooting.*[2]

And so we have the group, gathering at the same house, with Roane stepping outside from time to time to do a little target practice. Bright dinner conversation must have been a trifle difficult to manage.

And the image Allsopp gives of Pike just prior to the first exchange of fire is almost painful—a sort of combination of Apollo and Groucho Marx.

Standing, unflinchingly and confidently, looking like a Grecian god, his long flowing locks being blown about by the breezes, Pike calmly enjoyed a cigar until the command was given to "fire."[3]

Lieutenant Colonel John Seldon Roane, Governor of Arkansas, from 1848 to 1852

Somehow the picture of a Grecian god puffing on a long, black stogie seems to be one only Dali could have painted.

Allsopp tells us that word had gotten out, and, since Pike and Roane were both well-known men, a crowd of some 200 or 300 had gathered. On a boat at the landing were Pike's sons, Hamilton and Walter, who were waiting to kill Roane's second, Colonel Johnson, whom they considered responsible for the duel, if anything had happened to their father. Allsopp provides some further details, not included in Mrs. Roome's account, of the end of the duel.

Doctor Burton said, "I am happy to state that I am authorized by Mr. Roane's second, Mr. Rector, to say that our principal has declared himself as having received entire satisfaction."

"That being the case," said Doctor Dibrell, "as Mr. Pike's second, I suggest that these two brave and honorable gentlemen shake hands."

Pike stood resolutely in his place until Roane advanced toward him with extended hand, when he met him and accepted his hand, with all the grace and dignity of a Chesterfield.†

The bearing of neither of the principals could have been more punctilious [exactly and carefully correct]. *In a few minutes they were conversing with each other and with the party as if there had never been the slightest difference between them. In a short while after the reconciliation had been effected, all parties adjourned to a banquet at Fort Smith, where there was something to drink and much merry-making.*

It looked as if neither wanted to kill the other. Roane was a good shot, who could kill a deer while running or hit a turkey on the wing; Pike was equally as good a marksman; so that all concerned had expected a

† Lord Chesterfield was famous for the excellence of his manners. A series of letters, written to his son, had been published and became a sort of book of etiquette for the well-bred and polished gentleman—or those who merely wished to be.

Albert Pike in an 1850 daguerreotype four years after his duel with John S. Roane

funeral, instead of a banquet, and the result could not be otherwise than surprising.[4]

Lest the speed of reconciliation make it appear that Roane and Pike were never serious, it should be noted that according to the *Code Duello,* it was an unthinkable social sin to continue a quarrel after fire had been exchanged. Both men probably thought they would be killed.

How on earth did Pike get himself into such a position? Both Mrs. Roome and Allsopp make oblique references to it. The reader will recall Mrs. Roome's line:

Shortly after the close of that war there appeared in the columns of a Little Rock newspaper an article written by him [Pike], severely criticizing the conduct of a part of the Arkansas regiment at the battle of Buena Vista, of which regiment John Selden Roane was Lieutenant–Colonel. The latter considered these criticisms as reflecting upon him personally, and immediately sent a challenge to Captain Pike.

Allsopp puts it a little more colloquially.

Pike resumed his law practice when he returned from the Mexican War in August, 1848. He came back to Little Rock with much to say. Not at that time owning a newspaper of his own, he took the columns of the Arkansas Gazette *to say it in the usual Pike way, which was heartily and frankly.*[5]

Really to understand why these two genuinely brave men beguiled a morning taking potshots at each other, we need yet a little more background. The data for the following is taken from Wallace Lee Brown.

Pike had commanded a regiment of Arkansas volunteers in the Mexican War. The battle of Buena Vista had been successful, but considerable mismanagement had been present, and Pike placed the blame squarely on the regimental officers, Archibald Yell and John Selden Roane. In a letter written on March 8, 1847, to the *Arkansas Gazette,* Pike remarked upon the action of the battle on February 23.

It is a sad thing that brave men, for they were brave, should be...destroyed for want of discipline. In the first place, the companies of our Regiment engaged there, had been hardly drilled at all, except what little the company officers had done. The Colonel and Lieutenant Colonel [Roane] had never drilled them since they left San Antonio. Their order once broken could not be restored, and a retreat was bound to be a rout.... Had they... possessed that mobility and facility of changing front which only discipline could give, they could not have been routed as they were. Poor Yell! He atoned for his error with his life, but other brave men died with him, who were not in fault.

General Archibald Yell

General Antonio Lopez de Santa Anna

It must not be understood that I intend to accuse any, much less officers, of a lack of bravery—on the contrary, the universal testimony is that the officers behaved with great gallantry—but the astonishing confusion for want of discipline, utterly broke up, dispensed and disorganized their commands, so that they could not be collected together. Many of the men behaved heroically, but their individual courage and conduct could not restore confidence or order to the mass.[6]

Considering the fact that Pike was accusing him of being so poor a leader that he was responsible for the deaths of several of his men, it is not too surprising that Roane "considered these criticisms as reflecting on him personally." Pike quite probably was a better leader—he never missed a chance to drill his troops, and they did very well indeed—but it is understandable that Roane did not find that comforting. Charges and countercharges grew so heated that Pike finally requested General Wool to appoint a court of inquiry to investigate the situation. Roane did not wish a full investigation, and the court was told that everything had been the result of a misunderstanding and that all was now well.

General John Ellis Wool

But Roane did not let the matter rest there. Pike had written a poem on the victory and sent it to the newspapers. The poem remained very popular for a long time after it was printed. Part of it reads:

Buena Vista[†]

From the Rio Grand's waters to the icy lakes of Maine,
Let all exult! for we have met the enemy again;
Beneath their stern old mountains we have met them in their pride,
And rolled from Buena Vista back the battle's bloody tide;
When the enemy came surging swift, like the Mississippi's flood,
And the reaper, Death, with strong arms swung his sickle red with blood.

SANTANA boasted loudly that, before two hours were past,
His Lancers through Saltillo should pursue us fierce and fast,—
On comes his solid infantry, line marching after line;
Lo! their great standards in the sun like sheets of silver shine;
With thousands upon thousands,—yea, with more than three to one,—
Their forest of bright bayonets fierce-flashing in the sun.

. . . .

Now, WOOL, hold strongly to the heights! for, lo! the mighty tide
Comes, thundering like an avalanche, deep, terrible, and wide.
Now Illinois, stand steady! Now, Kentucky, to their aid!
For a portion of our line, alas! is broken and dismayed;
Great bands of shameless fugitives are fleeing from the field,[‡]
And the day is lost, if Illinois and brave Kentucky yield.

Battle of Buena Vista
Engraving from J. Frost, *The Mexican War and Its Warriors,* 1849

[†] At the Battle of Buena Vista (Feb. 22–23, 1847) General Zachary Taylor, with an army of 4,700, defeated Santa Anna's Mexican force three times that size.
[‡] The rout Pike complained of and which he blamed on Yell and Roane

Ride! May!—To Buena Vista! for the Lancers gain our rear,
And we have few troops there to check their vehement career.[†]
Charge, Arkansas! Kentucky!, charge! Yell, Porter, Vaughan, are slain,
But the shattered troops cling desperately unto that crimsoned plain;
Till, with the Lancers intermixed, pursuing and pursued,
Westward, in combat hot and close, drifts off the multitude.
. . . .
And thus on Buena Vista's heights a long day's work was done,
And thus our brave old General another battle won.
Still, still our glorious banner waves, unstained by flight or shame,
And the Mexicans among their hills still tremble at our name.
So, honor unto those that stood! Disgrace to those that fled!
And everlasting glory unto BUENA VISTA'S DEAD![7]

When Pike returned to Little Rock he discovered that Roane and one of Roane's officers had written letters to a newspaper stating that Pike's regiment did not take part in the Battle of Buena Vista at all. Since Pike's regiment had not only been in the battle but had fought with great credit, this was a flat lie. Pike, as a result, challenged Roane to the duel.

However general the rejoicing may have been that the duel was concluded without bloodshed, the rejoicing was not universal. One of those who had come to witness the duel, a Cherokee named Bill Fields, was simply disgusted. He remarked, in broken English, that with either of the pistols the combatants used, he could have killed a squirrel every time at 75 steps. He had a little trouble understanding how two large men—both supposed to be good shots—could repeatedly miss each other at ten steps.[9]

Albert Pike

[†] A full-speed charge, not one's life work.

XI

The Pleasures Of The Flesh, The Balance Of The Spirit

On Physical And Spiritual Joys

It's probably part of the "plaster saint" effect, but for some reason, it always seems to surprise people that Albert Pike liked food, wine, dancing, and the company of beautiful women.

He did.

Pike remembers, with what really seems to be a little nostalgia:

> The mad bouts of our younger years, when we were somewhat noted for our qualities as boon companions and spoken of far and wide for our capacity as wine-bibbers† and were foolishly vain of it ourselves.[1]

In fact Pike was rather hard on his body. In his later years reflecting back on his earlier life and on the dual, body–spirit nature of man, he concluded that his body had come out with the short end of the stick. Pike continued his comments, noted above, saying:

> I rather think that if either portion of me has just cause of complaint, it is my body. If it has vexed me some fifty times with bilious fevers, I have permitted divers [various] disciples of Aesculapius [doctors] to afflict it grievously with nauseous medicines; and if it confined me to my room and the sight of the brick walls cross the street during four months of the dead year 1872, I am its debtor for its persuading me to engage in studies of interest and profit, and still more for the visits of friends, and the frequent presence of one sweet face [Vinnie Ream, see Chapter XIII] which otherwise I should never have learned to love so well.
>
> I have exposed it to many hardships, and privations, and been greatly careless of its comfort, and well-being, starved it for many

---

† Per capita consumption of alcohol in the 1800s in America was more than three times what it presently is. Like most of his contemporaries, Pike drank heartily. It should be noted, though, that his friends commented they had never seen him "under the influence." The Scottish Rite, then as now, has always prohibited use of alcohol in any of its facilities.

days together, and famished it with thirst, and worn it with fatigue, in the great deserts where Red River and the Brazos have their sources. I have not been over temperate in eating or drinking, and have never hesitated to rob it of its needed hours of sleep, whether for profitable or unprofitable purposes. What was the suffering I caused it, when I compelled it to cross the snow covered Sierra east of Taos, its extremities freezing in the intense cold; what weariness and aches in the long journeys on foot through the deserts of the Red River, the Brazos, the Cimarron and the Canadian!

Ah! We have endured many hardships and much fatigue and had many pleasures together with adventures and mad-cap follies this body of mine and I; and if I do sometimes wish it were younger, I am well enough content with it as it is, and begrudge the worms the privilege of fattening on it, when I and it shall part company. If it is not part of myself, I love it as much as if it were, and wish I could know that it would be burned to ashes, and could believe as my ancestors did that it would be transmuted into Light, ascend by the three steps of Vishnu to the highest heaven, and there add new brilliance to the radiant stars.[2]

Stars aside, Pike had known what it was to be thirsty and hungry. A few of the lines from his prairie days make that clear. It's no wonder he enjoyed food when he could get it.

I got very thirsty once, went without water three days and starved three days. I tried everything to appease my hunger, I even tried chewing on a bullet. Then we got the Mesquite bean, which helped out some, but I did not find any relief from chewing bullets or anything of that kind.

Pretty soon after leaving the main party we got on the head borders of the Brazos river. And every one of us, the whole party, worked for water. The bed of the stream was dry. We dug all night with our knives in the bed of the river for water. We finally got water, but it was so salt that we got no relief from it.... I used to think on that trip that if I ever got back to the United States,[†] I would go from one hotel to another, eating and drinking.[3]

And when he got back from the war in Mexico, he wrote:

I had not had anything to eat or drink fit to eat for six months. We had nothing to drink in Mexico but mescal[‡]—and I tell you it was

[†] It's sometimes hard to remember that what would become Oklahoma and New Mexico were not in the United States at the time.

[‡] Mescal is a cheap potable by-product of the manufacture of tequila.

caution. Our satisfaction was to go where we could get something to drink. I think I got six mint juleps[†] in less than half an hour.[4]

It would be unfair to Pike to leave the suggestion that he was an indiscriminate boozer. He had, in fact, a finely developed palate, both for food and wine, and was a rather moderate drinker for his time. Allsopp quotes an unpublished manuscript by Col. J. N. Smithee:

In the hotels, old French restaurants and coffee houses in New Orleans and Washington, it was the fashion to duplicate the dishes of Captain Pike. There are few people who know how to order a dinner, usually being content with what the waiter chooses to set before them. Pike was fond of a good dinner, good wine and genial companions, and he knew how to select each. Often he visited the national capital to appear as an attorney before the Supreme Court of the United States. There Pike's dinners became famous and he drew around him a jolly set of companions and bon vivants as ever graced the board of Lucullus.[‡] *Among them were the brightest, brainiest and wittiest men in the nation's capital. They included editors, poets, authors and statesmen.*

An old friend said that he met him at a dinner party given in his honor by a well-known citizen at New Orleans. When he was introduced to make a speech, as usual, the guests were struck with admiration at his noble and commanding appearance, and charmed by his affable and courteous demeanor,—so much so that he was lionized during his stay in that city. In his speech on that occasion, he narrated incidents of his life, but in a quiet and modest manner, dwelling more on the acts and doings of companions and associates than of himself.[5]

Smithee was not the only one to be impressed. A traveler from England by the name of Alfred Bunn wrote an article when he returned to England about his travels in America. Of Pike, he said:

We had the further pleasure of becoming known to one whose literary and social qualifications are of the most enviable distinction—we allude to Albert Pike, of Little Rock, Arkansas, one of America's distinguished poets, whose name heads the list of chiefs. To his brilliant conversation the table owed a great part of its diversion, and to his wit the fullest amount of its hilarity.[6]

[†] A book on mixed drinks (kept on hand solely to research such questions, of course) suggests that a mint julep in Pike's day was four ounces of bourbon, ice, and sugar mixed with mint that has been crushed in a little hot water. Assuming that to be the case, the young Pike made it through 24 ounces or a pint and a half of alcohol in half an hour. It's a wonder all that ice, sugar, and mint didn't have an adverse effect.

[‡] Lucius Licinius Lucullus, Roman Consul and General, c. 117–56 B.C., known for lavish and convivial dinners

Pike had an appreciative eye for beauty and, as has been shown earlier, a really keen sense of humor. Those come together in a rather strange way in one of the essays he wrote to Vinnie Ream, "Essay IV—Of Man's Opinions of Women," quoted below.

As you can see from this fashion drawing of that day, it was the mode to wear dresses, as the French would say, décolleté, barely covering the bosom. Obviously, the fabric in formal evening dresses was not evenly distributed.

It was the literary fashion at the time for the newspapers to cover dinners and receptions in Washington in elaborate detail, spending hundreds of words describing the dresses. This is a stanza from "A Dollar or Two" which is quoted in Chapter XII, "General Pike Was Not Wanting In Humor."

Do you wish that the Press should the decent thing do,
And give your reception a gushing review,
Describing the dresses by stuff, style, and hue?
Hand Jenkins in private a Dollar, or two.

Pike, writing to Vinnie, suggests that the newspaper writers have the wrong idea. Instead of describing the dresses, they should be describing the ladies' décolletage. (Lest anyone get upset, remember that one of Pike's favorite styles of satire is in the tradition of Jonathan Swift—writing outrageous things in a perfectly serious and dead-pan fashion.)

I am no ascetic, and should prefer it, if poetically done, to... stupid details of the dress and its material. I have pleasant recollections of more than one fair bosom that I have had ample opportunity to feast my eyes upon, standing behind and looking down upon and between the snowy globes that were revealed by the dress in all their charming symmetry.

Only I do not understand by what dexterity of feminine reasoning the conclusion is arrived at that it is modest and becoming to bare the bosom to lewd eyes, and not allow a glimpse of the ankle to be had.[7]

Although, in point of fact, Pike thought some of the concerns people had about modesty to be a little overdone.

We are the only living creatures that God made, to be ashamed of being seen by its kind as He made it. What, after all, is modesty in dress, but mere habit? It is not deemed necessary to clothe the statues of men or women, and there may be more immodesty in dress than in nakedness.... We believe in the resurrection of the body...and would not wish to believe that we shall not see in heaven the eyes and faces and loved bodies of those dear to us here; and we do not expect to avail ourselves, there, of the art of the tailor or milliner. It would be an immense relief to men of slender incomes if the female dress were worn only for the purpose of hiding and concealing that which our Maker must have thought not unfit to be seen, the human person. But it is worn for the purpose of adornment, of display, of extravagance, to gratify vanity and to enhance the value of the unseen. The savage is actuated by some of the same motives, when he sticks a red feather in his hair.[8]

Pike understood how easy it was for people to focus too completely on the body and the things of the flesh. But while he firmly believed in the spiritual and knew that the spiritual was much more important than the body, he had little patience with those who attempted to deny their physical being.

Those who despise and mortify their bodies are in the right to do so, if they think them worthless, or impediments to the aspirations of the soul. But as without bodies, we should be without sins, so also we should be without any human virtues. We should be subject to no pains, but also we should have no human pleasures; and to the very sensual appetites, to revile which is deemed to be a duty of religion, we owe all the noblest energies and virtues of man and woman. The human being is a unit, altogether the work of God, and not in part that of the devil. The appetites and passions are forces, that God has given to us, to be the springs and creative causes of energy and excellence. If we had not these forces, our moral sense and reason would be inactive, torpid, and barren. The more energetic and powerful the appetites and passions are, the greater excellence, is there in due proportion between these and the moral sense and reason. For they are the inciters to most human action and endeavor, though they are consequences of the organization of the body only; and the admirable harmony of excellence results, if the senses of right and wrong and the reason keep them in due control, not mortifying and denying them, but tempering and regulating their forces, and so maintaining a due equilibrium between the opposing forces of body and soul resembling that which is found in the Deity between the infinite power and the infinite wisdom, the infinite justice and the infinite mercy, the almighty Will and infinite beneficence, makes the sublime and eternal harmony of the Universe.[9]

Balance. Equilibrium. Those two great concepts appear again and again in the Degrees of the Scottish Rite and in the other works of Pike. Nowhere, perhaps, is that balance more important than in the great conflicts between the body and the spirit.

It should be realized at once that Pike did not want to "deny" the body or its appetites. His teaching was that they must be controlled, not eliminated. In Freudian terms, the Superego must control the Id.

If the body—which is to say the appetites of the body—are left without control, the result is selfishness, at best. Rather like a child who has not learned self-control, the body wants what it wants when it wants it, and if others are hurt and inconvenienced, so be it. The mind and spirit must take control of the appetites and channel them into useful energy.

That can be quite a fight.

That which is the greatest battle, and in which the truest honor and most real success are to be won, is that which our intellect and reason and moral sense, our spiritual natures, fight against our sensual appetites and evil passions, our earthly and material or animal nature. Therein only are the true glories of heroism to be won, there only the successes that entitle us to triumphs.[10]

This concept of virtue as the triumph of the mind and spirit over the animal and sensual is so central to the development of a spiritual life as Pike saw it that he returns to the topic again and again.

Virtue is an attribute and disposition of the mind, from which flows effort to overcome or govern the appetites and passions.... The man is *virtuous*, who is not *without* desires, appetites, instincts, and passions; but who is master of, and controls them. For virtue to exist, there must be a struggle and a warfare. The tame, spiritless, passionless, negative being is not virtuous.... Virtue is strong, vigorous, active, impassioned, more sublime in proportion to the energy of the passions it overcomes.[11]

But Pike makes it clear that the passions, while animal, are not evil. They cannot be evil, since they were given to people by God. They are great blessings and the means of enjoying pleasure. The secret is: use them, but control them; do not abuse them nor be used by them.

All the attributes and capacities of a human being are given it by a beneficent God, for wise and beneficent purposes. This is our Masonic faith. In every human being, as in all the universe, He has implanted conflicting forces, by the opposite action of which to produce harmonious results. The appetites and passions are not given by a malicious demon, for the misery of the child, the man, or the woman, as a curse; but by God our Father, in the exercise of His infinite beneficence and love. They are necessary to the enjoyment of the means of gratification and pleasure which He has poured out around us in such endless profusion. To be capable of use, in any being less than perfect, they must necessarily be capable of abuse; and to create a *perfect* being, if *possible*, would be for the Deity to reproduce Himself. A creature in whom the soul is united to a body of flesh and blood, and gifted with human senses, is in part of an animal nature, and is necessarily imperfect.

Albert Pike

The appetites and passions are necessary to the existence of man, and ministers or sources of lawful pleasures. The desire to gratify them produces the necessity for labor and exertion. Abused and unrestrained, they become low and base, and causes of vice and crime. Used and gratified in moderation, they are the springs and sources of all heroic, manly, and noble actions, the very life-blood of the affections of the heart, and the best aspirations of the soul.[12]

Spirituality and faith are essential to us. We are so constructed that we simply cannot be happy and complete without them.

No man can suffer and be patient, can struggle and conquer, can improve and be happy, otherwise than as the swine are, without conscience, without hope, without a reliance on a just, wise, and beneficent God. We must, of necessity, embrace the great truths taught by Masonry, and live by them, to live happily. "I put my trust in God," is the protest of Masonry against the belief in a cruel, angry, and revengeful God, to be feared and not reverenced by His creatures.[13]

Faith in moral principles, in virtue, and in God, is as necessary for the guidance of a man, as instinct is for the guidance of an animal.[14]

And this awareness of God resulting in the ascendancy of the spiritual over the animal is, as Pike points out, what Masonry is all about. This is the great recurring lesson from the first Masonic degree to the last.

For the Apprentice, the points of the Compass are beneath the Square. For the Fellow–Craft, one is above and one beneath. For the Master, both are dominant, and have rule, control, and empire over the symbol of the earthly and the material [the Square]....

To achieve it, the Mason must first attain a solid conviction, founded upon reason, that he hath within him a spiritual nature, a soul that is not to die when the body is dissolved, but is to continue to exist....

Every Degree of the Ancient and Accepted Scottish Rite, from the first to the thirty-second, teaches by its ceremonial as well as by its instruction, that the noblest purpose of life and the highest duty of a man are to strive incessantly and vigorously to win the mastery of everything, of that which in him is spiritual and divine, over that which is material and sensual; so that in him also, as in the Universe which God governs, Harmony and Beauty may be the result of a just equilibrium.[15]

XII

"General Pike Was Not Wanting In Humor"

On Pike At Play

General Pike was not wanting in humor. No truly great soul is. In his collected poems, the reader may enjoy that capital song known as 'The Fine Arkansas Gentleman,' which is unsurpassed. . .for Falstaffian fun."[1]

That's a little like saying that Niagara Falls is not without moisture. Pike was famous for his sense of humor, and it is a great misfortune that most people know him, if they know him at all, by the most serious of his writing, *Morals and Dogma*. It's a great and rewarding book, but it fails to reflect the total richness of Pike's output.

This was the man famous for always having a new joke or story to tell. Friends wrote home about evenings spent in Pike's company and of the mirth, laughter, and good fellowship which were always part of such evenings.

There are other quotations scattered throughout the book which could have gone just as easily in this chapter, but the purpose here is to focus on the sheer fun in which Pike invited his readers to share.

Sometimes the humor is very dry and understated, and Pike leaves the reader to do the work of imagination. In this short passage, for example, simply consider the image of Pike, riding on a mule, and trying to run down a buffalo, rather like Sancho Panza trying to catch up with the good Don Quixote.

> We approached warily to within a hundred yards of the animals, and then rushed upon them; and had I been mounted on anything but a slow mule, the chase would have been exciting. As it was, I was soon distanced; for though a buffalo appears, both standing and running, to be the most unwieldy thing in the world, I can assure my reader that they get along with no inconsiderable velocity.[2]

Mules appeared again in Pike's sketches of his early explorations in the West. Read this, close your eyes, visualize it, and see if the Keystone Kops don't come to mind.

None of the men knew how to manage the animals, and they were generally no sooner on than off. One poor fellow was no sooner on his mule's back than he was seen describing a somerset [somersault]—pitching in his fall plump upon his head. Another would go up in the air as straight as an arrow, and alight on his feet. Others would stick on, and the mules taking the bit in their teeth, would run a mile or two with them like incarnate fools.[3]

The mule which we had packed was a little, ungainly wretch, of a most crooked and morose disposition. To speak the simple truth, though somewhat irreverently, she was a perfect devil incarnate. About four miles from Santa Fe I rode aside from the path to obtain a near view of a singular hill to the left, and while delaying there, heard my squire raising a most terrific whoop, with as much earnestness and repetition as though a bunch of Flat Heads had attacked him. I hastened to the rescue, at the utmost speed of which my mule was capable—which was but slow withal—and found my paragon of squires busily attempting to disencumber *Mulita* of her packs. She had lain down out of sheer obstinacy, and refused to budge until we took off the packs and assisted her to regain her legs. We soon discovered that a

Pike, a New Englander, was caught off guard by the adobe houses in New Mexico, which contrasted strongly with the Newburyport, Massachusetts, houses he had left not long ago. This painting by Will Hurd is typical of the people and architecture Pike encountered on the trip in which one particular mule was to prove so frustrating.

mule is not exactly the animal to humor in that way. Afterward, and as soon as she came in sight of a hill, down she dropped, and the same farce of unloading was again to be enacted. My patience at length failed me—with which I was never overstocked—and I resolved to try my obstinacy against hers.[†] Down she fell again, set her ears forward, with a mulish expression of countenance which seemed to say, "get me up if you can." I dismounted, took my rope of plaited hide from my saddle bow, and directed Manuel to do the same. Each of us applied to the gourd[‡] for resolution, and then standing, one on each side of *Mulita*, commenced beating her where she lay, with the knotted ends of our ropes.... After bearing it until the patience of a mule could endure no longer, she sprang up with one jump, and trotted on. She went on for about six miles without again taking lodgings, until we arrived at the little town of which I before spoke. In order to reach the village we had a broad ditch, about three feet deep, to cross, dug for the purpose of conveying water to irrigate the fields. Into this I drove *Mulita*, but she had no sooner got fairly in than down she dropped, on one side, covering one trunk entirely, and after remaining so for a moment, rolled over on the other side. I was strongly tempted to murder her, but though greatly enraged, could not help being amused at the diabolical revenge she had taken. Everything was thoroughly wet.[4]

Pike was fascinated by the people of the frontier, and he captured the expressions and rhythms of their speech with his famous memory and with the "ear" which had made him an accomplished violinist. It helps to read the next passage aloud, listening to the differences in the formal rhythms and rather strained tone with which Pike opens the narrative and the language which is to follow.

Reader, didst ever see a shooting-match in the west? I dare swear you never have, and therefore there may be no tediousness in a description of one. I hate your set descriptions, laid out, formally, in squares and parallelograms, like an old-fashioned garden, wherein art hath not so far advanced as to seem like nature. You can just imagine the scene to yourself. Conceive that you are in a forest, where the huge trees have been for ages untouched by the axe. Imagine some twenty

---

† Trying to out-stubborn a mule is an awesome task!

‡ Pike has earlier mentioned that the gourd was "shaped like an hour glass, and holding, at a moderate computation, about half a gallon, filled with a liquor some scores of times stronger than spring water."

men—tall, stalwart, browned hunters, equipped in leather, with their broad knives by their sides, rifles in hand, and every man with his smoke-blackened board in his hand. The rivals in the first contest were eight sturdy fellows, middle aged and young men. The ox for which they were to shoot was on the ground, and it was to be the best six shots out of eleven. The four quarters, and the hide and tallow, were the five prizes; they were to shoot off-hand at forty yards, or with a rest, at sixty, which is considered the same thing. The judges were chosen, and then a blackened board, with a bit of paper on it about an inch square, was put up against a tree. "Clar the track!" cried the first marksman, who lay on the ground at his distance of sixty yards, with his gun rising over a log. The rifle cracked, and the bullet cut into the paper. "Put up my board!" cried another; "John, shade my sight for me!" and John held his hat over the sight of the gun. It cracked, and the bullet went within half an inch of the center. "My board!" cried another; "I'll give that shot goose!"[†]—and he did, fairly boring the center with the ball. The sport soon became exciting. It requires great steadiness of nerve to shoot well, for any irregularity in breathing will throw the bullet wide of the mark. The contest was longer than I anticipated; but was decided without quarrel or dispute. The judges decided, and their decision was implicitly obeyed. The whole eleven shots of one man, who won two quarters, could be covered by a half dollar.[5]

Pike was justly famous for the eulogies he delivered for his friends. He was often called upon to provide them (and they are things of great beauty—collected in a book entitled *Ex Corde Locutiones: Words From The Heart, Spoken of Dead Brethren by the Grand Commander of the Supreme Council of the 33D Degree for the Southern Jurisdiction of the United States, 1860 to 1891* and published after Pike's death), so there is a little hit at himself in this passage.

After praising each other all our lives, there are always excellent Brethren, who, over our coffins, shower unlimited eulogies. Every one of us who dies, however useless his life, has been a model of all the virtues, a very child of the celestial light.[6]

Pike's self-deprecating humor can be very dry indeed; you have to think about this one for a while. Readers familiar with Mark Twain's explanation of his own vices and why it was so important to have several well-cultivated bad habits (so that one could give them up in an emergency) will notice a certain similarity of outlook.

† Your guess is as good as mine.

I have never feared any indulgence so much as to make myself the slave of an oath never to enjoy it. I prefer to be master of it by my own free will. I have not lived in obedience to any rigid rules, for these make a species of servitude, even when they are our own enactments. An inditement [sic] against me for irregularities would be proved with a multitude of counts.[7]

Pike even made fun of himself as a lawyer, and he was proud of his success in the law and of the important cases he had won. Still, he knew that many people truly believed that lawyers were incapable of simply saying what they meant.

Now it happened that some hogs were getting into his garden in Little Rock, and he fully intended to shoot the next one that did. And so he inserted a notice to that effect in the newspaper, *The Advocate*, May 22, 1835, using legalese at its finest.

Whereas certain unprincipled hogs have contracted a vile habit of making forcible entry into my garden, by demolishing the fence—to the great injury of the vegetables therein—And whereas, also, I have read the riot act to them sundry times without its producing any salutary effect—This is to give notice, that after tomorrow, I shall be in the habit, for my own recreation, of discharging sundry guns, pistols, etc. on my premises—loaded with shot and powder—and that it is very possible that some of the said shot might by accident hit some of the said hogs, unless the owners should take care of their four-legged property.[8]

The law comes in for its fair share of Pike's humor.

A lawyer now is one who works for fees, defending the wrong as readily as the right, and supposed to be unscrupulous as to the intellectual means and devices by which to achieve success. If he is admitted to be honest, and regarded as respectable, he is rather thought to be so notwithstanding his profession; and if sufficiently plausible and unscrupulous he may become a legislator; and there are yet a few states wherein, if really eminent in his profession, he may become a judge.[9]

There is another type of lawyer, intellectually so constituted as to be incapable of appreciating and understanding a closely logical argument. They provoke an antagonist beyond endurance, by this imperviousness and invulnerability, which the keenest shafts of logic cannot penetrate. They hear all with a stoic complacency, and reply, not to your argument, but to something else that you have not said or thought. They are unconvincable, and equally incapable of themselves arguing logically. They can no more distinguish the true from the false, than a man colorblind can believe a red light *is* red and not green. They are habitually lost, like a man in the woods or a cane-break, who incessantly travels round in a circle. They can no more tell in what quarter the truth lies, than a man can tell in which direction the North lies, when he is enveloped in a fog on the prairie.† And points of the intellectual compass can no more get right for them than those of the physical compass can, to us, in a place where we were, at the beginning, turned round; as the sun rises for me in the West, at New Orleans, and in the North at Washington, and as one will be so completely reversed in railroad travel, that he cannot force his sense to understand that he is not going eastward when going westward, and so that he has to ignore the evidence of his senses, to believe that his berth is not on the opposite side of the car.

So there are judges who, as the speckled denizens of the dark pool "rises" only to a gaudy and glittering fly, listen with weary indifference to the reading of the law, to elaborate discussion of its analogies, to the interpretation of it by the old law, to illustration and explication, and "rise" only to the fallacy or a phrase, by which they are inevitably hooked.[10]

That humor takes another form in his "Essay VII—Of Habits and Their Slaves," where Pike lists some bad habits which are especially annoying.

What habit is so irksome as that of the habitual punster, always lying in wait for you to entrap you and insensible to your misery. You wish that some serious calamity might be visited on him; and yet, to pun is no crime; but only a misdemeanor.‡ The propounder of conundrums is even less tolerable,§ for he always

† Pike is poking a little fun at himself here. When he and his companions were returning from their original trip to Taos, decades before, when Pike was a very young man, they had intended to go to South America and seek their fortunes there. They got turned around in the fog in the prairie, which lasted more than a day, and went in exactly the wrong direction, ending up in Arkansas. Pike's whole career as a lawyer, a general in the Civil War, and all his Masonic activities, were a result of getting lost in a fog. No further editorial comment is offered.

‡ Pike is, of course, making an atrocious pun on "demean" and "demeanor." Also there seems to be an echo of the line by Charles Lamb (whom, we know from Pike's essays, Pike read and enjoyed). Asked to make a pun, Lamb replied, "Upon what subject?"

"The King," his listener replied.

"Impossible," said Lamb, "the King is no subject."

§A conundrum is a riddle or question whose answer is a pun—just like the first sentence of this passage endeavors to make you his accomplice. Who makes you so uncomfortable as the habitual grumbler, at his luck, at the weather, at the short-comings of his inn, the scant and poor fare of the way-side eating-houses, the discomforts traveling, the rudeness of landlords and servants? What ill habit is more disagreeable than that of censoriousness [finding fault]? Unless, perhaps, that of flattery.

And what habit so detestable as that of cant [hypocritical talk]? What more unfortunate than that of disputation,† the fruitful mother of quarrels and intolerance? The habit of intolerance, in religion and politics grows upon a man, and if he cannot gratify it,‡ makes him miserable. "He will hardly get to heaven," it is said, "who desires to go there alone;" but he in whom intolerance has become a fixed habit thinks heaven hardly worth the trouble of getting there, if one of a rival sect is to go with him. He might not misdirect one seeking to find his way there, if he knew the road, and the other, of a different belief, did not; but he would be sure "never to show the way to anyone at the same shrines not worshipping."[11]

His humor could have more than a little bite.

A peacock is not half as vain of his tail as a man is of being loved.—at first. Afterwards————![12]

Consider the value of Nonsense. In Congress or before the people, it is more convincing than an oration of Demosthenes. On stage it attracts larger and more delighted audiences than the plays of Shakespeare, and no books sell better or are more read than those that contain nothing else than nonsense. In the pulpit, the empty declaimer wins more applause than the golden-mouthed Chrysostom§ could. Our modern poets, with a few exceptions, eschew nonsense, and are intelligible, and some, like Tennyson, teach the highest philosophy in stately and melodious verse. I believe that a Scotsman once defined metaphysical discussion as being, "when the chief ye're talking to disna ken what ye mean, and ye dinna ken yerself."[13]

---

† Disputation, argument and discussion for the sheer love of the clash of ideas, was one of Pike's favorite pastimes.

‡ Obviously, anyone can gratify an urge to be intolerant at any time he wishes; all he has to do is not tolerate something. But Pike is suggesting here that intolerance is like the habit of drinking—when someone has a habit of drinking, wants a drink and can't get one, it makes him miserable.

§ St. John of Chrysostom (fl. 3rd century), known for the beauty and elegance of his sermons

Sometimes, Pike's "bite" was more like that of a shark. Consider his attack on the Reconstruction government of Tennessee.

"There was, thank God, not the least chance that wisdom would rule in the counsels of the State, control the course of the lunatic who is Governor, or influence the extraordinary zoological collection called by courtesy a legislature."[14]

Or reflect on these passing shots at Congress.

Some men seem to have borrowed their manners from the gaming-dens, the prize rings, or the House of Representatives.[15]

A lingering reverence or affection for the Law, and fear of the censure of a respectable judge, are seldom wholly without effect to restrain the lawyer inclined to stray into evil courses; but the great majority of legislators are under no restraint whatever.[16]

The harangues of stump-orators in the Southern, Southwestern and Northwestern states of the Union, have wrought incalculable mischief. They are incomparably greater afflictions than epidemic diseases. As a lie has more legs than a centipede, and the antagonistic or contradictory truth is snail-paced, and never overtakes it, so Error in matters of policy and legislation, rarely succumbs to the Truth, but clad in triple-brass is invulnerable, even in the heel.† So the prophets of Baal of the press outnumber those of the Truth, twenty to one; and to them, in a great measure, all the follies and calamities of the country are owing. And if no human being had ever heard or read a single speech ever made in Congress, the balance of profit to the Country though it would have lost many utterances of wisdom, would have been enormous, for Error is always more persuasive and acceptable to the people than truth.[17]

Sometimes, the bite sneaks softly up, wearing a smiling face. In this passage, Pike takes devastating blows at social conversation, small talk, and his favorite target, Congress.

No one can reasonably object to nonsense, in its proper place. We are a nonsensical race. In after-dinner speeches it is eminently appropriate and acceptable. In fashionable conversation it is indispensable. It is the fractional currency of the polite world; and without it, most men would be reduced to monosyllables in chatting with women. These chatter it with a charming volubility, and to talk it well is the most desirable of accomplishments. If we had in our fashionable coteries, "the sparkling nonsense of educated and intellectual trifles" of the modern French *salon*, it would not be

† The reference is to Achilles, who could only be wounded in the heel.

without actual value; but the "*peine forte et dure*" ["pain, strong and lasting"; torture] of our fashionable small talk, is worse than the incessant dropping of water on the head of a criminal.

Let nonsense be endured in its place; but against judicial and Congressional nonsense all who have a regard for the public welfare ought emphatically to protest. In it and cant there is incredible power for evil. Plausible nonsense is more dangerous to republics than foreign wars. It is a fatal mistake to suppose that fallacies and plausibilities are harmless, so long as Truth is left free to combat them. For Truth to be unhorsed in the lists† is not of rare occurrence. We reaped the fruits of nonsense, when the Northern and Southern States tore each other's throats for four wretched years, and that code of the devil, Martial Law, shook its bloody scepter over states.[18]

And at one point, tired and frustrated because his efforts to bring about investment in education and infrastructure were producing nothing, he wrote:

I am weary of Arkansas—weary and worn out, and must get out into the world, somewhere. It is nothing to me that I am in a minority here; because I have no tendency towards office; but I am sick of the constant squabbling and snarling that goes on around me, and of the antediluvian notions of Boobydom. The government of the State is in the fullest sense of the word a Boobyocracy,‡ and itself lies supine like a lean sow in a gutter, "with meditative grunts of much content," waiting for the good time to come when railroads, school houses and other public improvements will build themselves, and nobody have it to pay for. That's their idea of the millennium.[19]

President James Monroe

It is often the little touches in Pike's work which suggest his sense of the absurd. Consider this paragraph.

I expected to see President Monroe when he came to New England, but something happened that night, no one knew what. Monroe the President made what they call now a

† "Lists" were the spaces used for jousting.

‡ Some sixty years later, 1922, H. L. Mencken, noted American satirist, coined the word *booboisie* to describe the same mental attitude; antediluvian means "before the Flood."

tour through that part of New England. He was to be in Newburyport, but he did not come. But they had a parade all the same, and we had an old fellow in the carriage who, they said, resembled Monroe. They paraded him through the streets.[20]

Pike loved satire, and he wrote it well. In the following poem he takes on several issues which were problems in his lifetime. It is rather saddening to see how little has changed. (It's also impressive to see how many rhymes he found for the word "two.")

AN AUNCIENTE FYTTE,[†]
Pleasaunte and full of Pastyme of
A DOLLAR, OR TWO

With circumspect steps as we pick our way through
This intricate world, as all prudent folk do,
May we still on our journey be able to view
The benevolent face of a Dollar, or two.
For an excellent thing is a Dollar, or two;
No friend is so staunch as a Dollar, or two;
In country or town,
As we stroll up and down,
We are cock of the walk, with a Dollar, or two.

Do you wish to emerge from the bachelor-crew,
And a charming young innocent female to woo?
You must always be ready the handsome to do,[‡]
Although it may cost you a Dollar, or two.
For love tips his darts with a Dollar, or two;
Young affections are gained by a Dollar, or two;
And beyond all dispute,
The best card of your suite
Is the eloquent chink of a Dollar, or two.

Do you wish to have friends who your bidding will do,
And help you your means to get speedily through?
You'll find them remarkably faithful and true,
By the magical power of a Dollar, or two.
For friendship's secured by a Dollar, or two;
Popularity's gained by a Dollar, or two;
And you'll ne'er want a friend
Till you no more can lend,
And yourself need to borrow a Dollar, or two.

[†] An Ancient Poem, Pleasant and full of Pastime—"Fytte," (later "Fit") was actually an old term for a division of a long poem. Via this archaic diction choice, Pike is having fun suggesting that the problems of buying justice, etc., for "a dollar or two" are so ancient in our history that a poem might have been written on the topic several hundred years ago.
[‡] "To do the handsome thing" meant to do the thing which was expected of a generous gentleman.

Do you wish in the Courts of the Country to sue
For the right or estate that's another man's due?
Your lawyer will surely remember his cue,
When his palm you have crossed with a Dollar, or two.
For a lawyer's convinced with a Dollar, or two;
And a jury set right with a Dollar, or two;
And though justice *is* blind,
Yet a way you may find
To open her eyes with a Dollar, or two.

Do you want a snug place where there's little to do,
Or at Government cost foreign countries to view?
A contract to get, or a patent renew?
You can make it all right, with a Dollar, or two.
For merit is proved by a Dollar, or two;
And a patriot's known by a Dollar, or two;
Civil service rules?—Oh, oh!
They're all humbug, you know;
Just use with discretion a Dollar, or two.

If a claim that is proved to be honestly due,
Department or Congress you'd quickly put through,
And the chance for its payment begins to look blue,
You can help it along with a Dollar, or two.
For votes are secured by a Dollar, or two;
And influence bought by a Dollar, or two;
And he'll come to grief
Who depends for relief
Upon justice not braced with a Dollar, or two.

Do you wish that the Press should the decent thing do,
And give your reception a gushing review,
Describing the dresses by stuff, style, and hue?
Hand Jenkins in private a Dollar, or two.
For the pen sells its praise for a Dollar, or two;
And squirts its abuse for a Dollar, or two;
As contractors sell votes,
And banks discount notes,
That are not worth a damn, for a Dollar, or two.

Do you wish your existence with faith to imbue,
And so become one of the sanctified few?
To enjoy a good name and a well-cushioned pew,
You must freely come down with a Dollar, or two.
For the Gospel is preached for a Dollar, or two;
Salvation is reached by a Dollar, or two;
Sins are pardoned, sometimes,
But the worst of all crimes
Is to find yourself *short* of a Dollar, or two.[21]

Though Pike had a high regard for humanity, that regard did not keep him for viewing man's shortcomings with more than a touch of sardonic irony.

There is nothing in human nature so curious to me as its perversity, moral and intellectual. Every man is familiar with perversity in others, probably in himself, which compels one, as it were, to do what he knows to be wrong, ungenerous, unwise. We share it with certain members of the animal creation, the mule, pig, and hen. (It is worthy of consideration, that we have not one good moral quality which some animal hath not in a superior degree; nor hath any animal any vice or base or violent passion, that is not to be found in more detestable excellence in human nature.)

There is a logical perversity also, in the human intellect, in a greater or less degree, observable in the large majority of lawyers and judges which compels them, occasionally, frequently, or in some, always, to prefer sophisms [a clever use of words to hide a logical error], solecisms [incorrect speech], paralogismal [argument false in form] fallacies, and every manner of illogicality, to sound, correct, just and fair induction and deduction, logical connection of propositions and ideas, and honest processes of reasoning. Distortion of the intellect, mental myopism, intellectual color blindness, are by far more common than physical defects. I have known lawyers, two especially, who became Senators of the nation, who always preferred the wrong side of a case to the right one. One of these was singularly dexterous and felicitous in misstating the facts of a case, so that it was common to say that if you, opposed to him, did not watch him carefully, he would state your case away from under you: and I heard him once, in the Supreme Court of the United States, so unfairly, untruly and intentionally misstate his case, as to confuse his opponent who could not detect the fraud which made his argument idle and lost him the case.[22]

Very near the beginning of his career, Pike wrote some essays for the *American Monthly Magazine*. They involved descriptions of different kinds of men. They are worth a look. He was young, about 21, when he wrote them, and he had not yet developed the subtleties and the sharp thrusts of wit which are typical of his later work. But Pike's early essays for the *American Monthly* give good promise of what is to come. Consider this excerpt from "The Philosophy of Bowling."

What a glorious place is a bowling-alley for observing characters and passions—there is no place like it; you may judge there of a man's manners, of his self-possession, of his ease, of

Albert Pike

his energy, of his temper, and in a single item, of his whole character. Like walking or smoking, bowling is a matter in which but few men arrive at any perfection....

There is a certain tall, broad-shouldered, graceless acquaintance of mine, whom you will see shambling about the street any day. I never knew him to roll a ball in my life without hitting it upon the board so that it bounded at starting; and it is one chance in three that he rolls off at the side of the board. The way in which he gets on the board too, and takes the ball, and recovers himself after throwing, are all ludicrous. He throws too with a vengeance; and I have known him follow the ball a rod after it left his hands. Now he does not enjoy bowling; how can he?—without using any grace or ease in it. And bowling is a perfect development of his character.

There is another;—he throws a curved ball—and that too with an impetus. In his own mind now, that man is superb at bowling, and you'll hear him ejaculate—exquisite! capital!—at any good hit, as though he were playing first trumpet to his own praises; and yet, withal, he is rather poor at it; to tell you the whole truth he is a collection of vanity—and in the same proportion as he prides himself on being graceful and elegant, is he distant from being either. I don't think he enjoys bowling—he is too careful—there is too much aiming—and he rolls too vehemently.

Then here is another who is continually changing. At one time he rolls a swift ball—then a slow one—now he stands to the right of the board—now to the left—and in consequence he will average eight† always—he is too uneasy to enjoy bowling—he is not well enough satisfied with himself—and he is the same everywhere. I never hew him to keep to one thing a week in my life—and for a friend, I would as soon choose a flying squirrel....

Here is another that tosses his ball half way, and then stamps and pulls his hair if it does not go right, as if a tossed ball could go right....

But here is a man to whom bowling is a luxury—he has every requisite for a bowler—he is a poet you may know by his eye; and lazy you may know by his motions. If you get him to write you some half dozen lines, Hercules' labors were nothing to it—but when you get it, it is superb. You may see by the way in which he goes on the board, and takes his ball, that he will enjoy it; there is a peculiar sway of body in his moving, that shows an indolent ease—and he rolls beautifully too—throwing his ball out, not letting it slide from his hands—rather swiftly, but not very, and always striking where he aims; he makes nothing of a double, and is sure of twelve and a half for an afternoon's average—and that after all is the poetry of bowling.

To a man troubled with gentlemen in blue [policemen, bailiffs, and debt collectors], your bowling alley is a specific [a remedy]—for indeed every toss of the ball throws out some portion of their influence at the finger's ends; it is infinitely better than suicide when you are in debt and cannot get out of it—a pistol is nothing to it—and a voyage of discovery among fishes, and lumps of gold, and great anchors, should not be spoken of in the same breath.[23]

As one can see, Pike was fond of the extended analogy as a means of satire. But a few words of explanation are in order about this next example. Pike is here striking out at a social fad in the United States, and especially in Washington which surfaced during the latter years of his life. It became fashionable for women, both young and old, to be—or at least to act—silly and stupid. This really annoyed Pike who had a high regard for the intelligence and ability of women. Writing to Vinnie Ream, a highly talented young woman who shared his disgust at the fad, he compares the women with hens—an animal for whose intelligence Pike did not have a high regard.

† The method of scoring has altered over the 160 years since Pike wrote this.

There is in fact, a great deal of feminine nature in a hen, as one will soon learn, who will devote himself to diligent study of their ways and perversities, their humors, tempers, fancies and frivolities. Some are vain, idle and whimsical, given to gadding and gossip; some ill-tempered, cross-grained, petulant and peevish; some sedate, industrious and given to meditation; and all are self-willed and perverse, pertinacious and pragmatical. Where a hen chooses to lay, she *will* lay; and where she chooses to sit, she *will* sit. Some are motherly and kind to their chicks, and will adopt little motherless ones of the same age; while others are cross to their own, and will bestow invective and spiteful pecks on the unhappy little orphans; and some will remain quiet, permitting their week-old progeny to have rest and peace, while others will keep their chicks racing after them all day, until the little legs that move so funnily when they run, are tired out, as she travels about from morning to night, without ostensible purpose, as if possessed with a devil of unrest.

You become attached to some of them, and other you detest. But you have one advantage of dealing with these. When they are perverse, refractory, ill-conditioned and devilish, and beating fails to reform them, you can cut off their heads and be rid of them.[24]

XIII

The Bright Side–The Battle–The Dark Side

On Love

I have nothing ill-natured to say of women. I love the sex, for the sake of the fair faces that I have liked and loved, the innocent lips that I have kissed, and the hearts that have been loving and true to me. They are at least better than men: and when I weigh impartially the joys and sorrows that I have owed to women, I find the joys vastly preponderate.[1]

Love was to play important roles at the beginning and the end of Albert Pike's life. The middle part of it was less filled with love than with endurance.

Pike's writings on love fall into three divisions—the bright side, or romance; the battle of the sexes, sometimes observed with telling sarcasm; and the dark side, or love which turns to pain.

Photo: Library of Congress

Vinnie Ream

He fell deeply, passionately in love several times early on, as only a young man or woman can, especially in the 19th century, the Age of Romance. He married, and married for love, but the personality of his wife, Mary Ann Hamilton, changed over the years so that he spent most of his time alone with his books or his children. Finally, Pike and his children moved out of the family house where his wife remained. Despite their separation, Pike saw to it that his wife was very well provided for until her death. They were never formally divorced. He makes only a very few references to it in his letters, but he longed for a happy home life, which he was not to have.

And then, when he was well advanced in years, Pike met Vinnie Ream.

In our cynical age, it is hard to believe or realize that a love between an old man and a 19-year-old girl can truly be pure and honorable in intent. But so it was. Pike was one of the great minds of his age, and Vinnie was attracted to that mind. They shared many things deeply, but there is no indication at all that the physical ever entered into the relationship in thought, word, or deed. Most of the biographical information we have about Vinnie was compiled by Walter Lee Brown in his 1955 doctoral dissertation. In addition, much of the detail of this chapter is drawn from Pike's original letters and his voluminous personal essays written for and to Vinnie.

Vinnie Ream grew up in Washington, D.C., and Missouri. During the Civil War her family returned to Washington, and she got a job as a postal clerk. She was 15. About 1864, she went with a friend to visit Clark Mills, a sculptor in Washington with a very considerable reputation. She was admiring his work, and he tossed her a piece of clay, telling her to do a portrait of him. He intended it as kindly jest, but she quickly produced a good likeness, to the surprise of them both. He recognized great talent in her, and she became his student.

Photo: Office of the Curator, U.S. Capitol

Abraham Lincoln

Vinnie Ream's most famous statue (marble, 6′ 11″) was commissioned by Congress in 1870 for display in the Rotunda of the United States Capitol.

Brown points out that, before a year had passed, she had done busts of Senators Charles Summer, Thaddeus Stevens, John Sherman, and E. G. Ross. She had also sculpted Generals McClellan and Fremont, not to mention Horace Greeley. She had started on a sculpture of Abraham Lincoln, which was not completed at the time of his assassination. When Congress voted to have a full-length statue of Lincoln made for the Rotunda of the Capitol, she won the competition.

Vinnie and Pike became very good friends who greatly enjoyed spending time together, talking, and sharing ideas. When Vinnie subsequently married, her husband became as much a son to Pike as Vinnie was his daughter.

And it is to Vinnie we owe some of Pike's most interesting writing. He apparently mentioned in passing that he was thinking of writing some essays, and Vinnie jumped on the idea. This is Pike at his most gallant.

Cicero tells us that the highest adornment of age is dignity: but to me it seems that its most worthy decoration is to be still able to love the young and beautiful, and to content and gratify the one who has the right to its obedience to her wishes, as the first consequence of love. I comply with the desire of one who is beyond measure dearer to me, and who for her excellencies and unvarying affectionate goodness to me, is entitled as sovereign to look for me to do the utmost in my power to please and serve her.

She was glad that I should love her, when I was one of those who could say with Ovid, "We have lost all: life only yet remains to give the sense and subject of new pains, why joy to stab the limbs of life bereft? For a new wound no room at all is left."† And during all the days of trial and of sorrow since then her true love has been "all my life and all joy of living," all that has given me hope, confidence and courage, and the treasure of a tranquil peace of mind. She has been always the same, never otherwise than loving, finding comfort mid her other troubles in my love; a woman, an artist, wise, resolute, brave, and also to me a little loving child, ingenious and innocent; and it is very glory and pride to love her with all my heart and soul. So that it is true to me to say; "These no Calliope nor Apollo‡ sings; she whom I love my inspiration brings."

For when I half-jestingly spoke of writing some such essays, she said they were to be written for her, and has since then with a sweet consciousness of sovereignty assumed that it is surely to be done.§ To resist her will is vain; and I have now begun them. And if she promises, and keeps the promise, to come once in every week and hear read that which I have written, they may reach in number to a score. If they should remains always unknown to everyone in the world but her, it will be enough that *she* has heard them, and thanked me for them with loving looks and gracious words.[2]

THE BRIGHT SIDE

Love is emphatically the physician of the Universe.[3]

In the latter half of the 19th century there was a rather strange religious revival movement in parts of the United States. It seems to have been largely spontaneous and essentially fundamentalist in nature. While the preachers didn't agree on much, they were in agreement that all the ills of mankind sprang from the body. The body, they taught, was evil, and everything associated with it was evil.

---

† Pike, who had been one of the wealthiest men in Arkansas, had lost virtually everything in the aftermath of the Civil War.

‡ Calliope, the Muse of eloquence, not the musical instrument made of steam whistles; Apollo, Greek god of poetry

§ Could anyone have found a nicer way of saying, "She said, 'Because I said to, that's why.'"?

Pike believed, as we have seen, that it was important that the spiritual control the animal in man, but he thought it pure nonsense to assert that the body was evil. We've seen part of this passage before, but it's interesting to put it into its context.

The body! Ah, do not tell me that it is a thing to be despised and mortified, a prison for the soul, the cause of all its stains and imperfections. You shall not thus libel the forms and faces of the beloved ones; and when you preach to me the hateful and hideous creed, I only need more fondly clasp the dainty little hand that comes to nestle in mine, only the more lovingly kiss its soft white palm, for it confutes all your theories. It is not merely an implement with which our darling does deftly and patiently her wearing artist-work, but verily a part of that unity that is the idol of our life, her very self.[4]

But it is in his poetry that Pike waxed most eloquent on the bright side of love. An example:

Song

Let the dreaming astronomer number each star,
  That at midnight peeps over its pillow of blue;
A pleasanter study to me is, by far,
  The orb that shines over a cheek's rosy hue.
Let the crazy astrologer search for his fates
  In the cusps and the nodes of his dim luminaries;
He is wiser, like me, who his fortune awaits,
  As told in the glance that in beauty's eye varies;
Who studies, as I do, the stars of the soul,
And cares not nor heeds how those over us roll.

I have studied them many a long summer eve,
  When the leaves and bright waters were quietly singing,
The science and learning that thence we receive,
  Is a joy and perfume to the memory clinging,
It is better than wasting the eyes and the brain,
  And youth's sunny season, intended for pleasure,
In delving for knowledge more useless and vain
  Than is to a squalid old miser his treasure.
I would give not one glimpse at the eyes that I love,
To know all the stars that are clustered above.

There was Lydia; no star was as bright as her eye,
  So soft, yet so proud, in its black, misty lashes;
While Harriet's, set in the clear summer sky,
  Would have shamed every orb in the azure that flashes;
There was Lizzy's, a gem 'neath her ivory brow,
  And Kate's, like Love's planet in still waters dreaming;
And Lilian, whose soul seems to shine on me now,
  As it shone of old time in her amber eyes beaming;
There was Mary, who kept me from conics and Greek,
While her eyes lit a love which the tongue could not speak.

There was Ann, whose dear smiles yet my visions inspire,
And whose eyes bless my dreams like a light in the distance,
That over rude waters shoots welcoming fire,
And to all good resolves and fair hopes lends assistance.
Let fate kindly light with such stars my dark way,
For the few fleeting hours of my life-dream remaining;
I'll ask not for science to help me grow gray,
I'll ask not for fame while my life-tide is waning;
I'll wish for no laurels, I'll ask for no prize,
But permission to study sweet lips and bright eyes.[5]

THE BATTLE OF THE SEXES

The term "battle of the sexes" almost always suggests humor more than conflict. And so it was with Pike. But he had grown old enough to see posturing for what it was, and it annoyed him. Speaking of the fashion of his day for young men to pay extravagant court to all women—whether they merited it or not—Pike shared a little of his cynicism with Vinnie.

Observe the pretentious, over-done, over-acted extravagant "politeness" of a group of young and middle-aged men to these over-dressed or well-dressed, ill-bred or well-bred, refined and delicate or rude and uncivil, beautiful or hard-featured girls and women. It is alike to all, for it is not for the woman's sake the part is played, but that the men may pass for well-bred, gallant gentlemen. They are practicing; you think it all real, and congratulate yourself on being a citizen of a country in which so universal a deference is paid to women.

Ring the alarm bell, cry "fire!" let the blaze be seen, and the one avenue of escape narrow, and you will see how much *true* chivalry there is in all the crowd. Or, overhear the same group of men talk among themselves of the same woman! Go even to a supper table, at a great crowded reception at Washington, and see the human cormorants and vultures feed, not more regarding the women. . . .[6]

Powerful image, that. The men shoveling food down their mouths like cormorants or vultures and ignoring or elbowing aside the ladies.

Pike was fully aware of the famous line: "The battle of the sexes will never be won—there is too much fraternizing with the enemy." And in much the same wry spirit he comments on men who poke fun at women. Remember, in the same essay, he is going to compare women and hens (Chapter XII, "General Pike Was Not Wanting in Humor," page 147), so he is including himself here in the activity he describes.

Men satirize women, for the most part, only because they are conscious that they cannot rebel otherwise than by words. A good, true and loving woman, will only laugh at their extravagant diatribes, professing that it is rare that there be not some truth at the bottom, however it may be exaggerated.[7]

Of course, there are some women who deserve satire. Pike continues:

There are women enough, to whom the bitterest do no injustice; and many to whom the least unkind [sarcasms] apply.[8]

Anyone who remembers the song "Let a Woman in My Life?" from *My Fair Lady*, may get the feeling they've heard the following sentiments before.

No one is ever wholly free of all servitude, nor in all things wise. It is in the matter of love and women that men learn the least and are least free. He who loves is a slave to his passion and its object.

Music and night and love are blissful to you; you are the very slave of her caprices and her whims and of your passions. She changes all the plans and purposes of your life. All its pursuits become insignificant and without interest to you. You change your home and all your course of living to be near her and to see her.[9]

THE DARK SIDE

Pike was very much aware of the dark side of love, and in the century before this, it could be very dark. A woman, once she married, essentially lost her identity. Economically, socially, and in almost every other way, she was at the complete mercy of her husband. If he beat her, or did not support her, there was very little she could do about it. A marriage really was a throw of the die for a woman.

In one of his essays, Pike provides long excerpts from letters he has received. They are worth looking at for several reasons. They give us an idea of the social conditions at the time. They cast a light on Pike's character—for he had a large correspondence. His advice was valued by many people, and even those who hardly knew him wrote to him to share their troubles. That which follows is depressing, but it is important for understanding the man and his times.

I never read of a marriage, without thinking of lotteries, of desperate commercial adventures by blockade-running and in seas infested by pirates, of diamond hunting in fields where one gem awaits one fortunate finder among a hundred that hope and are disappointed, of the search for an adept in financial wisdom among national legislators, and the little chance there is that such an investment [marriage] will prove profitable and pay dividends of content and happiness. The subject has a melancholy interest for me because of those whom I have cared

Vinnie Ream, the celebrated young sculptress, and Albert Pike became very good friends who greatly enjoyed spending time together, talking, and sharing ideas. When Vinnie subsequently married, her husband became as much a son to Pike as Vinnie was his daughter. Note in the background Ream's bust of Lincoln. It was the last statue of Lincoln modeled from life and was one of many such studies Ream did of historical figures at that time. Among them is the life-size standing statue of Admiral David G. Farragut, now in Farragut Square in Washington, D.C. Also see Ream's bust of Albert Pike, page 227.

for, who have married, not more than two or three have been fortunate; and of these whom I like and who are married or widows, every one has reaped of marriage much sorrow and grievous disappointment. (Is it a vague presentiment of coming ills, that so commonly makes tears the companions of bridal robes? I know that sadness at marriages would be often more appropriate than gladness, and tears than laughter.) Do you think I have no reason to say this and that the marriage of one possessing my affection would be to me an occasion for rejoicing? Let me show you why I ever find excuse to remain, or to be suddenly called, away, when one in any way a degree dear to me is to enter into the "bonds" of matrimony and would almost as soon witness an execution as a wedding.

I take two or three letters from a package, laid away and labeled "to be buried with me," and read them with a heavy heart and tearful eyes. If I read to you a few sentences, do not think harshly of the writers because they told me of their afflictions, nor of me because I read also the words of love for me that they wrote in their grief; for it was because they loved me and I loved them, with a love of which neither I nor they needed to be ashamed, that they had a right to tell me all their troubles.

No matter how long or little a while ago these letters were written; nor who the writers were, nor where they lived, nor whether they are now dead or living. It is enough for you to know that the letters are real and true.

By this one, a wife, who was but three years before a brilliant girl, whom I had loved when, ten years earlier, she was but of the age of eighteen, and still loved when she married, to all appearance fortunately,—a woman wonderfully beautiful, of a bright and animated intellect, thoughtful, often sad and yet often charmingly enthusiast, wayward, frank, free, independent and brave both to do and to endure, wrote me these words, which have not yet been written long enough for me to read them without tears:

"I am glad to be able to think, in all trials of heart and soul, that there is one who will always love me, and care for my welfare; and it may be a source of consolation to *you* to know that I look to you for the only love I can safely and surely count upon. There is no possible happiness for me in this world; and I have no wish to hope for anything beyond. The utter desolation of my heart, as *I* know it, would be too appalling for any to contemplate. My heart is dead: it has not died a natural death: it has been murdered. You can see it is better for me not to speak; only to say I love you."

And this is from one, gentle, affectionate, of equitable sweet temper, patient, prudent, once a gay girl, charmingly unaffected, bright, glad, sparkling, well-bred, accomplished, witty, written to me when she had been ten years married; and loved by me from young girlhood.

"I have been of late reduced to so much indignity, and maltreatment, that I am determined to struggle for myself, if I will but be assisted by friends and relatives, to get me another home. I have tried and tried to bear up, dear friend, but I see that endurance ceases to be a virtue. I have no means, and my husband gives me no means of support. I am unable to put up any longer with all these trials. My husband is recreant to every feeling of consideration and tenderness to me and my helpless little ones. I am wearied and find that when locked out I am at a loss where to go with my children. I beg your kind advice; for I am so poor that I have no means to apply legally to anyone in the city. Write to me soon, and tell me how must I do. Speak to me as you would to your own child; for am I not your dear daughter, and have I not loved you as one for years? I am half crazed, and I call on you for advice."

And this letter, blotted all over with her tears, was signed, "Devotedly, your child."[10]

But men could be hurt by the dark side of love, too. Pike had been, and he describes the experience in Essay to Vinnie number VIII—"On the Death of Love."

I think there is nothing in this life so cruelly sad as to have been beloved, and while your own love has become a worship and an idolatry, suddenly to find that which you fondly thought was unchangeable, succeeded by a wearying indifference and so to go mournfully away and see the loved face, more loved than ever, no more, or only as that of a common or casual acquaintance. That woe has once fallen to me, and the wounds bleed yet.

You had seen the signs of change, the disuse of certain fond words and tokens of affection; the little hand no longer stealing into yours, but only permitting itself to be imprisoned, and gladdening you no longer with its answering pressure; the little form no longer nestling close to you, but only permitting your caresses; the wandering eyes, showing that those thoughts, once all yours, were elsewhere; the little fair head, no longer seeking to rest against your heart; the notes that brought you words of love, coming now at rarer intervals, with excuses for their infrequency that once would have been made; but she protested that her love would never, never, never change when it had already changed and waned; and you would not believe in the unfailing signs of the approaching calamity.

She did not wish to worry you perhaps, and so deceived you, until she could dissemble no longer, to spare you pain, as it was necessary to prove to another that you had no right to say she loved you, and the whole truth flashed upon your soul like a blaze of lightning in the night, and you staggered away, dazzled and blinded, to suffer and shed passionate tears when no human eye could see the agonies of your misery.

Perhaps having assured you, but a day or two before that you were as dear to her as ever, and that she could not change, she undeceived you civilly in the presence of others, whom she had invited you to meet, as if she had planned it before hand to mortify you. Gracious to all the rest and especially to one, she hardly spoke to you and when once she came to sit near you, on the same sofa, made the distance between you as great as possible; and so remained, until she rose and went away without a look or a word, and you, as soon as possible, escaped from the scene of torture, that she might no more have opportunity to say by her actions to others or another, "Behold! And know that he is less than nothing to me."

So you went home alone, put her picture, always at your right hand on your table, on the mantle, and wrote on the back, with black lines drawn round it, the date and the date when she died to you; and during the long hours of the night you sat and continually thought the same, only the same thought. You were stunned, stupid with astonishment, and lay writhing in pain like a branded dumb animal. . . .

But you will, nevertheless, go and come by the house in which she lives, hoping to see her, and yet wishing that you may not, and sometimes foolishly thinking that perhaps she was only offended, and loves you still, and only waits for you to come to her. If she loves you still, she would not wait for you to come. Why, she was gayer that evening, after you went away, than before. Do you think your going grieves her? Psha! She sees you pass, and laughs at you, and men whisper it about and pity you.[11]

There are many facets to love, and Pike had experienced them all, ecstasy and pure intellectual love and wild passion and calm devotion. He knew rejection and hurt and acceptance and joy. And he telescopes all those feelings into a poem simply titled:

Love

I am the soul of the Universe,
 In Nature's pulse I beat;
To Doom and Death I am a curse,
 I trample them under my feet.

Creation's every voice is mine,
 I breathe in its every tone;
I have in every heart a shrine,
 A consecrated throne.

. . . . . .

I kiss the snowy breasts of the maiden,
 And they thrill with a new delight;
While the crimson pulses flush and redden,
 Along the forehead's white.

I fill the restless heart of the boy,
 As a sphere is filled with fire,
Till it quivers and trembles with hope and joy,
 Like the strings of a golden lyre.

I brood on the soul like a golden thrush,
 My music to it clings,
And its purple fountains throb and flush,
 In the crimson light of my wings.

Deep in a lovely woman's soul
 I love to build my throne,
For the harmonies that through it roll
 Are the echoes of one tone.

The sounds of its many perfect strings
 Have but one key-note ever,
Its passions are the thousand springs,
 All flowing to one river.[12]

XIV

"What We Have Done For Others"

On Social Reform

"What we have done for ourselves dies with us. What we have done for others and the world lives on and is immortal."

These are probably Pike's best-known words, and, most likely, the words by which he would have wished to be remembered. Pike was deeply committed to reform; he was a reformer all his life, fighting for tax-supported education, economic development, justice for women and minorities. He incorporated social reform into the very fabric of the Scottish Rite, Southern Jurisdiction, he wrote editorials supporting social justice and equality, he defended average men and woman again and again as a lawyer, often with no hope of a fee, when they were caught up in the machinery of the law.

This portrait of Albert Pike, originally owned by the Scottish Rite Bodies of Billings, Montana, is believed to be the work of Charles Loring Elliott.

It's hard for most people to think of serious, staid, bearded, portly, old Albert Pike (whose pictures, often make him look like a stuffed owl) as being a social activist.

Bearded he was. Serious he could be. Portly—some of us would prefer to say "reasonably proportioned." Staid or a stuffed owl, not likely! Albert Pike was a man of passion, strong passion. And passion, for him, meant action. As Walter Lee Brown points out:

He was greatly respected and admired in Arkansas for learning and scholarly attainments and for his zeal in working for civic and internal improve-

ments in the state during the 'fifties. He repeatedly though unsuccessfully advocated the establishment of a system of free, tax-supported public schools in Arkansas. He helped organize an "Industrial Association" at Little Rock in 1852 in an attempt to encourage the development of manufactures in the town and state, and he worked for and secured increased and improved mail service for Arkansas the same year. And he labored to bring railroads to Arkansas.[1]

Pike understood, as few did at the time, that there was an important relationship between education, infrastructure, economics, and justice. And he was profoundly frustrated by people who said that education, or roads, or other improvements were "too expensive."

Within two miles of this very town, this place called in mockery a city, the great Southern Road is in winter an almost impassible bog.... So is the old military road from Little Rock to Ft. Smith. It is a perfect miracle if a man gets a hundred miles on any road in the State, without breaking his carriage to pieces, or laming the horses. Last spring, I lamed three, upon old rotten causeways, in one trip, at a cost, in the long run, of over four hundred dollars:—a tolerable large tax, one would say, to pay in a single year on account of bad roads.[2]

Pike believed in the importance of justice: economic, social, and political. He held two truths to be paramount when it came to his fellow humans. The first was that everyone's welfare was the concern of everyone else. No one, especially a Mason, ever had the right to say that what happened to someone else was not his concern. For Pike, there was no such thing as "not wanting to be involved," simply because he knew we were all part of one organic society. What affects anyone affects everyone.

God has ordained that life shall be a social state. We are members of a civil community. The life of that community depends upon its moral condition. Public spirit, intelligence, uprightness, temperance, kindness, domestic purity, will make it a happy community, and give it prosperity and continuance. Wide-spread selfishness, dishonesty, intemperance, libertinism, corruption, and crime, will make it miserable, and bring about dissolution and speedy ruin. A whole people lives one life; one mighty heart heaves in its bosom; it is one great pulse of existence that throbs there. One stream of life flows there, with ten thousand intermingling branches and channels, through all the homes of human love.[3]

The second great truth, according to Pike is one which was hardly believed, much less accepted, during his lifetime, and really did not come to full flower in the United States until the 1960s.

> Truths are the springs from which duties flow; and it is but a few hundred years since a new Truth began to be distinctly seen: that MAN IS SUPREME OVER INSTITUTIONS, AND NOT THEY OVER HIM. Man has *natural* empire over *all* institutions. They are for him, according to his development; not he for them. This seems to us a very simple statement, one to which all men, everywhere, ought to assent. But once it was a great new Truth—not revealed until governments had been in existence for at least five thousand years. Once revealed, it imposed new duties on men. Man owed it to *himself* to be free. He owed it to his *country* to seek to give *her* freedom, or maintain her in that possession. It made Tyranny and Usurpation [unlawful seizure of power] the enemies of the Human Race. It created a general outlawry of Despots and Despotisms, temporal and spiritual. The sphere of Duty was immensely enlarged. Patriotism had, henceforth, a new and wider meaning. Free Government, Free Thought, Free Conscience, Free Speech! All these came to be inalienable rights, which those who had parted with them or been robbed of them, or whose ancestors had lost them, had the right summarily to retake.[4]

With a few important exceptions, the churches in the 1800s were not really committed to the problems of the society. It was rather generally believed that the churches should focus on the world to come, not this world. That attitude persisted well into this century. While the New York Association for Improving the Conditions of the Poor had been founded in 1843 and the Charity Organization Society would be founded in 1877, most of the charitable work of individual churches focused not on solving the problems of the poor, but on the creation of soup kitchens and orphanages as a means of evangelizing. This attitude was brilliantly satirized by George Bernard Shaw in his play *Major Barbara.* Many ministers opposed any efforts to help the poor, commenting that their poverty was the result of God's judgment on them for their sins. To do anything to alleviate those conditions, they insisted, was to oppose the will of God. The speeches of Russell Conwell, perhaps, most clearly typified the position.

Pike had nothing but contempt for that viewpoint.[†] He insisted that it was not only right, it was essential that Masons try to make the lives of others better. He saw poverty as being a result of powerlessness. Masonry, Pike believed, had an absolute responsibility to make this world a better, happier place.

> [Freemasonry] has at heart the welfare in this life of the people among whom it exists,—in this life for its own sake, and not merely as a term of probation, and of preparation for another.

[†] For an excellent overview of the conditions and attitudes of the time, see Kathleen Woodroofe's *From Charity to Social Work in England and in the United States.*

This field of labor and exertion is large enough for it. To set free the captives of power, and deliver those who are imprisoned in the houses of bondage of craft, to make the life of the poor less a burden to them and some human hearts happier, to teach men their rights and enlighten those whom Ignorance and Error hold in fetters, is the work that it requires of its Initiates.

And it thinks that every man that works to benefit others, earns the right to have, and is worthy of, honour and reward. It holds that no creed is of value, except as it bears fruit in action; that what those learn that sit at its feet and listen to its teachings is chiefly valuable because it enables them to enlighten others. It is the Advocate and Defender all the world over, of free government and Liberty of Conscience; its Mission the Apostolate of Truth, Justice and Toleration.

It constitutes a great Brotherhood, of men of many tongues and races, cherishing for each other a warm affection, cultivating the sympathies that make the hearts of thousands beat in unison, thrilling with the same emotions, inspired by the same impassioned aspirations, the leaves upon the one great tree of the Scottish Free Masonry, that still continues to grow, though they, one after another, their destiny fulfilled, drop upon its roots.[5]

In a really remarkable insight for his time, Pike realized that most social ills are environmental or economic, not moral, in their origins. We simply must not judge a person—we may judge an act if necessary, but not the person who committed it. Pike reminds us that we have little right to the luxury of moral indignation.

We are all men of like passions, propensities, and exposures. There are elements in us all, which might have been perverted, through the successive processes of moral deterioration, to the worst of crimes. The wretch whom the execration of the thronging crowd pursues to the scaffold, is not worse than any one of that multitude might have become under similar circumstances. He is to be condemned indeed, but also deeply to be pitied.

It does not become the frail and sinful to be vindictive toward even the worst criminals. We owe much to the good Providence of God, ordaining for us a lot more favorable to virtue. We all had that within us, that might have been pushed to the same excess. Perhaps we should have fallen as he did, with less temptation. Perhaps we *have* done acts, that, in proportion to the temptation or provocation, were less excusable than his great crime. Silent pity and sorrow for the victim should mingle with our detestation of the guilt. Even the pirate who murders in cold blood on the high seas, is such a man as you or I might have been. Orphanage in childhood, or base and dissolute and abandoned parents; an unfriended youth; evil companions; ignorance and want of moral cultivation; the temptations of sinful pleasure or grinding poverty; familiarity with vice; a scorned and blighted name; seared and crushed affections; desperate fortunes; these are steps that might have led any one among us to unfurl upon the high seas the bloody flag of universal defiance; to wage war with our kind; to live the life and die the death of the reckless and remorseless freebooter. Many affecting relationships of humanity plead with us to pity him. His head once rested on a mother's bosom. He was once the object of sisterly love and domestic endearment. Perhaps his hand, since often red with blood, once clasped another little loving hand at the altar. Pity him then; his blighted hopes and his crushed heart! It is proper that frail and erring creatures like us should do so; should feel the crime, but feel it as weak, tempted, and rescued creatures should....

On all accounts, therefore, let the true Mason never forget the solemn injunction, necessary to be observed at almost every moment of a busy life: "JUDGE NOT, LEST YE YOURSELVES BE JUDGED: OR WHATSOEVER JUDGEMENT YE MEASURE UNTO OTHERS, THE SAME SHALL IN TURN BE MEASURED UNTO YOU."[6]

Good people could be put into bad situations by the sheer force of necessity. In the Seventh Degree of the Scottish Rite, Pike's lecture reminds the candidate that, however ready he may be to sneer at or feel superior to those who have fallen into crime, he would do well to put down the stone he just picked up. It is, Pike remarks, one thing to be strong, moral, and upright when you are comfortable.

There is scarcely one of us who has not, at some time in his life, been on the edge of the commission of a crime. Every one of us can look back, and shuddering see the time when we stood upon the slippery crags that overhung the abyss of guilt; and when, if temptation had been a little more urgent, or a little longer continued, if penury [poverty] had pressed us a little harder, or a little more wine had further disturbed our intellect, dethroned our judgment, and aroused our passions, our feet would have slipped, and we should have fallen, never to rise again....

When we condemn or pity the fallen, how do we know that, tempted like him, we should not have fallen like him, as soon, and perhaps with less resistance? How can we know what *we* should do if we were out of employment, famine crouching, gaunt and hungry, on our fireless hearth, and our children wailing for bread? *We fall not because we are not enough tempted!* He that *hath* fallen may be at heart as honest as we.... Wisely are we directed to pray that we may not be exposed to temptation.[7]

And Pike recognized that the economic problems which could lead to temptation did not center in the production of wealth, for the country produced a great deal. It was, rather the distribution of wealth.

Unfortunately, every age presents its own special problem, most difficult and often impossible to solve; and that which this age offers, and forces upon the consideration of all thinking men, is this—how, in a populous and wealthy country, blessed with free institutions and a constitutional government, are the great masses of the manual-labor class to be enabled to have steady work at fair wages, to be kept from starvation, and their children from vice and debauchery, and to be furnished with that degree, not of mere reading and writing, but of *knowledge*, that shall fit them intelligently to do the duties and exercise the privileges of freemen, even to be entrusted with the dangerous right of suffrage [the vote]?[8]

The problem, as Pike saw it, was that the people who had the power didn't have the compassion. Jobs could be created. Schools could be funded. There were answers to problems if men would be a little more caring and a little less greedy. Again, remember that he is writing at a time when it was your own "fault" if you were poor. Poverty, ignorance, and crime were, in the common opinion, *facts*—ordained by God and unchangeable. Pike saw them as *problems,* not as facts, and as problems which could be solved.

There are certainly great evils of civilization at this day, and many questions of humanity long adjourned and put off. The hideous aspect of pauperism, the debasement and vice in our cities, tell us by their eloquent silence or in inarticulate mutterings, that the rich and the powerful and the intellectual do not do their duty by the poor, the feeble, and the ignorant; and every wretched woman who lives, Heaven scarce known how, by making shirts at sixpence each, attests the injustice and inhumanity of man.[9]

Photo: Library of Congress

In the mid-19th century, women, often immigrant labor, toiled at sewing machines in the intense heat of garment district workrooms, known as sweatshops, to earn a profit for their employer or "sweater."

He was a firm believer that "from whom much is given much is expected." Pike felt that an employer owed a very great duty to those who worked for him.

In these days when jobs are exported to sources of cheaper labor and the "bottom line" is used as justification for plant closings, relocations, or major workforce reductions, Pike's words may seem hopelessly idealistic. But he meant every word, and no one can doubt that our economic situation would be far less of a burden if employers were to accept the responsibility which, Pike insists, is inherent in the employer-employee relationship.

Albert Pike in the 33rd Degree regalia of the Scottish Rite of Freemasonry, S. J.

[Masonry] teaches to the employers of other men, in mines, manufactories and workshops, consideration and humanity for those who depend upon their labor for their bread, and to whom want of employment is starvation, and overwork is fever, consumption and death. While it teaches the employed to be honest, punctual and faithful, as well as respectful, and obedient to all proper orders, it also teaches the employer that every man or woman that *desires* to work, has a *right* to have work to do; and that these, and those who from sickness or feebleness, old age or infancy, are not able to work, have a right to be fed, clothed, and sheltered from the inclement elements; that he commits an awful sin against Masonry and in the sight of God, if he closes his workshop or factory, or ceases to work his mine, when they do not yield him what he considers sufficient profit, and so dismisses his workmen and workwomen to starve; or when he reduces their wages to so low a standard that they and their families cannot therewith be fed and clad and comfortably housed; or by over-work must give him their blood and life in exchange for the pittance of their wages; and that his duty as a Mason and a Brother peremptorily requires him to continue to employ those who else will be pinched with hunger and cold, or must resort to theft and vice; and to pay them fair wages, though it may reduce or annul his profits, or even eat into his capital; *for God has but* LOANED *him his wealth, and made him His almoner and agent to invest it.*[10]

And the illustrations Pike gives were vivid.

Everywhere in the world labor is, in some shape, the slave of capital; generally, a slave to be fed only so long as he can work; or, rather, only so long as his work is profitable to the owner of the human chattel. There are famines in Ireland, strikes and starvation in England, pauperism and tenement-dens in New York, misery, squalor, ignorance, destitution, the brutality of vice and the insensibility to shame, of despairing beggary, in all the human cesspools and sewers everywhere. Here, a sewing-woman famishes and freezes; there, mothers murder their children, that those spared may live upon the bread purchased with the burial allowances of the dead starveling; and at the next door young girls prostitute themselves for food.[11]

The work of the Scottish Rite Mason is not to avoid helping the poor, but to do what he can, however little or however much that may be.

The world is the work of God, and he who belittles and reviles it belittles and despises Him. The word of God is revealed in the intellect of Humanity; and to libel humanity is to insult the Deity.

The field of labor of the Scottish Free-Masonry is a vast one, and most of the workers must do in it the work that lies close at hand, each in his own little plot or corner of it. Only few can occupy the area of a larger circle. There is no law that limits the consequences of a good action; and if the honest motive be the same, the earnest purpose and the brave endeavor, the work of the simple laborer may count for as much as the work of the Leader, in God's estimate and summing-up of results. It is not little or contemptible in His sight.

There is work for the Labourer and Leader everywhere. We go no-whither without finding penury [poverty] and destitution to be relieved, strifes and dissensions to be allayed, sorrows to be alleviated, wrongs to be redressed, errors to be put to rout, the Right and Truth to be vindicated, lives to be made better worth prolonging, neighborhoods to be made better worth living in. It is by faithful work in this field only, that men can prepare themselves for another life, not working for that, but working to do good here.[12]

Considering the fact that some people try to insist Pike taught "works righteousness," the idea that salvation is gained by good works, it's important to notice what he actually said. He did not say that by working to do good here one could *earn* salvation and another life. He said that good works here *prepared* one for another life. It's a matter of having some kind of answer when the question is asked, "Have you done it even unto the least of these?"

For his time, Pike has an extraordinary sensitivity to and understanding of the problems of women. There was, quite literally, no forgiveness for a woman who had sex outside of marriage. In some states it was a crime (and in New England, in the days of the early colonies, it had been punishable by death). And even if the law did not exact a penalty, society did. "Nice" girls did not do that sort of thing, and certainly girls who broke these rules were not proper prospects for marriage.

That was the sort of double standard which infuriated Pike. He attacks it in a passage which is remarkable for its time in several ways—not the least of which is his suggestion that the sexual act is "natural and innocent." That statement alone would have sufficed to get him condemned from many pulpits in the United States. Everyone knew that sex was, for a woman, a duty—but it was certainly nothing in which she was to find pleasure. The books of psychology of the day even listed such pleasure as proof of a mental disorder in women. Pike's suggestion that it was society and the law which were wrong was as radical as anything which came out of the 1960s.

> The laws of society as well as the world's ways, sadly need mending. It is the fashion, now, to say that the worst use to which you can put a man is to hang him. I am not so sure of that; but I am sure, that the worst use to which you can put a woman is to condemn her to a life of shame, because she has once done amiss, not by the act, which is natural and innocent, but by the absence of the law's sanction for it. Nothing is so heartlessly cruel as to interpose an insurmountable barrier, to make her return to respectability impossible.[13]

No, there was nothing staid or "stuffed-owl" about Albert Pike. He was a man of powerful passions and of strong convictions. Those convictions surrounded the great questions of human happiness, and he fought for them all his life, from his earliest newspaper editorials to the books he was writing at his death. More than a century after his death, society has caught up with and passed him in some areas; in others he is still in the vanguard. Most of us would not care to think how little of our own thinking would hold up, judged by the standards people will use 100 years from now.

But Pike probably would not have cared one way or the other. He was a rebel all his life, and his years as a general in the Civil War were the least of his rebelliousness. Remember that long hair—at a time when short hair was the fashion. Yet, impatient as he could become with a society which refused to see what was clearly right and which held on so tightly to fears and superstitions and hatreds and ways of thinking which did only harm, he knew that change was slow. He knew how often reformers were hated and reviled in their own lifetimes.

He who endeavors to serve, to benefit, and improve the world, is like a swimmer, who struggles against a rapid current, in a river lashed into angry waves by the winds. Often they roar over his head, often they beat him back and baffle him. Most men yield to the stress of the current, and float with it to the shore, or are swept over the rapids; and only here and there the stout, strong heart and vigorous arms struggle on toward ultimate success.[14]

But that didn't mean you could give up.

Is it true that Masonry is effete [no longer able to produce]; that the acacia, withered, affords no shade; that Masonry no longer marches in the advance-guard of Truth? No. Is freedom yet universal? Have ignorance and prejudice disappeared from the earth? Are there no longer enmities [anger and hatred] among men? Do cupidity and falsehood no longer exist? Do toleration and harmony prevail among religious and political sects? There are works yet left for Masonry to accomplish, greater than the twelve labors of Hercules; to advance ever resolutely and steadily; to enlighten the minds of the people, to reconstruct society, to reform the laws, and to improve the public morals. The eternity in front of it is as infinite as the one behind. And Masonry cannot cease to labor in the cause of social progress, without ceasing to be true to itself, without ceasing to be Masonry.[15]

And he boiled down the whole essence of his philosophy into a single sentence:

What we have done for ourselves dies with us. What we have done for others and the world remains and is immortal.[16]

XV

"Defunct Was Remarkably Well-Behaved— For A Corpse"

On Albert Pike Attending His Own Wake

Col. Albert Pike.—This gentleman has been announced dead again by one of the Mobile papers, and the usual honors to the departed duly attended to. This is the third attempt during the year 1858, to "kill him off." At last accounts Col. Pike was in the enjoyment of reasonable health, and about to engage in a Buffalo hunt, in the wild region west of Fort Smith.[1]

Far from dead, Pike had just finished the final successful work of seeing a claim by the Creek Nation against the federal government paid. He had been working very hard, and decided to remain for a few weeks of hunting and camping with his Indian friends.

The story was corrected in Arkansas quickly. But the news of his death reached Washington just days before he did, in January 1859, and no word of the correction had been received. The first Pike knew of the story was when he walked into a meeting of the Roast Oyster Club, a group he had helped to form the year before which enjoyed dining and spending convivial evenings together, and shocked the socks off all present.

Pike was a greatly loved man in Washington, and his friends had been deeply upset by the news. The next day, on the street, he met his good friend John F. Coyle, the editor of the *National Intelligencer* and a man deeply proud of his Irish heritage. As Pike tells us in Essay XIV to Vinnie ("Of Shattered Idols"), Coyle looked at him and, when he could finally talk, asked, "What right have you to be walking about, looking for all the world like a live man, when you're d— d— dead?" Pike replied, "Because I've not been waked—and until that how could I keep quiet in the grave?" "Then," said Coyle, "you shall be waked."

Coyle then planned a great "wake" at his house and invited about 150 people to a banquet. But one or two days before the wake took place, Pike was invited to another banquet in his honor. All of these things were heavily covered in the Washington press, and one of the participants collected the stories, poems, etc., which were part of the event and had them privately printed, bound, and distributed to the participants. The book is entitled *The Life–Wake of the Fine Arkansas Gentleman Who Died Before His Time*, and most of the information which follows comes from that book.

Dr. R. Shelton Mackenzie was invited to the banquet noted above. A few days before the wake, he wrote a letter to a friend about it, and it's well worth the reading.

My dear Colonel: Among the curiosities of this great metropolis, its architectural wonders, its mingling of various nationalities and intellects, its aggregation of "fair women and brave men," its political intrigues, its ambitions, its defeats, its loves, its hates, nothing has astonished me more than a dinner at which I had the pleasure of assisting yesterday. I have partaken of many a banquet with the living, but never, until yesterday, sat down to table, aye, and fairly hobnobbed, with a dead man.

You will ask for particulars, and inquire in what mausoleum did the repast take place? Whether a tomb stone did duty for the table, and a shroud was the substitute for a tablecloth? No. My legs were under a living host's mahogany, and several other living people formed the company, But among them, towering alike in physical and mental force, appeared what unquestionably must have been an apparition—for I read a newspaper account, with full particulars of his death, and I had mourned very sincerely over the extinction, by the common catastrophe of mortality, of as genial a nature, as flashing an intellect, and as fine a genius as ever adorned the social circle or shed grace and luster upon the literature of his native land, as well as upon that antiquated spot which he affectionately speaks of as "the old country." . . .

But—for the festival with the Dead ... there was nothing sad, except some melancholy attempts at punning.... There was no crepe worn on the arm. No expression of grief, whatever may or ought to have been felt—on the whole, a subdued resignation. That secret grief existed might be inferred only from the circumstance that the company was unusually thirsty. But that might have been the effect of our host's exquisite vintage, liberally dispensed, and affectionately done justice to.... Grief is proverbially dry, and all of us had just such a decent amount of thirst as must have convinced the departed that he was deeply lamented.[2]

After describing the guests at the table, Mackenzie continues.

The parlor door opened, and a stalwart figure, large and lofty, with keen eyes, a nose reminding one of an eagle's beak, a noble head firmly placed between a pair of massive shoulders, and flowing locks nearly halfway down his back, entered the apartment, looking as like a living man as anything I had ever seen. But the company, who did not appear frightened in the least, at this apparition, one and all assured me that he was dead, that he had been killed in the newspapers, that he was wandering about, wishing some one to say, "Rest, perturbed spirit!" . . .

He behaved remarkably well—for an apparition. A good spirit in his way, he naturally took a nip of "old rye!"—Not the "J.B." brand, but a curious, well-flavored liquid, which Berks county had sent to our host. When we went in to dinner, the Defunct accompanied us, and dropped into a vacant seat. All through the evening, the Defunct endeavored to behave like a living man. When Mr. Coyle sang a touching melody, narrating the adventures, at home and at New Orleans, of a fine Arkansas gentleman, the Defunct politely informed him that he had better make himself more fully master of the words which he (the Defunct) had an interest in.†

We took wine with him, conversed with him, enjoyed his stories, anecdotes and songs; but strictly under protest. A departed man could not be recognized in any other capacity.[3]

Albert Pike
Portrait by Charles Loring Elliott

A few days later came the wake. It was quite a production. There was even a printed program for the evening. It lists the Mourners in Chief, some 13 of Pike's special friends, and adds, *"The corpus of Albertus Magnus, in charge of the Superintendent of Ceremonies, Geo. S. Gideon, Esq."*

And thus began an evening of the sort of really atrocious puns men of literary inclination can get up to. "Albertus Magnus" of course, means "Albert the Large" or "Albert the Great," and Pike could hardly be described as "willowy." But it went further. St. Albertus Magnus was one of the greatest minds and thinkers of the Medieval Church. He wrote many volumes, as did Pike. He defended the importance of human reason in faith, as did Pike. He saw nature as proof of God, as did Pike. Dubbing the defunct "Albertus Magnus" was an auspicious beginning to an awesome evening.

The feasting and drinking were well under way (and the consumption of those 150 guests was measured in gallons). Professor Dimitry, one of the leading intellects of the time, read the obituary he had written about Pike for the newspapers before it was discovered not to be needed, yet. It really is a masterpiece of sincere praise. Pike then arose to speak. It is beautiful and pure Pike (the impure Pike came a little later in the evening, as we'll see).

† The reference, of course, is to Pike's poem "The Fine Arkansas Gentleman." See Chapter II, "The Motives That Aggravate Him," page 37.

My Friends—the old whom I have known so long, and the new whom I am glad to know.

I was in due time advised by our host, that during the ceremonies of this evening, I should be called upon to answer for myself, and give assurance that my mortal body was not yet tenantless. Knowing that something of humor would be looked for in what I might say, and that anything partaking of the serious would perhaps be regarded as out of place, I endeavored to prepare myself beforehand to conform in that to your natural expectations.

It was in vain. Besides that, I have not the gift of wit or humor.† I knew that my friend Dimitry was to read what he had written of me, when he really believed me dead; and though I could not anticipate a eulogy so infinitely beyond my deserts [deserved rewards], I did know his kindly feelings for me, and that he had spoken of me in terms of affection and regard. Indeed, I could not find it in my heart to prepare to respond with jest and levity; as if it were a thing to be ashamed of, to be touched and affected by a tribute offered by generous sympathy and kindness, that would, it seems to me, touch and affect the most callous heart.

Nor could I fail to know that, on the part of my host and old friends, there was, in originating these ceremonies, and would be in conducting them, something more than mere fun and frolic; and that in the merriment would mingle kindness and affectionate regard for myself. To respond to this with a jest, would be something like an insult. I am too much moved to attempt that, and you will pardon me, I hope, for not pretending to a stoicism that I do not possess; and for the serious tone, not, I hope, inappropriate, of the little I am able to say, in the way of acknowledgment and thanks for the touching testimonials of friendship and esteem.

When one who has been adjudged by the Grand Inquest of the Press to have departed this life, ventures again to revisit the glimpses of the moon, and to intrude among the living, a decent respect for the opinions of mankind‡ requires him to declare the reason that impels him to demand a new trial and the reversal of the verdict.

---

† Ironic understatement, indeed!

‡ Pike may strike a serious tone in this speech, but that wry sense of humor is never far under the surface. Compare the line "A decent respect for the opinions of mankind requires him to declare the reason that impels him to demand a new trial..." with "When in the course of human events, it becomes necessary for one people to dissolve the political bands which have connected them with another...a decent respect to the opinions of mankind requires that they should declare the causes which impel them to the separation."

That such a conclusion was not warranted by the facts, has not always been held a sufficient ground for such reversal; since in my own state once, one upon whose estate, on a false rumor of his death, administration had been granted, was gravely informed[†] by the judge, when he presented himself in person, that he could be re-possessed of his estate only by claiming it as his own heir, since the law had adjudged him dead, and the administration being bound to proceed.

Reason perhaps teaches, and every one of us, no doubt, when encompassed with trouble, weary of the struggles of life, sick with disappointments, and disgusted with enmities fraught, that if we were indeed laid away to rest where the wicked cease from troubling and the weary are at rest, in the quiet grave, on which the hands of affection would plant a flower, and friendships drop a silent tear; if one had indeed reached the end of all the toils and heartaches, the regrets and discomfitures of life, it would be most unwise in him to return if he could, again to mingle in the contests, the rivalries and the animosities—again to count the errors, to suffer the wrongs, and to do the injustices, that once embittered his existence.

"For death," it has been said, "is the harbor whither God hath designed every one, that there he may find rest from the troubles of the world. When therefore, he calls us, let us lay our heads down softly, and go to sleep, without wrangling like forward [stubborn] children...."

I might be willing to let the judgment stand, and claim as my own heir, if I could inherit as a present estate all that wealth of kind recollection and charitable opinion that has been so unexpectedly, and so gratefully, to me, bestowed upon my memory; if I could be thus enriched beyond all measure and estimation, by the kind regrets that from so many hearts rained upon the grave in which my mortal body was imagined to be laid.

For if one dies lamented by his friends, and none think his faults, his follies, and his errors worthy to be any longer remembered; and if they mourn for him and miss him, and their regrets go with him to the grave, their sorrows continuing after he has departed, what would it add to his epitaph to say that he died possessed of a large estate, or that he held high office and sat in the councils of the nation?

That has chanced to me which has come to but few men—to have read, while living, the judgments passed upon myself as dead. I have found men more generous than I believed, since far more good has been said of me than I deserved, while much of ill that might have been truly uttered, has been kindly left unsaid. Life in my eyes has assumed a new value, and the world is brighter

[†] "Gravely informed" after presumption of death!

to me than it seemed before, for I am wiser than before, and know men better. I know them better, and therefore love them more, and would fain do the world and my fellows some service before I die. All the discontents and enmities that lingered in my bosom, and they were not many, have disappeared.

I detain you too long. May the memory of each of you, when it comes to you to die, be as highly cherished and as gently dealt with, as mine has been; and if you, like me, should have the good fortune to read your own obituaries, may you have as good cause to be grateful for the consequences of the mistake as I have! You deserve no less fortune, and I could wish you none better.[4]

John Coyle than sang a set of verses written by one of the guests. You'll remember Pike's poem about Rector, "The Fine Arkansas Gentleman." Taking the same structure, the guest (probably a Dr. Burwell) had written a parody. It's too much fun not to include, and it shows more clearly than the eulogy the love in which the group held Pike.

The Arkansas Gentleman Alive Again

The fine Arkansas gentleman restored to life once more,
Continued to enjoy himself as he had done before;
And tired of civilized pursuits, concluded he would go
To see some Indian friends he had, and chase the buffalo,
This fine Arkansas gentleman
Who died before his time.

The rumor of his visit had extended far and near,
And distant chiefs and warriors came with bow and gun and spear;
So when he reached the council grounds with much delight he sees
Delegations from the Foxes, Sioux, Quapaws, Blackfeet, Pottawottamies, Gros Ventres, Arapahoes, Commanches, Creeks, Navajoes, Choctaws, and Cherokees,
This fine Arkansas gentleman, etc.

They welcomed him with all the sports well known on the frontier,
He hunted buffalo and elk, and lived on grouse and deer;
And having brought his stores along, he entertained each chief,
With best Otard and whiskey, smoking and chewing tobacco, not forgetting cards, with instructions in seven-up, brag, bluff and euchre, till they drank themselves dumb and blind, having first war-whooped till he was deaf,
This fine Arkansas gentleman, etc.

He went to sleep among his friends in huts or tents of skin,
And if it rained, or hailed, or snowed, he didn't care a pin;
For he had lined his hide with whisky and a brace of roasted grouse,
And he didn't mind the weather any more than if he slept in a four-story brown stone front, tin-roof, fire-proof, Fifth Avenue house.
This fine Arkansas gentleman, etc.

Now whilst he was enjoying all that such adventure brings,
The chase, and pipe, and bottle, and such like forbidden things,
Some spalpeen [rascal] of an editor the Lord had made in vain,
Inserted in his horrible accident column, amongst murders, robberies, thefts, camphene accidents, collisions, explosions, defalcations, seductions, abductions, and destructions, under a splendid black-bordered notice, the lamentable news that—he was dead again.
This fine Arkansas gentleman, etc.

The other papers copied it, and then it was believed
That death at last had taken him so recently reprieved;
They mourned him as a warrior, a poet, and a trump,
And with elegies, eulogies, biographies, reviews, articles, criticisms on his productions, doubts whether he had ever fought, wrote, hunted buffalo, or indeed lived at all—And one incredulous pagan, "Johnse Hooper," of the Montgomery Mail, always—denied his dying plump.
This fine Arkansas gentleman, etc.

The Masons and Odd Fellows prepared to celebrate
His obsequies with every form of grief appropriate,
So sad the tavern-keepers and the faro-dealers feel,
They craped† *the bell a half an hour and intermit a deal.*
This fine Arkansas gentleman, etc.

But far above the common grief—though he was good as gold—
His creditors, like Jacob's wife, refused to be consoled;
They granted him a poet and a warrior, if you will,
But said they had extensive experience in generals, commodores, orators, statesmen, Congressmen, actors, and other public characters—who rarely paid a bill,
This fine Arkansas gentleman, etc.

Behold in this excitement our distinguished friend arrive,
We "knew from a remark he made" that he was still alive;
Then every journal joyously the contradiction quotes,
The tailors take his measure, and the banks renew his notes,
This fine Arkansas gentleman, etc.

But Johnny Coyle—an Irishman—the news refused to take;
He swore "no gintleman alive should chate him of his wake."
So he called his friends together, as here you plainly see,
And he has set out spirits and the tabaccy jar to lay the body under the table dacently.
This fine Arkansas gentleman, etc.

So now when he must surely go the way that all must pass,
Don't hold a feather to his lips, nor yet a looking-glass;
But whisper that a friend's in need of either purse or hand,
And he'll make a move to aid him—if they haven't got him damned.
This fine Arkansas gentleman, etc.

Or try another certain test, if any doubt remain;
Just put within his pallid lips a drop of whiskey—plain,

† They draped the bell with black crepe in token of mourning.

And if he makes no mortal sign, just put him in the ground,
And let his Maker raise him at his final trumpet's sound.
This fine Arkansas gentleman, etc.[5]

But Pike had prepared a song of his own, telling of his (supposed) adventures in the underworld during his (supposed) death. It was sung by Mr. Savage, to the tune of "Benny Havens, Oh!" (You have to repeat "One Spree at Johnny Coyle's" several times in the chorus to make it work.)

Benny Havens, Oh!

One Spree at Johnny Coyle's

A gentleman from ARKANSAS, not long ago 'tis said
Waked up one pleasant morning, and discovered he was dead;
He was on his way to Washington, not seeking for the spoils,
But rejoicing in the promise of a spree at JOHNNY COYLE'S;
    One spree at Johnny Coyle's, one spree at Johnny Coyle's
    And who would not be glad to join a spree at Johnny Coyle's?

He waked and found himself aboard a rickety old boat;
Says the ferryman when questioned, "on the Styx† you are afloat;"
"What! dead?" said he:—"indeed you are," the grim old churl replied;
"Why, then I'll miss the spree at Coyle's" the gentleman replied.
    One spree at Johnny Coyle's, &c.

Old Charon‡ ferried him across the dirty, sluggish tide,
But he swore he would not tarry long upon the further side;
The ancient ghosts came flocking round upon the Stygian§ shore:—
"But," said he, "excuse me; I must have at Coyle's one frolic more."
    One spree at Johnny Coyle's, &c.

Horace and old Anacreon†† in vain would have him stay;
From all those ancient fogies he made haste to get away;
For his Majesty, King Pluto, he was bound at once to see,
And at Johnny Coyle's, on Friday night, alive or dead to be.
    One spree at Johnny Coyle's, &c.

Old Cerberus‡‡ growled savagely, as he approached the gate;
"But," said he, "I've seen too many dogs for you to make we wait;
"If you show your teeth at me, my dog, your windpipe I shall twist;
"For if I were not to be at Coyle's, I'm sure I should be missed.
    One spree at Johnny Coyle's, &c.

He crossed that adamantine halls, and reached the ebon throne,
Where gloomy Pluto frowned, and where his queen's soft beauty shone.
"What want you here?" the Monarch said: "Your Majesty," said he,
"Permission at one frolic more at Johnny Coyle's to be."
    One spree at Johnny Coyle's, &c.

---

† The River Styx, in classical mythology, formed the border of Hades (not to be confused with Hell), the land of the dead.

‡ Charon was the ferryman on the river Styx.

§ Usually a synonym for "dark" or "fearful," here used literally as "pertaining to the river Styx."

†† Pike is having some fun at his own expense here. Horace was a classical poet who primarily wrote serious and elevated verse of the sort Pike attempted in *Hymns to the Gods.* Anacreon, who died 488 B.C., was a Greek poet who wrote primarily satires and short poems on love and wine. These are the two who entreat Pike to stay. Another factor may be at work here, too. "To Anacreon in Heaven" was a famous British drinking song (we use the tune for "The Star-Spangled Banner"), and it is more than probable that a fair amount of conviviality was accompanying the singing of "One Spree at Johnny Coyle's."

‡‡ Three-headed dog who guarded the path to Hades

"As Orpheus came, and yet returned, to breathe the upper air,
"So I your royal bounty crave, once more to venture there;
"Give me one night—no more;—Alas! Such nights are all too few!
"One more refection [meal] of the Gods; and then, good world, adieu!
One spree at Johnny Coyle's, &c.

"'Tis not to power, or wealth, or fame, I hanker to return,
"Nor that love's kisses once again upon my lips may burn;
"Let me but once more meet the friends that long have been so dear,
"And who, if I'm not there, will say, 'Would God that he were here!'"
One spree at Johnny Coyle's, &c.

"Are you not dead?" the King then said. "Well, what of that?" said he,
"If I AM dead, I've not been WAKED, and buried decently."
"And why," the Monarch cried, "desire again to share life's toils,
"For the sake of one good frolic more, even at Johnny Coyle's?"
One spree at Johnny Coyle's, &c.

"We've Nectar and Ambrosia here; we do not starve the dead."—
"Did you ever sample canvas-backs and terrapins?" he said:
"The table of your Majesty well served is, I dare say;
"But I wish you were at Johnny Coyle's, to taste his St. Peray."
One spree at Johnny Coyle's, &c.

If its good company you want," the King said, "We've the best—
"Philosophers, Poets, Orators, Wits, Statesmen, and the rest;
"The courtiers of the good old times, the gentlemen most rare."—
Says he, "With those I'll meet at Coyle's your folks will not compare."
One spree at Johnny Coyle's, &c.

Pike then goes through 12 stanzas dedicated to naming and describing the various friends he will meet at Coyle's.

"Enough!" old Pluto cried; "the law must be enforced, 'tis plain;
If with those fellows once you get you'll ne'er return again;
One night would not content you, and your face would ne'er be seen,
After that spree at Johnny Coyle's by me or by my queen.
One spree at Johnny Coyle's, &c.

"And if all these fellows came at once, what would become of us?
They'd drown old Charon in the Styx, and murder Cerberus
Make love to all the women here[†], and even to my wife,
Drink all my liquor up, and be the torment of my life.
One spree at Johnny Coyle's, &c.

"They'd laugh and sing and rollick here, and turn night into day;
While every one his best would do to drive dull care away;
We'll take them by installments, sir; so you may e'en remain,
And dismiss all hope of visiting the upper world again."
One spree at Johnny Coyle's, &c.

[†] "To make love" in this context does not have the common current meaning of "to have sex with"; it means to court, flatter, or flirt with.

Now something rash would have been said by Arkansaw, no doubt,
But the Queen winked at him, as to say, "take care what you're about!"
For very much elated was the fair Proserpine,
At the promise of unbounded fun with this good company.
One spree at Johnny Coyle's, &c.

So then she hung round Pluto's neck, and to her snowy breast
She clasped the cross old vagabond, and fondly him caressed;
And while her kisses warm and soft upon his lips did rain,
She murmured, "Let him go, my love, he'll surely come again."
One spree at Johnny Coyle's, &c.

Said he, "I won't;" said she, "Dear Lord, do let me have my way!
Let him be present at his wake! How can you say me nay?
I'm sure you do not love me; if you did, you'd not refuse,
When I want to get the fashions, and you want to hear the news."
One spree at Johnny Coyle's, &c.

And so at last the Queen prevailed, as women always do,
And thus it came that once again this gentlemen's with you;
He's under promise to return, but that he means to break,
And many another spree to have, besides this present wake!
One spree at Johnny Coyle's, one spree at Johnny Coyle's
And who would not be glad to join a spree at Johnny Coyle's?[6]

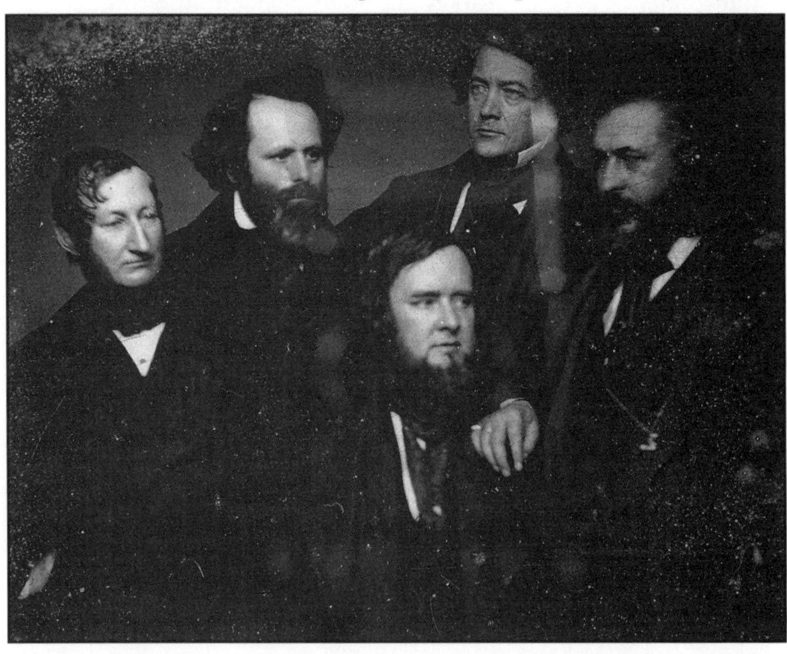

As the material in this chapter demonstrates, Pike enjoyed the company of friends. In this daguerreotype from 1849, Pike (at far right) is shown with (from left) Charles L. Elliott, John A Haggerty, William T. Porter, and J. R. Clark.

There was more, much more, to the evening. One guest offered a set of verses to be sung to the same tune used for "The Star-Spangled Banner," which began:

Oh! say, can you see by friend Coyle's festive light,
The proud form we've oft before hailed by its gleaming,
Whose pen and whose sword have fought many a fight.
And who comes with his beard patriarchally streaming?
While his jokes fresh and rare—and his love for the fair,
Give proof that when Death called—no victim was there,
Tis Pike of Arkansas—and long may he wave,
The delight of good fellows—true, jovial, and brave.[7]

A few hours (and libations) later, one of the "mourners" offered a poem which begins:

When Pike appeared at heaven's gate,
And rang with hearty pull the bell,
Saint Peter turned his hoary pate,
And gruffly answered, "go to hell!"
"If I do," says Pike, "then I'll be d—d,
For every corner there is crammed."

A passing angel interfered,
And plucked the porter by the beard;
Says he, "Saint Peter, hold your jaw—
That's Captain Pike of Arkansas!"

"The d—l it is?" said Peter, quick,
And wide the golden wicket flew;
"You're welcome, Pike! walk in, old brick!
I'm glad to see you—how do you do?"[8]

According to a newspaper reporter who was among the guests, the "wake" finally broke up in the small hours of the morning, with the 150 guests boiling out of the house and dispersing in sundry directions, offering each other mutual support and singing, each in his own key, the songs which had been offered during the evening.

All in all, a highly satisfactory time for all concerned—with the possible exception of the neighbors.

XVI

Images

On Painting With Words

"I wish I could do with oil what Pike could do with words." These are the words spoken in 1994 by Will Hurd, a painter known nationally as the "New Mexico Colorist." His comment is quite a tribute to Pike, considering what Hurd can do with oil paints. But more than one writer has observed that Pike's greatest poetry is written in the form of prose.

The materials in this chapter, by and large, do not relate to each other. They are here simply as examples of the sheer descriptive power Pike could call upon. Some are dark and depressing, some are nostalgic, some are wry, some are filled with light. They span more than 60 years of creative effort.

THE BEAUTIES OF NATURE

Sunrise is a stirring and beautiful sight even in the prairie. You lie down, the broad bed of grass and flowers beneath you, and the pure dew bathing your forehead during the night. Day light spreads over the heaven, and you awake—you dash your hands in the grass and with the dew you wash yourself—you are on your horse—and then up comes the sun—broad, bright, and like a sphere of white fire—unaccompanied with the gorgeous heralding of the colored clouds. He sets in his own simple and stern majesty—the king of heaven—no pompous heraldry announces his death to the earth below—but he sinks to his grave like a warrior, silently, and in quiet calmness. You see no flushing of the sky—no piling together of the red clouds—and yet there is something indescribably grand in a sunset on the prairies of Missouri. It has always seemed to me like the burial of a conqueror—in his naked, simple glory—undirged—unglorie d—buried with his own grandeur—and it alone—about him—and then if from some simple cottage—half hid—in the green prairie, you hear the tones of a lonely flute[†] ringing over the plains which is almost a desert, the charm is complete.[1]

[†] I can't escape the belief that Pike was "waxing an elephant" for the readers of the article. Somehow the chances of finding a lonely—or even a sociable—flutist in a simple cottage half-hidden in the green prairie seem remote.

We were now fairly in the broad open prairie, and among the buffalo; and to the wanderer in the prairie, nothing is so inspiring as the thought of the immense herds of these animals which are found on its broad bosom. Their numbers are truly astonishing. You may see them for whole days on each side of you as far as your sight will extend, apparently so thick, that one might easily walk for miles upon their backs, listlessly feeding along, until they take the wind of you, and then moving of a speed, of which the unwieldy animals seem hardly capable. Wherever they have passed, the ground looks as if it had been burnt over.[2]

I have seen the prairie, and lived in it, in summer and in winter. I have seen it with the sun rising calmly from its breast, like a sudden fire kindled in the dim distance; and with the sunset flushing in its sky with quiet and sublime beauty.... I have seen the *mirage*, too, painting lakes and fires and groves on the grassy ridges near the bounds of Missouri, in the still autumn afternoon, and cheating the traveller by its splendid deceptions. I have seen the prairie, and stood long and weary guard in it, by moonlight and starlight and storm. It strikes me as the most magnificent, stern, and terribly grand scene on earth—a storm in the prairie.

We may speak of the incessant motion and tumult of the waves, the unbounded greenness and dimness, and the lonely music of the forests, and the high magnificence, the precipitous grandeur, and the summer snow of the glittering cones of the mountains: but still, the prairie has a stronger hold upon the soul, and a more powerful, if not so vivid an impression upon the feelings. Its sublimity arises from its unbounded extent, its barren monotony and desolation, its still, unmoved, calm, stern, almost self-confident grandeur, its strange power of deception, its want of echo, and, in fine, its power of throwing a man back upon himself and giving him a feeling of lone helplessness, strangely mingled at the same time with a feeling of liberty and freedom from restraint.[3]

In sober truth, there is to me, when I wander among the kingly cones of the mountains—those giants, wearing their stainless mantles of white snow over their broad shoulders of element-defying granite—there is something like a lifting in the mind of itself from and above the enthralling cares and the enslaving contingencies of the world, like that which we feel when we move like unimportant motes over the limitless desert of the ocean-like prairie, but with this one difference. In the prairie we are alone; we have that same desolate, companionless feeling of isolation, so well expressed by Coleridge. We separate ourselves from our companions, and turning our mind inward to a consideration of its own hidden joys or miseries—its memories or anticipations, we pass over the desert as men pass through a glimmering and lonely dream. But the mountains are our companions. We lose that feeling of solitude and oppression at the heart, and in its stead is an expansion and an elevation of the mind, as though the great spirit which, as Fancy might imagine, inspires the mighty mountains, was entering into the heart and abiding there. You will understand all this, however, to refer to a time when I was roaming about over these mountains, with the cool air that came down from their icy foreheads tempering the heat of summer—when I was perfectly at my ease, and had no other care than to pass off an hour or so, and take my fill of enjoyment from the glorious scene around me—and not to that time when I made my first ingress into the Province of New Mexico, starving, and through snow three feet deep. At that latter time, that hideous old maid, Reality, clasped me to her cold bosom, and her cry was, "aroint thee, Romance"—and so she did, unless there might have been romance in the sober and sad thought of bread, a fine fire and a blanket.[4]

This is a good example of Pike's use of allusion to create a multiple set of images in the mind of the reader. Readers of Pike's time, more familiar with Shakespeare than we tend to be, would have recognized the allusion to a line from *Macbeth*. The three witches are catching up on gossip, and one tells of an encounter with a sailor's wife who was eating chestnuts. "'Give me,' quoth I. 'Aroint thee [scram], witch,' the rump-fed ronyon [a scurvy person] cries." So Pike not only creates the image of Reality as an old maid, driving off Romance, he also calls to mind the witches, images of desolation and cruel fate. Not bad for a single sentence.

THE WAYFARING MEN

On the 10th we reached Fort Smith, and we must have made a most ludicrous appearance. Falstaff's ragged regiment was nothing to us. I had a pair of leather pantaloons, scorched and wrinkled by the fire, and full of grease; an old greasy jacket and vest; a pair of huge moccasins, in mending which I had laid out all my skill during the space of two months, and in so doing, had bestowed upon them a whole shot-pouch; a shirt, which, made of what is commonly called counterpane, or a big checked stuff, had not been washed since I left Taos; and to crown all, my beard and mustachios had never been clipped during the same time. Some of us were worse off. Irwin, for example, had not half a shirt. In short, we were, to use another western expression, "as pretty a looking set of fellows as ever any man put up to his face."[5]

NIGHT THOUGHTS IN OLD AGE

It is after dark, on the last day of the year 1873. I will converse no longer for the little residue of this year, with the dead wrecks and waifs [the dead and forgotten poets of earlier days]! I wish I had not chanced upon so sad a subject to end the year withal. I wish my darling's [Vinnie Ream's] sweet, bright face were here to cheer me now, as it was yester-eve, for I am alone, and it is very lonely. It is not quite still. The clock counts on with solemn regularity and the impassiveness of inflexible inexorable destiny, the passing moment; and except this beating pulse of time I hear only the retreating roar of the railroad train, rushing off northward with its freight of human hopes and interests, through the cold darkness of the night. How it reminds one of death and separation from friends taken leave of with wishes of safe journey and safe return, and never seen again; of parting on the pier with one [Vinnie] who, sailing to Europe, carried your heart with her and made a great blank in your life until she returned; of another who, with eyes full of tears, wrung your hand at the window of the railway carriage, and went away to the other side of the continent, to die insane in an asylum for lunatics [person unidentified]; of your own journeyings and accidents and escapes; of trains leaping in the river, precipitated into the abyss with rotten trestles, rolling over and over down embankments, crashing together in the night time and reddening the sky with the glare of their flames that devour the dead and the living alike.[6]

CHILDHOOD REVISITED

I returned, a year ago [1872], to the old town in New England where I grew up to the age of manhood [Newburyport, Massachusetts], and went about with a friend of my boyhood to find others whom I knew when a youth. And I rode also round by the old country-road, and through old town, by Parson Whittinglaw's church, and by the little goose-pond, and over fern-rock bridge, and so along the old winding road over Parker River, and by Drummer Academy, and along the neighboring avenue of great elms, and at last by the meeting-house, built on the site of the old one burned, in which Elijah Parish, whom I remember, preached vehemently against Madison and the war with England, (he was quoted for it by Mr. Hayne, long, afterwards, in his great debate with Daniel Webster), and then up Warren street, to the house in which my grandfather lived and my father was born; and I found all but the house unchanged, and it only in part altered. The chamber, a great spacious room, was there still, in which I had laid so many nights and heard the steady ticking of the tall old clock in the room below, where I had so often seen my grandmother, a little old bent woman, over ninety when she died, sit all day spinning flax on the quaint little wheel, turned by her foot.

All along the road were the same old stone walls that were there when I walked the road every week or two, more than fifty years before. Even the old posts and fallen rails, that had been placed at intervals at the sides of the road were there, precisely as they had been so many long years before. The country was the same, the old well-known red-painted houses seeming to have grown no older in half a century, and I carried away with me three or four little hard sour apples from the same tree, seemingly no older, which bore them when I was a boy.

But of the people there, I knew not a single soul, and if any whom I saw had ever known me, they had lost all memory of me. But in the old sea-port town, I found many whom I knew. But all grown old, old, and most of them very strange to me; and the young girls whom I had known, were all old, faded, women, tempting though the lips and eyes of some of them had once been to me. The old houses in which my father had lived were all there, unchanged, and seemed old dear familiar friend, I dare say the inmates wondered why I stood and gazed so long at them—an old man with long white hair on his shoulders, and a great, gray beard. If they had come near, to me, they would have wondered more, to see that I could hardly descry the houses through my tears.

I hardly think that I shall go to see the old town and houses, and see the changed faces, and miss the many dear friends, ever again. I hardly think that the people of the old town consider that I have done it much honor; for, living in a Southern state, I followed its fortunes in the war, held a military and a civil commission in the service of the Confederate states; and the war made shipwreck of my fortune. Surely I do not blame them or reproach them, and I am quite content they should think of me as they will; but the invisible threads of sympathy are the nerves of friendship, and when these are severed, those whom they bind together become simply strangers.[7]

MEMORY OF A BEACH

This passage is a good example of Pike's ability to use word pictures to create a memory so strong that we can almost feel it is our own memory, and then to use that memory to lead into his topic (in this case the way that ideas and issues which seem so important at one moment in time can be so utterly irrelevant to the next generation).

When I was growing out, as I thought, of boy-hood, and enjoying the golden years that filled the space between it and manhood, I loitered often on the sea-beach of Plumb-island, listening to the grand, solemn harmonies of the never silent sea, watching the white sails far-off upon its bosom, going to and coming from foreign lands that I longed to see, watching the waves that, when the sea was placid, followed each other in long wrinkles up the broad gentle slope of hard sand, and rising higher and higher as they glided up, into long ridges, with combs of white foam, curled over and fell, with deep grave resonant intonation on the beach, and still ran up it in shallow sheets of liquid crystal, until it flowed around my feet.

Here I carefully and with great interest scrutinized the waifs brought up from the sea-depths, by the waves or from mid-ocean or far lands, and deposited among the long lines of sea-weed on the beach. I never found anything of such a value as to make me care to keep it, but often things that, if they had had tongues, could have told me, I imagine, many a thrilling and a wondrous tale.

This piece of hard old oak, worn by the waves to a flat smooth disc, part of some ship, no doubt, that went to the bottom of the sea long years before, foundering, perhaps, in a gale, or struck by lightning, or crashing suddenly against an ice berg; shells whole and broken, brought up from unknown regions in the mysterious sea-depths; this green branch brought by the gulf-stream from some tropical island,—why have they not voices to tell us what they know?

Time, also, is an ocean, that casts up its wrecks and waifs upon the shore, where, after a time, they are buried under the sand. Among these are the writings of many of the old English poets, forgotten, little more known to us beyond their names, (if even these are known) than the dead of the last generation, in their coffins, under the ground.

I read these, now and then, and it seems strange and a wonder, that the men and things in which they took so living and eager an interest should have been as actual as we and the things of this day are, and that they should have passed away, and all the hopes and fears and loves and hates and vanities and ambitions and the questions and interests in which the fate of the world and of coming generations seemed so to depend should so utterly have come to naught, and be as though they had never been at all, and no more to us than the story of a dream, which interests only him who tells it, and wearies everyone who hears it.[8]

Sometimes a writer can use the same early memory in more than one context. We're fortunate to have such an example. In the passage above, Pike develops the image to compare the scatterings on the beach to represent the surviving bits and pieces of old poetry.

But in *Morals and Dogma* he uses a shortened version of the image to recall the philosophies and religions of the past.

We stand upon the sounding shore of the great ocean of Time. In front of us stretches out the heaving waste of the illimitable Past; and its waves, as they roll up to our feet along the sparkling slope of the yellow sands, bring to us, now and then, from the depths of that boundless ocean, a shell, a few specimens of algae torn rudely from their stems, a rounded pebble; and that is all; of all the vast treasures of ancient thought that lie buried there, with the mighty anthem of the boundless ocean thundering over them forever and forever.

Let us once more, and for the last time, along the shore of that great ocean, gather a few more relics of the Past, and listen to its mighty voices, as they come, whispering to us from the great bosom of the Past.[9]

THE CITY BY THE SEA

The description of a seaside city in Peru from the following poem always reminds me of Edgar Allan Poe's "The City in the Sea." True, Poe's poem is hallucinatory and frightening in its nightmarish power, whereas Pike's poem is a romantic postcard of sorts. Yet both poems, aside from their urban focus, have similar rhyme schemes and flowing rhythms with haunting images of considerable power.

Fragments
From "The Brigand," A Poem

There is an old walled city standing near
The broad Pacific's curving, sandy verge;
Whose very walls are sometimes, by the surge,
Whitened with foam. Great palaces are there,
That glitter in the clear Peruvian air;
And grand cathedrals, with old towering spires,
Reflecting from gold ornaments the fires
Of the eternal sun. Along the streets
By day and night without cessation beats
The pulse of life, and flows the living tide,
Of pomp and poverty, and woe and pride.
There shaven monk and proud Hidalgo walk,
Or roll in state; and like the lamp-eyed flock
Of Houris that in Paradise are met
By all who truly worship Mahomet,
Fair women congregate, on pleasant eves,
When the bland sea-breezes stirs the orange leaves,
With delicate ankles, round, full, graceful forms,
And eyes as deeply black as midnight storms,
Lighten by lightning; and a gait that shames
Old Andalusia's slender-footed dames.

On all sides of the city, far and near,
Tall mansions, rich with Spanish pomp, appear;
And promenades, o'erarched with flowering trees,
Dropping their blooms at every passing breeze,
Or bent with olives. All the air is sweet,
For the light sea-winds, with their fairy feet,
Go in and out the honeyed orange-blooms,
And through the thick pomegranates, purple glooms,
Becoming partners with the thievish bees,
In bearing off rich odors.[10]

OUT FOR BLOOD

When Pike chose to go on the attack, he could create a powerful image to do the attacking for him. His relations with the press were a combination of love and contempt. Pike owned and worked for newspapers during his career. And he certainly knew how to use them effectively. His editorials before the Civil War exhorted the citizens to social reform and the support of education. He could write stinging attacks when he wished to do so. But, in general, he strongly disapproved of newspaper reporters "digging out dirt" on people. The following example is from *The Meaning of Masonry*. Pike is exhorting his reader to ignore anything base or ignoble he knows about another, for a man's sins should be known only to God. He then contrasts that position with the ethics of reporter.

It is no more honorable now than heretofore, for one to become a perpetual spy upon the actions of other men, and a general tale-bearer, even if one is fortunate enough to own a press and types, and so can retail his scandal to a multitude instead of one. Imagine only, a gentleman, making it his trade whereby to earn a living, to fish in all the moral sewers of a city for all the instances of low vice and disgusting depravity, that for the credit of human nature ought to be ignored; and then to stand at the street corners and retail them orally to all the prurient and bestial who would listen, and for his trouble deposit in his palm a sixpence![11]

A second example of Pike's comments on reporters comes from his poem, "A Dollar or Two" which is given in full in Chapter XII, page 142.

Do you wish that the Press should the decent thing do,
And give your reception a gushing review,
Describing the dresses by stuff, style, and hue?
Hand Jenkins in private a Dollar, or two.
        For the pen sells its praise for a Dollar, or two;
        And squirts its abuse for a Dollar, or two;
                As contractors sell votes,
                And banks discount notes,
That are not worth a damn, for a Dollar, or two.

THE IDEAL LIFE

I should better like to live with my books in the secluded nook among the mountains of the little Missouri, where with a handful of them I dwelt secluded during ten months, with but two neighbors in the whole valley, each more than a mile distant, one above and one below, and write undisturbed by anyone. Among the great oaks and beeches, caring for my little wheat and corn fields and abundant garden, with a little low, rude log cabin [see page 114] for home, and clear springs to drink from, while the beautiful stream ran like liquid crystal by my door and I studied at my leisure the habits of the turkeys, ducks, chickens and pigeons that multiplied and filled the woods around me. One in a city longs again to be where he passed so many long quiet hours!

Even more I should like to pass what remains to me of life in the bosom of one of the great oak groves on the undulating prairies, that slope down to the broad, level fertile alluvial plains in the country of the Choctaws and Chickasaws, the fairest country that I have ever seen; and like the old patriarch own my flocks and herds and go in the pleasant months of the year, beyond the river, to sleep in my tent or in the open air, and live on game, and drink the health-giving waters of the mineral springs, and forget that there were such things as governments and laws and taxes, follies and knaveries, passions and newspapers.

But, after all, the city has its comforts and advantages, especially when one is subject to rheumatoid gout,—ice and fruits and the markets, in the summer; the street-cars, and coal and the bookstores, with endless supply of books and magazines. I have from my windows looking northward a view of the distant ridges that sweep round the basin, with its groups of unsightly hovels, and can see the somewhat stately pile of the university beyond the dull red brick abomination of the government printing office, and crowning the ridge, fancy it to be an Athenian temple of the gods. In summer the north wind comes fresh and cool to me over this expanse, and I do not need to envy the idlers who infest the watering-places and display the tawdry glories of their wealth and state honors, to be catalogued and chronicled by the chattering reporters.

But I like my library best, during the winter, and of the long evenings when the wind, whistling shrilly in the chimney, rattles the loose windows, and I close the shutters and let the curtains fall, and with the coal fire glowing and the lamp softly burning, I lounge and smoke my pipe—indispensable and most faithful companion of all but my eating and sleeping hours or read or write or muse in the great leather-cushioned chairs.[12]

THE REACHES OF TIME

Most of us have trouble visualizing time, especially long reaches of time. Pike, in an extended metaphor, helps the reader of *Morals and Dogma* to comprehend the great time needed for changes in human affairs.

Many years ago, before the Norman Conqueror stamped his mailed foot on the neck of prostrate Saxon England, some wandering barbarian, of the continent then unknown to the world, in mere idleness, with hand or foot, covered an acorn with a little earth, and passed on regardless, on his journey to the dim Past. He died and was forgotten; but the acorn lay there still, the mighty force within it acting in the darkness.

A tender shoot stole gently up; and fed by the light and air and frequent dews, put forth its little leaves, and lived, because the elk or buffalo chanced not to place his foot upon and crush it. The years marched onward, and the shoot became a sapling, and its green leaves went and came with Spring and Autumn. And still the years came and passed away again, and William, the Norman Bastard, parcelled England out among his Barons, and still the sapling grew, and the dews fed its leaves, and the birds builded their nests among its small limbs for many generations.

And still the years came and went, and the Indian hunter slept in the shade of the sapling, and Richard Lion-Heart fought at Acre and Ascalon, and John's bold Barons wrested from him the Great Charter; and lo! the sapling had become a tree; and still it grew, and thrust its great arms wider abroad, and lifted its head still higher toward the Heavens; strong-rooted, and defiant of the storms that roared and eddied through its branches; and when Columbus ploughed with his keels the unknown Western Atlantic, and Cortez and Pizarro bathed the cross in blood; and the Puritan, the Huguenot, the Cavalier, and the follower of Penn sought a refuge and a resting-place beyond the ocean, the great Oak still stood, firm-rooted, vigorous, stately, haughtily domineering over all the forest, heedless of all the centuries that had hurried past since the Indian planted the little acorn in the forest;—a stout and hale old tree, with wide circumference shading many a rod of ground; and fit to furnish timbers for a ship, to carry the thunders of the Great Republic's guns round the world.

And yet, if one had sat and watched it every instant, from the moment when the feeble shoot first pushed its way to the light until the eagles built among its branches, he would never have seen the tree or sapling *grow*....

So it is with the aggregate of Human endeavor. As the invisible particles of vapor combine and coalesce to form the mists and clouds that fall in rain on thirsty continents, and bless the great green forests and wide grassy prairies, the waving meadows and the fields by which men live; as the infinite myriads of those drops that the glad earth drinks are gathered into springs and rivulets and rivers, to aid in levelling the mountains and elevating the plains, and to feed the large lakes and restless oceans; so all Human Thought, and Speech and Action, all that is done and said and thought and suffered upon the Earth combine together, and flow onward in one broad resistless current toward those great results to which they are determined by the will of God.[13]

In a speech delivered in Little Rock in 1854, at the laying of the cornerstone for the Masonic–Oddfellows Hall, Pike uses the image of a book to suggest the reaches of time.

The Past is a great book; open, it is true, but too far from us to allow our reading more than here and there a word of two, printed in larger letters than the general text, on here and there a leaf blown open by the wind of accident. Yet, even of these, there are more than enough to occupy a life of study, and to afford conclusive evidence that one great law, an emanation from omnipotence, has ever governed, and will continue to govern this material and intellectual world, the law of steady though slow progression and advancement towards perfection.[14]

THE "GLORY" THAT WAS WAR

Until the Civil War in the United States, the general attitude of the upper classes toward war that it was more like a noble excursion than anything else. People got killed, of course, but rarely anyone who mattered. In Europe, it was quite generally held that there were only two occupations in which a gentleman could engage without dishonor—War and the Church. In England, rather typically, the eldest son inherited the estates and managed them, the second son went into the Military (as an officer, of course), and the third son became an official of the Church of England. Wars were generally fought according to established rules (a gentleman did not attack at night, for example) and they were, on the whole, regarded as interesting diversions—especially if the war were not being fought in your country.

Pike had a different view.

At times, the baleful fires of war light up half a Continent at once.... At times, the storm, revolving, howls over small areas only; at times its lights are seen, like the old beacon-fires on the hills, belting the whole globe. No sea, but hears the roar of cannon; no river, but runs red with blood; no plain, but shakes, trampled by the hoofs of charging squadrons; no field, but is fertilized by the blood of the dead; and everywhere man slays, the vulture gorges, and the wolf howls in the ear of the dying soldier.[15]

Fragments
Of An Unfinished Poem

The battle!—Listen to the musketry!
    While even and anon amid its roll,
Roars the loud cannon: now the cavalry
    Dash down, like waves against a rocky mole,†
Built strong and far in the bosom of the sea.
    The stern battalions charge as with one soul;
And now, like waves breaking in spray and rain,
The shattered ranks go floating back again.

The fight is over: misery scarce begun!
    Count, if you can, the multitude of slain;
The hoary head lies glittering in the sun,
    Pillowed upon the charger's misty mane;
And here, with hair like delicate moonlight spun,
    A boy lies dying, with the crimson stain
Around his nostril and upon his lips;
While just below his heart the red rain drips.

The banner of your state in the dust lies low,
    Rebellion draws to an untimely end;
Fair girls amid the horrid carnage go,
    And anxiously above the corpses bend,
Seeking among your dead or those of the foe,
    A father or a brother, or dear friend;
And constantly upon the tortured air
Rings the loud wail of agonized despair.

Where are your leaders, they who madly led
    Your feet to this deep perilous abyss?
There lie the best and noblest, with the dead,
    Happy in their entire unconsciousness;
The noisiest, like cowards, far have fled,
    Pursued by scorn's indignant, general hiss,
To distant lands, that liberty disowns,
And crouch there in the shadows of old thrones.[16]

And in a beautiful passage, he puts a simple human face on those left behind.

Far in the woods of Arkansas, or on a prairie in Texas, in the dark years not long past, in a little square cabin of round rough logs, without a window, and the rifts between the logs filled with clay, the floor of rough-hewn planks, a feeble old woman plies, night and day, her constant toil at the spinning-wheel and loom,—a little, poor, thin, pale, plain old woman, that went

† A large dam or earthwork at a harbor

there, years ago, from North Carolina, with her husband, who lies buried, out there, on the little knoll where the ragged peach trees stand, and where more than one of their children lie by his side. There is nothing of what is ordinarily called sentiment and poetry in that old heart; though, as she toils patiently alone, she does think dreamily of the old homestead and the cool spring, where he who lies buried out there first met her, in the good old north state.

It is very ordinary work, that, my curled and perfumed friend, on which her old and crooked fingers are painfully employed. The squadrons of the northmen cover all the seas, and their trumpets ring everywhere in the southland, except in Texas. Never had war a more cruel heart. With ports blockaded and all the avenues of commerce hermetically sealed, the South cannot clothe her soldiers, and they shiver in the winds that herald the coming of winter,—of winter, a word of which the Confederate soldiers learned the full and fearful impact.

Albert Pike, The Poet

Night comes; and still the old mother toils. On the hearth her frugal supper waits,—a bit of meat, a pone of corn bread, some beverage in a tin-cup,—is it "tea" of sassafras or blackberry leaves? or "coffee," of parched rye or okra seeds?—without sugar, at any rate, whatever it may be.

Some night her toil ends. The product of many long days labor with her old trembling hands is a pair or two of coarse stockings of wool, and a man's suit of clothing, of a coarse cloth, half-wool, half-cotton, dyed with a decoction of barks and mosses. You would not give much for them, my friend in broad-cloth. Coarse and common, they appeal to none of *your* sympathies. They represent only so much labour, some sleepless hours, and a few Confederate paper dollars.

Nevertheless, when the suit has been made up, not after any recognizable fashion, the whole is tied up in a package, with a few words of love, on a leaf torn from the old dog-eared Bible, and the state sends the whole to the widow's only son, whom she has not seen for three years, beyond the great river, beyond the old homestead, to the delivered to him, marching and fighting there, under Lee, in the army of the Potomac.

It is little she could do for her last child and the cause that is dear to her; but it is the widow's mite; and during the stormy winter-days and long bleak nights it will protect him against the cold, and save him from the dreaded pneumonia, to do battle again in the Spring, and help win victories or delay defeats that involve no dishonor; to save him, perhaps, from death by exposure, and bring him back to her when all is over and the cause is lost, to work for her, and keep the wolf of hunger from her door. That mother's pin-offering on the altar of Love and of her state and southernland had a value far beyond the value of pearls and diamonds.[17]

ONE-LINERS

Pike can create a powerful image in one or a few lines when he wishes, and they often come in the middle of other works. Here are a few "one-liners" in which Pike creates the power and "swift kick" of poetry, whether the passage is poetry or prose.

> Disgrace and Danger, like two hungry hounds
> Run ever on the track of those who do
> Good service to their country....[18]

> Praise has fed his eager spirit with her rain
> of dangerous sweetness.[19]

> The silver horn of the advancing tide
>   Had ploughed its highest furrow in the sand,
> And was retiring.[20]

...and dost maintain thyself aloof from the monotonous din of the old twirling oak leaves, from the moan of the gray weeds, the dull monotony of the harsh winds, and the dead limb, that, lone and dry, swings creaking from the leafless tree.[21]

Thy wife shall wait
Many long days for thee;
and when the gate
Swings on its unused hinges, she,
Opening her dim and grief-contracted eye,
And still forbidding hope to die,
Longing for thee will look;
Till like some lone and gentle summer brook,
That pineth in the summer-heat away
And dies some day,
She waste her mournful life out at her eyes.[22]

The great truths of philosophy and religion are, for most men, like the sun's rays which strike upon the arctic snows—they glitter and are reflected, but they do not penetrate or warm.[23]

Am I to be a slave forever?
To stay amid mankind, and die
Like a scorched river,
Wasting on burning sands away?[24]

Still as infant death,
The broad and heavy forest sleeps beneath
The white foam of the Galaxy...[25]

How ungratefully he slinks away, who dies, and does nothing to reflect a glory to Heaven! How barren a tree he is, who lives, and spreads, and cumbers the ground, yet leaves not one seed, not one good work to generate another after him![26]

Thou wast too full of uncontrolled romance,
Too full of Poetry's impassioned trance,
Too full of soul, to live amid the world.
Thy body to thy soul was like a cloud,
In which the silver arrows of the sun
Stay not, but pass wherever they are hurled;
'Twas like the clear transparent element,
That shows the emerald beneath it pent,
Nor robs one ray. Thy soul breathed in thy face,
And lay upon it like a visible mist.[27]

THE URGE OF POETRY

Of Pike's "serious" poetry, undoubtedly the best known is the poem, "Every Year." It was extremely popular during Pike's life, printed not only in book form but in illustrated sheets to be framed and hung on the wall. (See following page.) The images are simple, but powerful.

Every Year

Life is a count of losses,
Every year;
For the weak are heavier crosses,
Every year;
Lost Springs with sobs replying
Unto weary Autumn's sighing,
While those we love are dying,
Every year.

It is growing darker, colder,
Every year;
As the heart and soul grow older,
Every year;
I care not now for dancing,
Or for eyes with passion glancing
Love is less and less entrancing
Every year.

The days have less of gladness,
Every year;
The nights more weight of sadness,
Every year;
Fair Springs no longer charm us,
The winds and weather harm us,
The threats of Death alarm us,
Every year.

There come new cares and sorrows,
Every year;
Dark days and darker morrows,
Every year;
The ghosts of dead loves haunt us,
The ghosts of changed friends taunt us,
And disappointments daunt us,
Every year.

Of the loves and sorrows blended,
Every year;
Of the charms of friendship ended,
Every year;
Of the ties that still might bind me,
Until Time to Death resigned me,
My infirmities remind me,
Every year.

Ah! how sad to look before us,
Every year;
While the cloud grows darker o'er us,
Every year;
When we see the blossoms faded,
That to bloom we might have aided,
And immortal garlands braided,
Every year.

To the Past go more dead faces,
Every year;
As the loved leave vacant places,
Every year;
Everywhere the sad eyes meet us,
In the evening's dusk they greet us,
And to come to them entreat us,
Every year.

"You are growing old," they tell us,
Every year;
"You are more alone," they tell us,
Every year;
"You can win no new affection,
"You have only recollection,
"Deeper sorrow and dejection,
"Every year."

The shores of life are shifting,
Every year;
And we are seaward drifting,
Every year;
Old places, changing, fret us,
The living more forget us,
There are fewer to regret us,
Every year.

But the truer life draws nigher,
Every year;
And its Morning star climbs higher,
Every year;
Earth's hold on us grows slighter,
And the heavy burdens lighter,
And the Dawn Immortal brighter,
Every year.[28]

But, to my personal taste, the most powerful and surprising image Pike creates in his poetry is of a just-past-new moon, with the faint circle of the full moon barely visible.

A Fragment

Like the young moon,
When, on the sunlit limits of the night,
Her white sheen trembles amid crimson air,
And whilst the sleeping tempest gathers might,
Doth as the herald of her coming, bear
The ghost of her dead mother, whose dim form
Bends in dark ether from her infant's chair.[29]

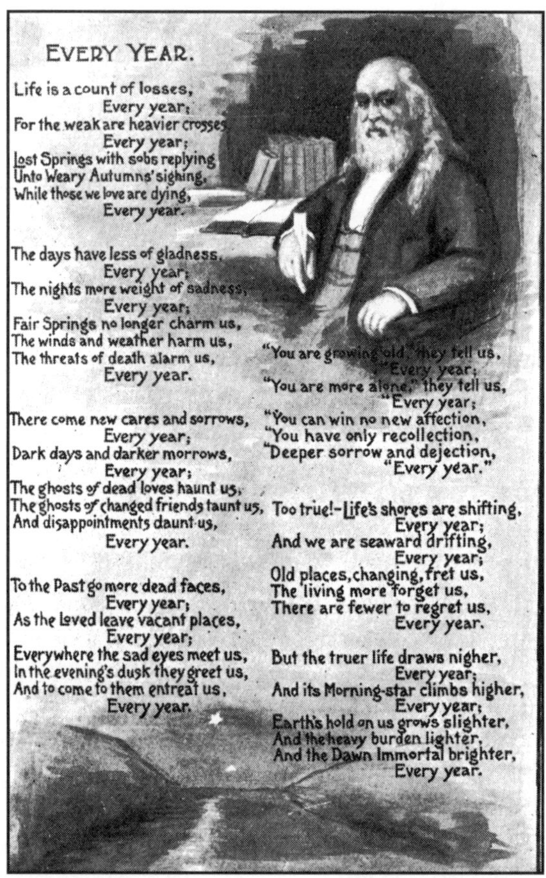

"Every Year," Albert Pike's most famous poem, was so popular it was printed in illustrated sheets to be framed and hung on the wall.

XVII

"The Horrid Blasphemy Of Thanking A God Of Love For Carnage"

On War

No city is not tortured by shot and shell, and no people fail to enact the horrid blasphemy of thanking a God of Love for victories and carnage.[1]

Strange words from a General? Not really. It is the men and women who stay safe at home, far from the battle, who sing of the glory of war and conflict. Those who have been in it know better. And Pike had been through the most bloody, horrible, destructive war the United States has ever fought. For sheer death and carnage, no American war has ever approached the Civil War.

Who can sum up the horrors and woes accumulated in a single war? Masonry is not dazzled with all its pomp and circumstance, all its glitter and glory. War comes with its bloody hand into our very dwellings. It takes from ten thousand homes those who lived there in peace and comfort, held by the tender ties of family and kindred. It drags them away, to die untended, of fever or exposure, in infectious climes; or to be hacked, torn, and mangled in the fierce fight; to fall on the gory field, to rise no more, or to be borne away, in awful agony, to noisome [dirty and stinking] and horrid hospitals. The groans of the battle-field are echoed in sighs of bereavement from thousands of desolated hearths. There is a skeleton in every house, a vacant chair at every table. Returning, the soldier brings worse sorrow to his home, by the infection which he has caught, of camp-vices. The country is demoralized. The national mind is brought down, from the noble interchange of kind offices with another people, to wrath and revenge, and base pride, and the habit of measuring brute strength against brute strength, in battle.[2]

War seems to be the natural state and element of man, and the appetite for blood a stern necessity of his nature. As in the

Brig. General Albert Pike

vegetable kingdom, one species thrives by the destruction and extermination of another; as in the animal kingdom, life maintains life; and the larger, by the law of their nature, pursue, capture and devour the smaller. As man himself in this respect ranks with the tiger and the eagle, and preys upon the harmless fish, the graceful deer, and even the bright-eyed singing bird, so until lately, it might almost have seemed that by a like unerring law of nature man's life maintained the life of man; that might made right, and the strong were made and meant to prey upon the weak, and secure their own fortune and luxury at the price of the pain, the misery, the torture and death of others, whose virtue and feebleness were their only protection.

Of the first two sons of Adam, eldest born upon our planet, when one would have thought the world wide enough, and causes of quarrel rare enough for them, at lest, to have lived in peace, the tiller of the soil rose up against his brother, the shepherd, and slew him; and in the days of Noah, crime, rapine [plunder], violence and murder had become so rife upon the earth, that saving only that patriarch and his family, God swept the whole population of the world with the besom [broom] of the deluge.

Long before the days of Abraham, war had again commenced; and from that time to the present there has probably never been a single hour when it has not raged on some portion of the earth's surface.[3]

War struck twice in Pike's adult life, with very different consequences and results. The first time was the War with Mexico. Part of the story has already been alluded to in the chapter about the duel between Pike and Roane. But a little more background is helpful. Walter Lee Brown writes:

Soon after the formation of the First Artillery, Pike was chosen captain to replace John T. Fulton, who had resigned. Equipped with rifles and two six-pounder field guns, the company was drilled in infantry as well as artillery tactics.... The company, known to the townspeople as "Pike's Artillery," became under his leadership expert both in mounted and foot drill, and much in demand for parades and displays on special occasions.[4]

If that sounds a little like a party, it was. Marching groups and military groups were very popular in the 1800s. In some ways, and meaning no disparagement, it was a little like an adult boy scout troop.

One didn't think of people getting killed. It was largely a matter of parades, firing salutes, and public festivals—with always the background reality that the home guard might be called upon.

General Robert E. Lee

And then the War with Mexico broke out, and calls went out for volunteers. It was very different than today. A man would form a company of volunteers and then go offer their services to the army. His group would elect their own captain, and they would march off to serve in the war—generally, at liberty to leave whenever they wanted. Richardson tells us:

In 1848 he [Pike] *raised a squadron of cavalry which he commanded with the rank of Captain, and served in the war with Mexico, having received special mention from Generals Taylor and Wool. Here he met Major Robert E. Lee, afterward General of the Confederate Army.*[5]

Pike was a good commander in the war, even though his private papers suggest he really didn't want to be there. But his volunteers had been eager to go. Pike was known as strict. We have already seen in the history of the Battle of Buena Vista what happened to troops who were not properly drilled. One man wrote home to a newspaper:

Pike is a strict disciplinarian, and in consequence, has incurred the dislike of several of his holiday soldiers, who have returned. But those who remain with him know and feel that he is not the man to undertake a thing without doing it well, and admire him for it.[6]

We won the War with Mexico. Nearly everyone came home and generally felt rather good about it.

They were soon to learn that they had no concept of what war was.

It is a truism that history is written by the winners. The North won, and Northern writers, especially, have condemned Pike for siding with the South. To do that is to assume he made a decision cheaply and easily. That is far from the case.

First of all, Pike genuinely loved both the Union and the Constitution. He wrote about that love many times before the war. He regarded the Constitution as the greatest legal document ever produced. He fought successfully to model the Constitution of the State of Arkansas on the federal Constitution.

Pike referred to the prospect of Secession as "a gulf of despair and horror darker and deeper than any that ever opened since the world began."[7]

In public speeches, editorials and letters, he examined the Southern cause over and over again, and pointed out that no sufficient reason existed for the Union to be dissolved. One common argument of the secessionists was that the South was a minority in the federal government and would never be able to control legislation or get legislation through against the efforts of the North. Pike pointed out how hollow that argument was.

I am in a minority here at home. For all practical purposes there might as well be a law in Arkansas that no Whig should vote at all. If the South should be justified in severing itself from the Union, because it is in a minority, so would a single state be justified in severing itself from the rest of the South; one county from the rest of the state, one township from the others of the county.[8]

It was not as easy to see the moral issues at the time as we think today it should have been. Pike was no friend of slavery. But he was realist enough to know slavery was deeply embedded in the economy of the South and could not be suddenly eliminated without terrible consequences to all. History proved him to be right. And while Pike saw slavery as a moral evil, he did not see it as a greater evil than starvation and wage exploitation which were merely conferred as the "benefits" of slavery upon the factory owner without any of the responsibilities which devolved upon the slave owner. George Williams, in his play *An Evening With General Albert Pike,* draws upon several of Pike's written statements for the lines:

I could not decide allegiance on moral grounds, either, for the scales would not balance. The South had slavery, and I hated it. But the North was no better. Scores of their factory and mill workers, women and children among them, routinely starved to death because they could not afford to buy food.

Neither side, for all their fine slogans, came with clean hands. No woman or child ever starved in the streets of a Southern city, but Southern plantation owners bought and sold other human beings. The Northern industrialists did no such thing, but they built and filled cemeteries with the women and children they had killed.[9]

Pike himself wrote:

I speak for the interest that I and my children have in this mighty question. They are natives of the South, but my heart-allegiance is divided. Born almost in the shadow of Faneuil Hall, educated in the free schools of Massachusetts; ...claiming, as a part of my inheritance as an American, an interest in the glories and the soil of all the revolutionary battle-fields of New England, owing all that I am, and all that I and my children ever shall be, to the institutions and influences of this Union, under whose flag I have fought, and its honor aided to defend; long denounced in the South...and almost odious there as an extreme Union-man, in times when those who loved popularity were not eager to be so classed; and my heart clinging alike to the North and the South—to the soil with which the ashes of my father, my brother, and my sisters have mingled and to the land to whose bosom I have committed the dead bodies of my children; how can I look upon the strife, the antipathies, the bitterness, and the hatred, ominous of disaster, of the North and the South, without the profoundest sorrow and the gloomiest apprehension?[10]

He hoped until the last that the conflict could be avoided. Allen Roberts, in his excellent book, *House Undivided: The Story of Freemasonry and the Civil War,* cites a speech Pike delivered to a meeting of the Grand Lodge in Little Rock, just six months and one day before Arkansas seceded from the Union.

These greetings that I convey to you are proof that the strong ties of Masonic obligations, Masonic affections and Masonic brotherhood, are not yet, like so many others, snapped asunder, but that they still endure and there is yet peace, and calm, and harmony around our holy altars, though the elements without are gloomily ominous of disaster and the atmosphere is oppressive as when an earthquake is near at hand. I am sure that all these brethren will unite with me in the earnest, anxious wish, that some power may say to the tumultuous waves, "Peace! be still!—that the bonds of friendship and good neighborhood may be re-knit and strengthened, and anger and recrimination cease, and that all the great moral and social influences of Masonry may be exerted, honestly and unceasingly, for the restoration of harmony, the maintenance of peace, and the performance of duty.[11]

He wrote, he editorialized, he spoke, he pleaded for reason to any audience he could find. It was simply too late. The Southern states started to secede, and Arkansas had to decide whether to follow them out of the Union or not. A desire to preserve the slavery tradition probably would not have been sufficient to take Arkansas out of the Union—only a part of the state was suitable for the kind of agriculture in which slaves were useful. A stronger impetus for secession was the fear of being required as Union soldiers to fight against their fellow Southerners.

Ultimately, for Pike it came down to a legal question. Was the Constitution a compact made by the States as the South believed, or was it an instrument created directly by the people of the United States as a whole as the North contended? If it were a compact made by the States, then a State had the right to withdraw from it. If it were made by the people as a whole, then perhaps a State did not have that right.

Pike believed that law was on the side of the South on that issue. Even the name "United States," he argued, suggested it was a compact of States. We did not call the country the "United People of America." The convention which created the Constitution was called by the States, and he argued that the resulting Constitution was a creation of the States.

> I was satisfied as to the right of secession, as an extreme remedy, fit to be used only in the last resort, and when all others should have failed. I did not think its exercise either wise or necessary in 1861. I consented to the secession of Arkansas, only when she was compelled to elect whether her sons and mine should take up arms for or against her sisters that had seceded—in vindication or denial of the right of a state peaceably to withdraw from the Union of the states.[12]

And so Pike cast his lot with the South.

President Jefferson Davis assigned to Pike the task of negotiating treaties with the American Indian tribes in what is now Oklahoma. But then a great tragedy occurred. Pike, now a Brigadier General, was ordered to take the Indian troops into battle in Arkansas, even though he had been promised (and he had promised them) that they would be called upon only to defend their own land. It came to a head at the Battle of Pea Ridge in Arkansas.

This detail of an imaginative Kurz and Allison print (1889) of the Battle of Pea Ridge, Arkansas, depicts Pike (left) leading his Indian troops.

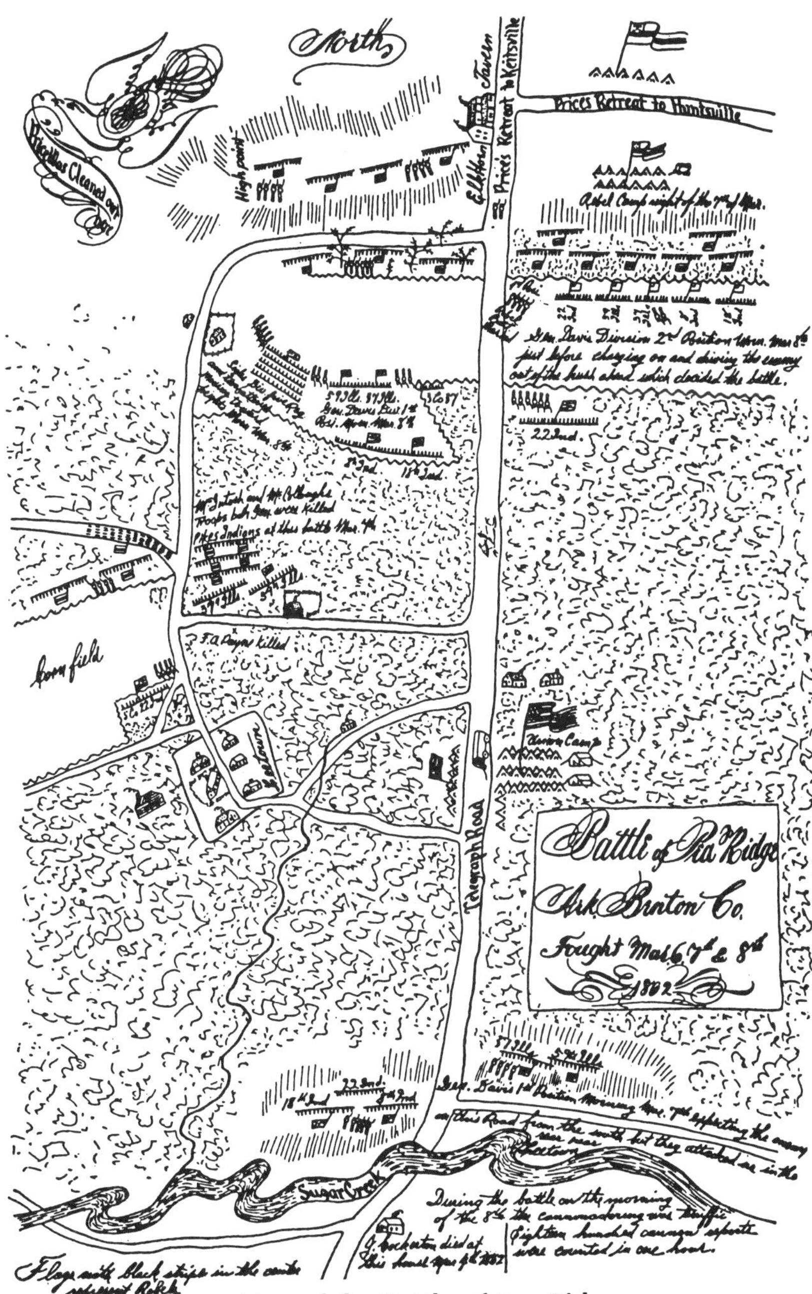

Map of the Battle of Pea Ridge

Charles S. Squires, a private in Company C., 37th Illinois Infantry Regiment during the Battle of Pea Ridge (March 6–8, 1862), drew this map of the battle. The position of "Pikes Indians at this battle Mar. 7th" is noted in the upper left quadrant of the map. The Battle of Pea Ridge and Pike's role in it are detailed by Michael A. Botelho in volume 2 of *Heredom*, the 1993 transactions of the Scottish Rite Research Society. Map courtesy: National Park Service

During the battle, it was alleged that some of the Indians under Pike's command scalped Northern soldiers killed in the battle. The fine ethical distinction between scalping a dead body and blowing a living man to bits with cannon is one I find hard to draw, but the Northern newspapers had no such problem. Subsequent reports indicated that there was actually very little scalping and that most of that was probably done by renegades and not by troops under Pike's command. Pike immediately sent a note of apology under a flag of truce to the Northern Commander, Brigadier General Samuel R. Curtis, when he learned of it, and did his best to find and punish those who had committed the act. But that made no difference to the press.

The National Park Service has created an noteworthy museum and preserved the battlefield at Pea Ridge. It's well worth a visit. A booklet, "The Battle of Pea Ridge, 1862" has been published by the Service. It contains several informative articles including one by Roy A. Clifford, "The Indian Regiments in the Battle of Pea Ridge." In it, Clifford sketches a comprehensive outline of the battle and Pike's involvement with it. It's clear that Pike fought well and valiantly, as did the troops under his command. But, in general, history *is* written by the winners, and this episode was portrayed as an atrocity. Clifford presents the following view of the battle and its aftermath.

Maj. General Earl Van Dorn

No apology need be made for the Indian behavior in this battle. If fault is to be found, it lies in the use of the troops outside of Indian Territory. By the treaties of alliance with the Indians, the regiments were not supposed to be used outside of the Indian Territory. Pike was rather bitter over the use of the Indians in the Battle of Pea Ridge and felt that they had had their treaties infringed upon. He also wrote to Secretary [of War, later Secretary of State, in the Confederate Cabinet, Judah P.] *Benjamin deploring the fact that* [the Commander of Confederate Forces at Pea Ridge, Maj. General Earl] *Van Dorn had made no mention of the Indians' part in the battle. Pike had ample reason to complain about this lack since his troops had behaved courageously in the battlefield and had given him trouble only when they became elated over the capture of three guns. At that time they had become excited and were uncontrollable for a time. It was during this time that the scalpings were supposed to have occurred. Even this incident was not caused by cowardice but rather by too much enthusiasm.*

It may be that Curtis feared a reprimand about the reported scalpings and, hence, refrained from all mention of the troops except to say that he had ordered Pike and his men to join the other forces. However, from the attitude taken by General Pike it would seem more likely that the General of the Southern army in this battle had little respect for the Indian troops and purposefully ignored any mention of their bravery in this battle. This would be strengthened by the fact that Van Dorn looked upon the Indians as being useful only as scouting parties. It is regrettable that Van Dorn felt this way.... It is little wonder that Pike was angry when Curtis sent page after page of detailed reports to the Confederate Adjutant with no mention of Pike's men.[13]

As a result of this dispute with General Van Dorn, Pike resigned his commission. But he was never ashamed of the war, his part in it, nor of the men who fought it. For instance, he has given us a wonderful character portrait of Robert E. Lee.

I think the country has produced no greater man than Robert E. Lee. I knew him, and served with him, was intimate with him and honored with his friendship.

He was of unstained honor and integrity without vices, and in every thing temperate. He never harbored an unworthy purpose. Scorning all falsehood, he was incapable of duplicity or disingenuousness. And no human creature could ever truly say that it had been deceived by him. Of unexcelled courage, heroic, constant, prudent, resolute, wise; anger, the professed enemy of counsel, never obscured his judgment and passion never alloyed his resolves. Sincerely religious, he was gentle, merciful, genial, kind and supremely generous. He did great deeds and was capable of greater.... He would have ruled a nation wisely, for he had a kingly and right noble nature.

He envied no one, hated no one, was jealous of no one, complained of no mistreatment, and in the modest brevity of his reports of the achievements of his army, has had no rival. Unaffected, simple in manner and kindly of temper, he had the love of his men, and never wounded the sensibilities of an officer. Cheerful under reverses, hopeful while hope was possible, he accepted defeat with equanimity, always generously imputing it to the faultiness of his own movements or arrangements, if it were not so inevitable as to admit of no censure at all.

With what simple dignity he surrendered his sword, and accepted the consequences of defeat! How touching his last words to his men! How noble, how glorious, how truly grand all the residue of his life![14]

It was of some comfort to Pike that Masonry had largely stayed out of the conflict. There were hundreds of stories from the Civil War of soldiers from the North and South gathering after battle to give burial or assistance to Masons from both sides who had fallen in the conflict.

One such incident is memorialized in the Gettysburg Friend to Friend Masonic Memorial Monument pictured on this page. Also, there were stories of soldiers from both sides sparing the lives of those they found to be Brothers, refusing to steal from Masonic widows, and sparing each other's homes and farms. Pike wrote:

> In time of war, here and in France, Masonic obligations have almost universally been regarded and remembered; which was not the case with those of any other society or association.[15]

Friend To Friend Masonic Memorial Monument

The Friend to Friend Masonic Memorial Monument in Gettysburg, Pennsylvania, dedicated on August 21, 1993, commemorates a Civil War incident of July 3, 1863. On that day, during the Battle of Cemetery Ridge, Confederate Brigadier General Lewis A. Armistead, dying from a battle wound, called out for assistance. Union Captain Henry H. Bingham, recognizing General Armistead as a Mason, asked, "How can I be of service to you, my Brother?" Bingham complied with Armistead's last request, that his personal effects, among them a Masonic Bible and a gold watch engraved with the Masonic Square and Compasses, be delivered to his wife.

The war ended, ultimately, and the healing process began. Pike had lost everything—all his lands, his money, virtually everything except his library and the clothes on his back.

The story of the library is interesting. Allen E. Roberts, in *House Undivided: The Story of Freemasonry and the Civil War,* points out that it was saved by a Masonic Brother—the Grand Master of Iowa and a Colonel in the Federal troops—who posted a guard around the building to keep it from being burned.[16]

Pike was a hard man to hold down. It seems fitting to include at least the last five stanzas of a poem he wrote after the war—a poem of reconciliation. It breaths the spirit of Masonry, which sustained him during those long and terrible days, and it breathes as well the optimism which was to characterize him until his death.

Re-Union

We see the faces of the Dead; they hover in the air,
And looking on us lovingly, our mirth they seem to share;
O dearly loved! though ye have gone to other stars or spheres,
We still have for you thoughts of love and consecrated tears.

Pour a libation rich with love upon the graves that hold
The ashes of the gallant hearts that long ago grew cold;
And swear that never party feuds or civil war shall break
Our bonds of love, and enemies of friends and comrades make.

The Dead are with us always, friends! let us their teachings heed!
"Forgive thy brother, if he err!" they eloquently plead:
"Let bygones be bygones!" they cry, "let the old love revive!
"And on the altars of your hearts keep Friendship's fire alive."

It is better far to love than hate, for Nations as for men,
Let us hope the good old humour soon will bless the land again;
But if the politicians still should wrangle, scold, and fight,
Their quarrels shall not break the ties that we re-knit tonight.

Our Autumn days of life have come, the frosts begin to fall,
Beyond the dark, deep river, hark! we hear old comrades call.
To the Dead and Living whom each loves, let each his goblet fill;
And the memory of the dead shall make the living dearer still.

WASHINGTON, D.C. JANUARY 1869[17]

For much of the rest of his life, Pike returned again and again to the war in his thinking. And his thoughts not only illuminate his own mental processes for us but also help us to understand the conflict. Most of us, now, do not understand the issues which loomed so large in the thinking of the men who fought the war. I have actually had some people tell me the Civil War was fought solely because the South wanted to keep slaves and the North wanted to free them. Let us listen to Pike on the causes and aftermath of the war.

After the Civil War, Pike's Little Rock, Arkansas, home was confiscated, along with nearly all his other possessions.

It was a war of opinions and convictions, and therefore there was a natural and just indignation on each side. We believed that we had the right to withdraw peacefully from a political connection created by a written compact between the States; that the attempt of the other States to prevent this by force was a flagrant outrage, and that it was an infamous thing to stigmatize us as rebels and traitors: and we also believed that upon the theory of our antagonists, the continuance of republican government was impossible. *We believe all this still more firmly now.* On the other hand, part of our opponents honestly believed that our view of the Constitution was utterly wrong; that it was not a compact between the States but a paramount law enacted by their superior; that we had no right to secede, and that Secession was rebellion and treason: and, moreover, they believed that our success would be fatal to the cause of republican liberty. They were, therefore, as indignant, and from their point of view, and with these convictions, as justly indignant as we were. There was a fiery and righteous wrath on each side; and each party was equally sincere. We did not believe that the Northern leaders of opinion really thought that we were rebels. We did not see how it was possible they could: and we thought that they called us so, to justify their war upon us, and to fire the popular heart with hate and the desire for vengeance. We still find it hard to believe that intelligent men could honestly have had a legal conviction that the act of a state, withdrawing from the Union, was the rebellion or treason of its people: for we think that if anything on earth can be demonstrable and certain, the contrary of that proposition is so.

But we know that there is no opinion so absurd, unreasonable, untenable, that it may not be hospitably entertained by intelligent and otherwise sane men; that we can never comprehend how men can believe that which we disbelieve.... The natural fruits of mutual rage and hate were atrocities and cruel outrages, wrongs and retaliations. These are of the Past, the bitter fruits of every civil war, and alien, in most cases, to the real nature of the men who committed them; for in war, when Hell legislates for humanity, men are insane for the time, and God save us from another Civil War! and efface the ghastly pictures of the last one, that have seemed so indelibly imprinted on the memory! May He teach us all the excellent art of forgetfulness!

Let us all admit, for it is true, that each party thought the course of the other utterly unjustifiable; and the inevitable consequences of its success, the ruin of the country and of republican government. To maintain that was and is the common object of all. If we differed as to the mode, we agreed as to the end; and as that one mode is now impossible, we *must* all unite in the effort to maintain one republican government over the whole country, if we claim any rights of citizenship at all.[18]

In one way, the story of Pike and the war did not end until after his death in 1891, twenty-two years after the poem "Re-Union" was written. As with many men who fought in the Confederate army, the United States government confiscated Pike's property after the war was over. Due to some legal precedents he was able to establish, some of it was returned to his heirs after his death, but some, he knew, would not be.

With that biting sarcasm he so well employed, Pike added a clause to his will, bequeathing to the United States government:

The indebtedness of the United States to me...for four horses lost to me in the military service of the United States in Mexico [and for] the moneys in the Treasury of the United States arising from the sale under process of confiscation of property belonging to me in Little Rock,—being some nineteen hundred and fifty dollars, in order that they may have an honest title thereto, and no longer hold them as the proceeds of plundering under the power of law.[19]

We do not know if the government ever acknowledged the gift or its own restored integrity.

XVIII

Aphorisms

On Pike's Piquancy

An aphorism is a short, pithy statement which catches and points out some truth, or gives one something about which to think. A truly great aphorism should provide, in just a few words, materials for hours or days of thought. Pike has some great aphorisms which capture and suggest a whole philosophy. These are given here without any particular order, because such lines are more effective when they are not grouped into categories. Each should stand on its own, not as a continuation of a topic or thought. A few of these are taken from longer quotations given elsewhere in this book, but most have not previously appeared in this work.

The man who wanders in the woods without an aim or purpose will be fortunate if he does not lose himself.

Essay XXIII—Of The Ability to Say "No"

Hypocrisy is the homage that vice and wrong pay to virtue and justice.

Morals and Dogma

To strive, to brave all risks, to perish, to persevere, to be true to one's self, to grapple body to body with destiny, to surprise defeat by the little terror it inspires, now to confront unrighteous power, now to defy intoxicated triumph—these are the examples that nations need, and the light that electrifies them.

Morals and Dogma

Every teacher of the Truth, in every age and among every people, has been inspired by God; and every True word, whensoever and by whomsoever spoken, has come to the speaker from God.

Lecture on Masonic Symbolism

Times change, and circumstances; but Virtue and Truth remain the same. The Evils to be warred against but take another shape, and are developed in a different form.

Morals and Dogma

If he is wealthy who hath large sums invested, and the mass of whose fortune consists in obligations that bind other men to pay him money, he is still more so to whom many owe large returns of kindnesses and favors.

Morals and Dogma

Duty is the moral magnetism which controls and guides the true Mason's course over the tumultuous seas of life.
Morals and Dogma

The great aim of reason is to generalize; to discover unity in multiplicity, order in apparent confusion; to separate from the accidental and the transitory, the stable and universal.
Morals and Dogma

A man would better hang himself with the garter of nobility, than wear it when he has not earned it.
Essay XXII—Of Values

If you seek for high and strained carriages, you shall, for the most part, meet with them in low men. Arrogance is a weed that ever grows on a dunghill. *Morals and Dogma*

No tower of Pride was ever yet high enough to lift its possessor above the trails and fears and frailties of humanity.
Morals and Dogma

Wisdom is that exercise of the reason into which the heart enters.
Reception of a Louveteau

No vice is more rare, for no task is more difficult, than systematic hypocrisy.
Morals and Dogma

Men may betray, but principles never can.
Morals and Dogma

The simplest thing in the Universe involves the ultimate mystery of all.
Essay XXI—Of Forces

When men begin to reflect, they being to differ.
Morals and Dogma

Nobody is very fond of listening to good advice.
Reception of a Louveteau

The well-informed man, only, is really free.
Legenda, XIX–XXX

We do not know, as yet, what qualifications sheep insist on in a leader.
Morals and Dogma

The grand objects of Nature perpetually constrain men to think of their Author. *Morals and Dogma*

It is only man who continues to accumulate after he has more than enough; and yet he fancies that God made him after His own image.
Essay XXIII—Of The Ability to Say "No"

God and Truth are inseparable; a knowledge of God is possession of the saving oracles of Truth. *Morals and Dogma*

Never was a human being sunk so low that he had not, by God's gift, the power to rise. *Morals and Dogma*

Albert Pike, Philosopher and Poet

In his influences that survive him, man becomes immortal, before the general Resurrection. *Morals and Dogma*

Honor and Duty are the twin stars, by which all men ought to steer their course over the stormy seas of life.
Essay XXI—Of Forces

Doubt, the essential preliminary of all improvement and discovery, must accompany all the stages of man's onward progress.
Morals and Dogma

The great problem is to find guides who are not willing to become tyrants.
Morals and Dogma

Selfishness is poverty; it is the most utter destitution of a human being.
Reception of a Louveteau

Men are great or small in stature as it pleases God; but their nature is great or small as it pleases themselves.
Morals and Dogma

To be ashamed of toil; of the dingy workshop and dusty labor-field; of the hard hand, stained with service more honorable than that of war; of the soiled and weather-stained garments, on which Mother Nature has stamped, midst sun and rain, mist fire and steam, her own heraldic honors; to be ashamed of these tokens and titles, and envious of the flaunting robes of imbecile idleness and vanity, is treason to Nature, impiety to Heaven, a breach of Heaven's great Ordinance.

Morals and Dogma

The subtle human intellect can weave its mists over even the clearest vision.

Morals and Dogma

There are no blessings which the mind may not convert into the bitterest of evils; and no trials which it may not transform into the noblest and finest blessings. *Morals and Dogma*

What is certain, even for science and the reason, is, that the idea of God is the grandest, the most holy, and the most useful of all the aspirations of man; that upon this belief morality reposes, with its eternal sanction.

Morals and Dogma

You can hardly get two men in any Congress or Convention to agree;—nay, you can rarely get one to agree with *himself*.

Morals and Dogma

He only who has borne the cross is worthy to wear it.

Essay XXII—Of Values

When we gaze, of a moonless clear night, on the Heavens glittering with stars, and know that each fixed star of all the myriads is a Sun, and each probably possessing it retinue of worlds, all peopled with living beings, we sensibly feel our own unimportance in the scale of Creation.

Morals and Dogma

Pride in unsound theories is worse than ignorance.

Morals and Dogma

Education, Instruction and Enlightenment are the only certain means by which Intolerance and Fanaticism can be rendered powerless.

The Meaning of Masonry

There are two natures in man, the higher and the lower, the great and the mean, the noble and the ignoble; and he can and must, by his voluntary act, identify himself with the one or with the other.

Morals and Dogma

In the rivalries of politics, the three things most especially useful are, in the order of their value, nonsense, humbug, lies.

Essay XIII—Of Rowing Against the Stream

Man has *natural* empire over *all* institutions. They are for him, according to his development; not he for them.

Morals and Dogma

Man is the child of his works.

Legenda XIX–XXX

Let man but be, as he is, a living soul, communing with himself and with God, and his vision becomes eternity; his abode, infinity; his home, the bosom of all-embracing love.
Morals and Dogma

I believe that a Scotsman once defined metaphysical discussion as being, "when the chief ye're talking to disna ken what ye mean, and ye dinna ken yerself." *Essay XXII—Of Values*

The Anti-Masons, traitors and perjurers some, and some mere political knaves, purified Masonry by persecution, and so proved to be its benefactors. *Morals and Dogma*

Epidemics of opinions are as irrestible as epidemics of disease, and their causes and laws are equally as inscruitable.
Essay XIII—Of Rowing Against the Stream

It is not beyond the tomb, but in life itself, that we are to seek for the mysteries of death. Salvation or reprobation begins here below, and the terrestrial world, too, has its heaven and hell.
Morals and Dogma

Almost all the noblest things that have been achieved in the world, have been achieved by poor men.
Morals and Dogma

To discover God's universal law of justice is one thing—to undertake to measure off something with *our own* little tape-line, and call *that* God's law, is another. *Morals and Dogma*

Let men be bribed and bought or paid, for unscrupulous service, with money, if you will; but not with place and honors.
Essay XXII—Of Values

Legislators may be very ordinary men; for legislation is very ordinary work; it is but the final issue of a million minds.
Morals and Dogma

You will no more make a statesman of a knave than a judge of an ass.
Essay XIII—Of Rowing Against the Stream

Knowledge is the most genuine and real of human treasures; for it is Light, as Ignorance is Darkness.
Morals and Dogma

Do thou what thou oughtest to do; let the result be what it will.
Morals and Dogma

It is prosperity, and not adversity, that is hurtful to a Commonwealth. *Essay XXII—Of Values*

The gleams and glitter of intellectual soap-and-water bubbles are mistaken for the rainbow-glories of genius; the worthless pyrite is continually mistaken for gold; even intellect condescends to intellectual jugglery, balancing thoughts as a juggler balances pipes on his chin.
Morals and Dogma

There is nothing so deplorable as the actions of men in public office, except the means by which they get it.
Essay XXIII—Of The Ability To Say "No"

Idleness is the burial of the living man.
Morals and Dogma

It is from the mutual action and re-action of antagonistic forces, that harmony, everywhere in the universe, results.
Essay XXII—Of Values

To write on rock is to write on a solid parchment; but it requires a pilgrimage to see it. *Morals and Dogma*

Thought is a force, and philosophy should be an energy, finding its aim and its effects in the amelioration of mankind.
Morals and Dogma

He who would attain to a reasonable degree of excellence, *must* form for himself an ideal beyond his reach.
Reception of a Louveteau

Each man has enough to do, to watch and keep guard over himself.
Morals and Dogma

We support ourselves only on that which resists.
Essay XXII—Of Values

He who *does* right is better than he who *thinks* right.
Morals and Dogma

Masonry is useful to all men: to the learned, because it affords them the opportunity of exercising their talents upon subjects eminently worthy of their attention; to the illiterate, because it offers them important instruction; to the young, because it presents them with salutary precepts and good examples, and accustoms them to reflect on the proper mode of living; to the man of the world, whom it furnishes with noble and useful recreation; to the traveller, whom it enables to find friends and brothers in countries where else he would be isolated and solitary; to the worthy man in misfortune, to whom it gives assistance; to the afflicted, on whom it lavishes consolation; to the charitable man, whom it enables to do more good, by uniting with those who are charitable like himself; and to all who have souls capable of appreciating its importance, and of enjoying the charms of a friendship founded on the same principles of religion, morality, and philanthropy. *Morals and Dogma*

XIX

"Hedged About With The Dignity Of Age"

On Pike's Last Years

When I became acquainted with General Pike, in January, 1880, he was already hedged about with the dignity of age, and no one ever wore that dignity more grandly or more graciously than he. Over six feet in height, straight and erect in carriage, and stout enough to be well proportioned, his broad shoulders surmounted by a large, well-formed head, to which his long, white hair and flowing beard imparted an almost leonine aspect, softened by his complexion, fair as a child's, and his beautiful brown eyes, in which the wisdom of age had supplanted the fire of youth, he was a poet's ideal of the "prophet, priest, and king." I found him then as I found him always to his death, a sweet and single-hearted man, loving and confiding in his friends to a most unusual degree, modest as a maiden, blushing and uneasy at merited praise, having no apparent thought of himself, but ever ready to lay aside the work in which he was interested to converse with a friend or a casual visitor.[1]

In some ways, age dealt kindly with Albert Pike. He had a home in the House of the Temple, then located at 433 Third Street, N.W., in Washington, D.C. He was greatly loved and admired, he had received just about every Masonic honor known to man (see Appendix), he had his books, his birds, and his flowers—and he was content.

Although The Supreme Council, S.J., relocated in 1870 from Charleston, South Carolina, to offices at Thirteenth and G Streets, N.W., Washington, D.C., the first true House of the Temple, formerly a private Victorian mansion, was located at 433 Third Street, N.W. This was Pike's home during his last years.

But had he chosen, he would have had plenty of reason for complaint. He had been, after all, one of the wealthiest men in his state—all gone in the Civil War. He had finally been forced to accept a salary as Grand Commander in order to live. His health was generally good, although interrupted by bouts of illness, but he was really no longer able to go on the hunting and camping trips he so much enjoyed.

His wife, Mary Ann Hamilton, from whom he had been separated for years, died on April 14, 1876. Suffering from a mental condition, possibly schizophrenia, she had made it impossible for either Pike or the children to live with her. Pike, however, gave her the big house in Little Rock and kept her very comfortably. Also, three of Pike's six children predeceased him.

He had had only marginal success in the social reform causes in which he so strongly believed (although, after his death, almost all would be accomplished in one way or another).

But he chose not to become morose or bitter.

Thank heaven! I am not soured by disappointments, nor because the glittering prizes of life have not fallen to my lot. I never envied those who win them, nor thought them more truly fortunate than myself. Nor can I now conceive why men should covet political honors, whether conferred by kings or by the people; nor why old men, or those of middle age, having already more wealth than enough to satisfy all the reasonable desires of a long life, should still be eager for more, and waste their lives in the struggle to increase their fortunes.[2]

He realized suffering was the common lot, and did not try to claim that his had been unique.

I have endured many hardships and much discomfort and deprivation, and been often in great trouble and great danger, and I have had great sorrows. This almost every man can say, for such is the tenure by which we hold our estate in life: that a great civil war swept from me my estate and left me poor, never caused me regret for the part I choose, nor cost me sleep. If I had been made poorer still, I hope I should have been able to say "great is this precept of the sacred books, wisdom is fortune's victim, but those who we fortunate call, who, taught, by life, have learned to be in life's woes and not cast off the yoke." And I hope, too, that if life could only have been saved by libeling the cause for which so many have, with the earnestness of conviction of its justice, bled, I could have said, with the same great satirist; "Think it most base, life to prefer to honor, and for life's sake to lose all cause for living."[3]

But even when discussing age, the wry Pike sense of humor couldn't be held in check for very long. He discusses the changes which come with age—but insists that one really doesn't miss the things of youth.

You almost believe him. You might have, if he hadn't included the part about the wine-bibber and the long haul up the stairs to the lodge room. Pike is poking very dry fun at himself, even if he is being serious at the same time.

It is not because we are wiser or better; for we remember and sometimes garrulously recount, the mad bouts of our younger years, when we were somewhat noted for our qualities as boon companions and spoken of far and wide for our capacity as wine-bibbers and were foolishly vain of it ourselves. If we have been epicures, and can no longer safely exceed the limits of temperance in eating simple food, we care no longer for the pleasures of the table. We do not envy the young, whirling in the gay dance, while we can only walk slowly and perhaps with pains; but we wonder how they can find pleasure in so frivolous an achievement. And if, as we slowly climb step by step, the long flights of stairs to our Lodge-room, someone passed us, taking two steps at every bound, we only think that if we could do it also, we should think there was no sufficient reason for the exertion.

And, in short, for all our bodily infirmities we console and even glorify ourselves by the thought, if not in the words, of Seneca; "Age has, especially when held in reverence, so great authority, that this is of greater worth than all the pleasures of youth." Do we think that the world has held our books and writing in insufficient esteem, we can say to ourselves in the words of Ovid; "Death is not wont to harm true geniuses, and larger fame comes after we are ashes." And he adds, which my shade may also say without untruth, "And I had a name, even while I was numbered with the living."[4]

He had a name, indeed. And if the advancing years meant less dance (and Pike had been famous in the society columns of the Washington newspapers for his excellence as a dancer) less food and wine (and we've seen his opinions on both in an earlier chapter) and less vigor and physical energy, it did not mean less intellectual activity.

But, although Pike probably had less reason to reproach himself with time lost than any other person, he was very much aware that more could have been done.

We think, at the age of twenty, that life is much too long for that which we have to learn and do; and that there is an almost fabulous distance between our age and that of our Grandfather. But when, at the age of sixty, if we are fortunate enough to reach it, or unfortunate enough, as the case may be, and according as we have used or wasted our time, we halt and look back along the way that we have come, and cast up and try to balance our accounts with Time, we find that we have made Life much too short, and thrown away a large portion of our days. We then in our mind deduct from the sum total of our years, the hours that we unnecessarily have spent in sleep; the waking hours each day, during which the surface of the mind's pool has not been stirred or ruffled by a single thought; the days that we have got rid of as we could, to attain some real or fancied object that lay beyond, in the way between which and us stood irksomely the intervening days; and the hours misspent and worse than wasted, in folly and dissipation; and we acknowledge with many a sigh, that we could have learned and done, in half a score of years well spent, more than we *have* done in our forty years of manhood.[5]

There was always more to learn. Pike loved information. He had an encyclopedic mind, and a memory at which his modern biographers still marvel. It simply never occurred to Pike to stop learning. He could as easily have stopped breathing.

After he was seventy years of age, he learned the Sanscrit language and translated from it into English the Veda, that source of the "World-Old" Philosophy of the Hindoos [Hindus].[6]

And he wrote—many volumes of works on Masonry and Masonic symbolism, articles, speeches, and hundreds of lengthy letters. The mind stayed active, even to the very end.

And there was one more and unanticipated gift which old age brought to him—it brought him love. We have already met Vinnie Ream. The love they shared was as powerful as it was pure, as supportive as it was Platonic. She was not yet twenty, he was in the declining years of a long life. And yet their minds connected at once and powerfully. The bond was so powerful and so pure than even when Vinnie married it was not disrupted, and her husband was as welcome as she at Pike's home.

Looking back, Pike decided that he had tasted life, and found it good.

Not every wine sours by length of time, nor does every old age, we are told by Seneca; and he will be far less likely to be sour and morose at three score and ten, who has passed much of his life away from the strife for wealth and place, in the companionship of a chosen friend or two, and of the plain rough men of the frontier, and the Indian, and of our old Mother Nature, than the center of power and fortune, however amply success may have crowned the latter's efforts.

And although even these pleasures, that for so many years gave life it's charm for me, are now no longer within my reach, and the rheumatic gout has put an end to my hunting and fishing, and the exposure of a life in camp would be imprudent, still I am content. I have had my full share of the enjoyment of that free life, and share a thousand pleasant recollections of it, that would be far less pleasant if there were not hardships and discomforts also to remember.[7]

Pike in old age, "waiting to be called to other duties"

He found contentment. And his sense of proportion never left him. Pike was accounted a great man during his life, but he denied that. Greatness, he felt, was limited to only a few—but he was aware that "friends and flatterers" could make a man lose his sense of balance and his own relative worth. And, as he wrote in one of his essays, greatness was not the important thing.

Thank heavens, greatness is no more essential to happiness, than excess or superfluity of the other gifts of fortune. Great wealth has, in my estimation, no advantages of a competency [a sufficient income]. I can enjoy the classics and the old oriental books, without being a great scholar, and be content with what books I have, without caring for a great library. The Great have not often been benefactors of their kind, and one content with the intellect that he has and with the path in which the duties of his life are to be done, may find the means and have the power, in one way or another to be of benefit to his fellows, and make his influences be felt for good, even beyond the seas.

Without being great, one may have the devotion of friends, and the love of women, the shade of his trees in the summer, and the warm fire and bright lamplight when the winter-winds blow cold around the corners. He may walk safely in the valleys of life, while those who climb the peaks are overwhelmed by the avalanche, or perish blinded by the snowstorm, or by a mis-step lose their footing and are lost in the rifts of the glacier.

I do not pretend to much philosophy, or that I do not sometimes wish for what I cannot have; but I have never coveted greatness.[8]

Pike's Last Hours

His love of nature and of birds and flowers and his thoughtfulness of his friends were constant with him until his last hours. During his health his room was always filled with birds of beautiful plumage or sweet song, and his writing desk covered with bouquets of flowers. He was accustomed to say that he could "write better when he could hear the singing birds, and was happier for their company." Many of them knew his voice and expressed their pleasure when he spoke to them by name or showed them any attention. When he was confined to his bed he had several of the cages brought into his bed-room, where they remained to the end.[9]

On the wall of the room in which Albert Pike died there is a small frame containing a half sheet of note-paper and a pencil, with which he wrote his last words after the power of speech had left him. He traced the Hebrew words Shalom, Shalom, Shalom—Peace, Peace, Peace. The name of the traditional founder of Freemasonry, Solomon, King of Israel, was derived from the same original and means "Peace." And so this great Freemason died as a citizen of the kingdom of Peace, and we are reminded of those words from the great Light of Masonry, so familiar to the Royal Arch, "Mark the perfect man and behold the upright, for the end of that Man is PEACE."[10]

The end was peaceful, but it was far from easy. Pike died as he had lived, fighting to the end. Undoubtedly he would have preferred to let go—he just didn't know how.

The winter of 1889–1890 was very hard on him. Pike, who had suffered rheumatism and neuralgia for some years, was subject to increasingly long and terribly painful attacks. And at that time there were very few effective painkillers and almost no anti-inflammatory drugs available. Even aspirin was not in widespread medical use until eight years after Pike's death.

He still read, and he tried to make notes and write, but writing caused him excruciating suffering. By the October, 1889, Biennial Session of The Supreme Council, 33°, it was obvious to everyone that Pike was failing rapidly. He was at the meeting, but his allocution had to be read

Albert Pike lying in state, Washington, D.C., Scottish Rite Cathedral, April 4, 1891

for him. As soon as the session was over, he became virtually bedfast, only managing to sit up for short periods of time. Walter Lee Brown tells us that his doctors diagnosed a stricture of the esophagus. Pike soon was able to swallow only liquids. This man who had so loved companionship and good food spent most of his time alone except for his books and his daughter, Lilian, who moved in to nurse him. Visits tired him rapidly.

In the last months of 1890 he suffered repeated attacks of gout and rheumatism. On March 21, 1891, his esophagus closed completely, and he was too weak for an operation. The doctors told him there was no hope. He could not swallow anything. He would starve to death.[11]

On March 31, the glands in his throat began to swell and to choke him. Shortly after 6 A.M. on April 2nd, he fell into a coma. At close to eight that evening, he died.

There was no suggestion during his last months that he feared the approach of death. He had written in the ritual of the Scottish Rite that "Death is that great friend who ushers us into the more immediate presence of God." He viewed it as a homecoming.

Death is the inexorable creditor, whose indulgence nothing in the world can purchase. Every moment that sees a new-born child laugh at the light sees also a man die, and hears the cry of a breaking heart, and the lamentations of those who sit lonely and in the desolation of affliction, no longer seeing the faces of dearly loved ones.

Round the little island of our being, on which we follow our various pursuits of toil or craft, of usefulness or mischief, throbs the illimitable ocean of eternity, upon which, round the isle, a broad circle of impenetrable darkness brooding lies. But beyond that zone the outer ocean sparkles, and its white-crested waves dance in the light, and somewhere in the distance the islands of the blessed are dreaming, girdled by the peaceful waters.

Here, in our present home, we live our little life, waiting to be called to other duties elsewhere, and one by one our loved ones and our cherished friends glide away from us unseen, and are swallowed up in the darkness which is the shadow of the broad wings of Death. Each of us belongs to some little colony of hearts that hath a life of its own, its private and inner life, apart from that of the mass of humanity which eddies round it in endless agitations, having with it no sympathies, nor any memories of association. When one of its members dies, it is as if a limb were severed from the body. The wound heals, but the limb is missed as long as the body lives.[12]

And, with faith in what he had built and was leaving behind, he wrote:

I also think that I may, without presumption, say, that I have so lived as not to have been born in vain. For I have endeavored to commend the truth to the members of a great brotherhood throughout the world, which is not destined to a speedy dissolution, but to endure and grow greater for ages; and I know that long after I am dead, the lessons that I have written will be read and heeded, and have the authority of the Master; and that wherever they are read I will be remembered and my memory held in grateful esteem. Surely this is enough for any man's consolation.

And when I die my children will not lay me in the grave with tearless eyes, nor soon cease to talk of me and be sorry I am dead; and she whom I love best, though her life is not such as she will refuse to be consoled, nor the world be dark and life a weariness to her will grieve for me a time, with tears, and remember me with a fond affection.[13]

And he wrote the words which were destined to become his epitaph:

When I am dead, I wish my monument to be builded only in the hearts and memories of my brethren of the Ancient and Accepted Scottish Rite, and my name to be remembered by them in every country, no matter what language men speak there, where the light of the Ancient and Accepted Scottish Rite shall shine, and its Oracles of Truth and Wisdom will be reverently listened to.[14]

So mote it be.

XX

Yesterday And Tomorrow

On Pike's Relevance Today

When I was attending the school, there were about seventy scholars, and we had to make fires turn about. My turn used to come pretty often. I would start out and come up into the school—a great big barn of a school building, and I had to strike fire in their tinder box, and make a wood fire in the stove, and then wait until the fire would get burning, before I could thaw out.

I recollect very well the first improvement that was made on the common tinder box.... The first improvement was a little affair that had a wheel at the end of it and a cord attached, so that we could wind the wheel and make it revolve against the steel.... The result was a great shower of sparks, and we lit the tinder with those sparks.[1]

Albert Pike
Photo Portrait by Mathew B. Brady

By one of those coincidences with which life occasionally thumps us on the nose when it finds our attention wandering, I was lighting my pipe with a disposable butane lighter when I first read that sentence. I scorched the pipe and burned my fingers. Nothing has ever brought home to me so forcefully just how much change has happened in the flash of history's eye which separates Pike's time from ours. The incident above must have happened around 1816.

Suddenly an aspect of Pike's work appeared to me which I had never considered before. The man was remarkably modern in his thinking. Pike's language is of his period. It is not the compressed outline prose we write today for people who have neither the time nor the inclination to read. But so many of the *ideas* expressed by Pike are far in advance of his time.

It's very hard to "think ourselves back" that far—not in time, but in change of background knowledge. Things which everybody knows now, and we assume everyone has always known, or which have "always" been a part of our lives, had just happened or were still in the future when *Morals and Dogma* was copyrighted in 1871 (and much of the material which follows in this chapter was written well before *Morals and Dogma).* Look at the changes.

Henry Ford was 8 years old, he would not build his first experimental car for 25 years.
Pasteur had suggested only 13 years before that diseases might be caused by germs—almost no one in the United States believed him.
Penicillin would not be developed for another 57 years.
Edison would not produce the prototype light bulb for another 8 years.
Bell's telephone would not transmit a voice for 5 more years.
Practical electric motors would not be developed for 17 years.
The first typewriter would not come on the market for 3 years.
The fountain pen would not appear for 13 years, and the ball point was 73 years in the future.
Hot dogs would not be sold in the United States for about 30 years.
Fifty years would pass before the marketing of toothpaste, and it would be 61 years before the patenting of the Zippo cigarette lighter.†
The first Elvis sighting was 64 years away.

Let's look at some of the areas in which Pike was well before his time, truly a man of today—and tomorrow.

ON SOCIAL AND CRIMINAL REFORM

Again and again, Pike tells the Scottish Rite Mason that his task is to make a difference in the world. Pike had some clear ideas of the areas in which reform was needed. In this one passage, he points out:

> The need to adjust the compensation of labor to account for automation
> The necessity for stable prices in the marketplace
> The need to understand and address the causes of poverty
> That alcoholism is a disease which requires "healing"
> The ineffectiveness of capital punishment and the need to change prisons so that they are places of reform and learning, not just graduate schools in crime.

The world is full of evils to be remedied, and miseries to be relieved. It is attempting to solve the great problem, whether national prosperity, wealth and power, high cultivation of leading

† Incidentally, matches became widely available in the United States about 1840. My thanks to the very kind folk at the National Lighter Museum in Guthrie, Oklahoma, who found the Zippo patent date for me.

intellects, abundant population, and the constantly increasing use of machinery must of necessity be accompanied by lessening the value of human labor to the starvation-point, making the life of the workman dependent upon the rise or fall of a penny a yard or pound in the price of the manufactured article; by the rapid increase of pauperism, and the degradation and living death of bestiality and brutality of the masses. This problem is not to be solved by the intellect, nor the evils that afflict society to be cured by ethics. Not the head, but the heart, must elevate the poor; must remove the causes of poverty by the charity that alleviates and the justice that cures; must heal the drunkard of his fiery thirst; must reform the criminal, instead of hanging him to save trouble; must cut down the gallows, and turn the prison into a school for the improvement of the heart, instead of leaving it as it is, the den of vengeance and of rage, that turns what once were little children into wild beasts; an institution for hardening the heart and utterly depraving the soul, in which the fiend would be the only fitting principal instructor.[2]

ON THE PUNISHMENT OF CHILDREN

At the time Pike was writing, "Spare the Rod and Spoil the Child" was received wisdom. It was generally the first resort, not the last resort, in correcting a child. Not until nearly a century later, would books on parenting appear, explaining to parents that punishment was rarely effective and that, when it was necessary, it should never be administered when the parent was angry. Here's what Pike had to say.

Punishment is seldom effectual. It is only legitimate when its purpose is to reform; never on the principle of compensation or equivalent. There is no common measure of wrong act and bodily pain, by which to determine how much pain is equivalent to so much wrong or fault. Revenge is nothing more than the infliction of so much punishment as *you* think the offense against you, the injury done you, deserves. If you punish in a passion, you do a greater wrong than that for which you punish the child. Punishment is only justifiable, and it is also wise, only as the ultimate argument to prove to the child that the act for which it is inflicted was wrong, and irrevocably determined to be so by your calm and deliberate judgment. It should be resorted to only when all other arguments have failed. Once tried, and ineffectual, it is too late to go back to those that should have preceded it. And we should always remember that the child also has its opinions, and may not always assent to the infallibility or our judgment, or admit the enormity of act for which we punish it. The parent, like the State, that punishes or legislates in a passion, or out of revenge, does so to little else than evil purpose.[3]

Albert Pike
Bust by Vinnie Ream

ON THE EDUCATION OF CHILDREN

Pike had served as a teacher several times, of course, and what little evidence is available suggests that he was a good one. In the following passage, he describes the ideal education of children. He places emphasis on the fact that learning needs to take place at its own pace, and should come from the self-motivation of the child. In the passage, he describes much of the attitude and structure of a Montessori school. But Maria Montessori was only one year old when *Morals and Dogma* was published, and she did not open her first school until 1907. Coming from the highly regimented learning structures of his day, Pike's attitude on education is remarkably modern.

In the young boy or girl, healthy growth and harmless passing of the time are more to be cared for than what are vainly called "accomplishments." The mind of the child is to be *forged* rather than *furnished*, and *fed* rather than *filled*. Exercise, the joy of interest, or origination, of activity, of excitement, the play of the faculties,—these, and not the accumulation of mere words, are the true life of a boy or girl. The self-teaching that a child gives itself, remains with it forever. It is of its very essence. What is given it from without, and received mechanically and without relish, and without any energizing of the entire nature, remains perfectly useless, or even worse than useless. The young mind must *grow* as well as *learn*; and the young child, playing in the lap of nature and out of doors, acquires for life an amount of objective knowledge marvellous beyond any of our mightiest marches of intellect.[4]

That wasn't the end of it. For pure, tub-thumping radicalism for his day, consider this (remembering that in most places schools did not exist, nor did the idea of compulsory education):

The primary school *obligatory* upon all; the higher school *offered* to all. Such is the law. From the same school for all springs equal society. Instruction! Light! all comes from Light, and all returns to it.[5]

The Albert Pike Monument was approved by Congress in 1898 and completed by 1901, ten years after Pike's death. The monument today is pictured opposite the title page, and a photograph of its dedication is on page 231. The bust of Pike (left) was sculpted by U.S.J. Dunbar in 1924 and is now part of Pike's crypt in the House of the Temple. See page 235.

ON ECOLOGY

Pike was perfectly prepared to use nature—he enjoyed hunting and fishing and camping, after all, but he did not appreciate the abuse of nature. For example, he insisted that the woods around his home remain undisturbed as a habitat for birds. Thinking that the natural world was the handiwork of God, it offended him to see that recklessly abused.

When the railroad crossed the West, many people found it sport to kill buffalo from the train. They did not stop the train to get the meat, of course. It was simply a matter of amusement to shoot the buffalo from a distance. Then leave them there. Millions of buffalo were killed that way, so many that the herds which had one taken days to pass any given point were virtually wiped out. Roundly condemning the practice, Pike contrasted it with the reverence the Indian tribes showed to nature and the buffalo, remarking:

> Few men killed buffalo then wantonly. Had they done so, it would have been a good cause for the Indians to kill them off if they could. We never killed any buffalo except just what we wanted to eat; no more and no less.[6]

ON THE ALLOCATION OF NATIONAL RESOURCES

One of the most vexing questions for any society is the division of resources between defense and domestic needs. There have never been any easy answers to this dilemma. Pike had lived through the horrors of war, and he repeatedly urged on Masons the importance of patriotism and the defense of one's nation. But he wanted to be certain no one ever forgot there were at least two sides to the issue.

> Treasures are expended, that would suffice to build ten thousand churches, hospitals, and universities, or rib and tie together a continent with rails of iron. If that treasure were sunk in the sea, it would be calamity enough; but it is put to worse use; for it is expended in cutting into the veins and arteries of human life, until the earth is deluged with a sea of blood.[7]

Although, over the years, many scientific breakthroughs have come from war efforts, they can never balance the devastation of war.

ON LANGUAGE, SEMANTICS, AND PSYCHOLINGUISTICS

Long before Noam Chompsky and S. I. Hayakawa, long even before Alfred Korzybski had uttered his famous dictum "The Word is not the Thing, the Map is not the Territory," Pike was concerned with words and symbols. In one place, he comments that "new words originating in California and Australia have found their way into general use,"[8] a pattern which continues to this day. For example, I have it on good authority that "tubular" in surfer slang means "excellent," not "like, of, or pertaining to a tube." But it was not the origin of words, but the tendency to confuse symbols with the thing symbolized that most concerned Pike. Style of writing and examples apart, his comments could form a chapter in any *General Semantics* textbook today.

There are, it is true, dangers inseparable from symbolism, which countervail its advantages, and afford an impressive lesson in regard to the similar risks attendant on the use of language: The imagination, invited to assist the reason, usurps its place, or leaves its ally helplessly entangled in its web. Names which stand for things are confounded with them; the means are mistaken for the end; the instrument of interpretation for the object; and thus symbols come to usurp an independent character as truths and persons. Though perhaps a necessary path, they are a dangerous one by which to approach the Deity....

The utmost which can be effected by human effort, is to substitute impressions relatively correct, for others whose falsehood has been detected, and to replace a gross symbolism by a purer one. Every man, without being aware of it, worships a conception of his own mind; for all symbolism, as well as all language, shares the subjective character of the ideas it represents.[9]

Because of the power of word symbols, Pike was fully aware of the danger of their misuse.

There are no idols so obsequiously worshiped by the people as words; and no craft is so fraudulent and useful at once as word-craft.[10]

ON "THE BURNING BED"

In recent years, we have become more sensitive as a nation to the problems of the battered or helpless wife, who finally murders or maims as the only way she can find out of an intolerable situation. While it seems to most of us as if she surely could have taken some lesser action, psychologists who are expert in the field tell us that the woman often literally cannot see those options. In many areas of life, men are just now beginning to understand that the opportunities and options which they take for granted are not always equally available to women. Our laws, social mores, and thought processes are still struggling to come to grips with this factor. Pike understood it perfectly well.

Men cannot appreciate the utter hopelessness and misery of a wife who is the victim of a brute's cruelty and cynical heartlessness, or a widow toiling with no possibility of better days, for the mere pittance that secures to herself and her children a precarious and meager livelihood. For men, there are always the chances of better conditions, and hope may, for them, gild the darkest clouds, but what can a woman, teaching or serving to keep her children from the fangs of the she-wolf Hunger hope for in this world? And what has she to relieve the horrible monotony of her daily life?[11]

An impressive assemblage attended the October 23, 1901, dedication of the Albert Pike Monument in what is now Judiciary Square, Washington, D.C.

THE PASSIONS AND HUMAN ACTIVITY

When *Morals and Dogma* was copyrighted in 1871, Sigmund Freud was 15 years old. It would not be for another 24 years that Freud would publish his theories, showing that the Id, the largely unconscious, animal part of man, his strongest drives and most powerful compulsions, actually formed the energy source which, sublimated, was responsible for creativity and the expansion of energy by the person in all fields of life.

Pike beat him by nearly a quarter of a century.

The appetites and passions are forces, that God has given to us, to be the springs and creative causes of energy and excellence. If we had not these forces, our moral sense and reason would be inactive, torpid, and barren. The more energetic and powerful the appetites and passions are, the greater excellence is there in due proportion between these and the moral sense and reason. For they are the inciters to most human action and endeavor.[12]

THE FUTURE OF RACE RELATIONS

There are times when Pike can simply astound the reader with ideas which were far in advance of his time. His concept of the future of race relations is a case in point. Before the term "melting pot" had been coined to describe the process of American immigration and naturalization, Pike used much the same image, calling it an "immense crucible" in which the nature of the American character was being forged.

That would have been remarkable enough, but the truly remarkable point is that Pike arrived at a conclusion which has only been popularly espoused in the last few years. For he did not believe that racial differences would disappear in the process. Rather, he believed that each race would keep its own special heritage—its roots—with its individual strengths, and that the American character which finally emerged would not be the result of the loss of the cultural traditions and characters but rather a combination of strengths, each retaining its original vigor but cooperating and interacting with all the others.

It was a formidable insight.

This latest of republics, this great country, in which, fortunately, there is ample scope and verge enough for the experiment, is, as it were, an immense crucible, wherein is now being carried onward to successful or unsuccessful issue, the grandest work of alchemy that a wondering world has ever fixed its gaze upon.

For here are flung together thirty-one millions of people, native and foreign-born, of many races, and speaking many tongues, of every creed and faith, of every phase of opinion, of many habits of thought, total strangers to each other; a vast mass of apparently discordant elements, hostile, heterogeneous, incongruous; to be, if possible by any chemistry, made in process of time to combine into one homogeneous whole.

Albert Pike about 1888

The antipathies that inflame and exasperate, and make our sky moody and threatening, are those of race and its instincts, and of opinions growing unconsciously out of ancient faiths and unfaiths. . . . .

The differences of race will never cease to produce their habitual effects. Opinions and faiths will never be moulded into one monotonous sameness. But a wise Providence will use and is using these differences as the very means of producing true unity and real harmony, by causing them to become like the instrumental divisions of an orchestra, which balance each other, and completely accord, without assimilation. It is some grand law of Heaven's enacting, that the universal harmony should flow grandly forth, from the clashing elements in all the worlds. . . .

Differences of opinion and apparent antipathies, often offensively expressed and embodied in aggressive political action, and even culminating in war, are yet manifestly seen to be, in God's providence, blessings, if wisely availed of and profited by, and the means which it suits His wisdom to use, in order finally to establish a new, distinct and grand nationality, a unit of force, power and action, ruled by the same great ideas of popular liberty and order, of brotherhood, and equality, in the eye of the law, with a national character, one, original, with no prototype; in which nationality and character all the varying shades of race, temperament and peculiarity are not to be obliterated or tamed down into one monotonous sameness, but blended, mingled and combined into one admirable harmonious whole.[13]

He was a remarkable man of great vision, drawing from the past, living in both the past and the future, he saw clearly the potentials ahead for society. Self-control, education, economic justice, human understanding—these could create a world of compassion and growth, a world of equality and brotherhood. It was—and is—just a question of will.

POSTLUDE

This book is down to the last few bars: the orchestra has that sense of urgency, not always restrained by the conductor, which communicates to the audience that things are about over. The listeners are straightening in their seats and looking covertly around to locate their gloves. Just about all "der vind" has been pushed.

But what is true of this book is not true of Pike or his story. Just when you hear what you're sure are final chords, you find it's an *aria de cappo,* the orchestra goes right back to the beginning and starts over.

Music seems a fitting analogy for the life and works of Albert Pike. There are the great solemn chords of his "serious" works, *Morals and Dogma* and the degrees of the Scottish Rite, S. J., at the head of the list, which strike such a profound resonance in the spirit that the body seems to vibrate with them as it does to the sound of a vast organ. Playing and above those great works are the skipping tunes of his comic verse and his lighter writing. While like the sharp accents and attacks of the percussion, his wit, his satire and his irony rush in, sting, and are gone before one can guard against them.

Yet the whole structure, just like a symphony, is based on strong and solid principles of logic and development. The only difference is that Pike uses the rules of rhetoric rather than those of musical composition and counterpoint.

And, like that aria, it does repeat. You can finish reading *Morals and Dogma,* for example, and then start over again at once, and it is as if you were reading an entirely new book. The insights gained the first time so change and modify the book that the second or third or eighth time through is as fresh as the first, although greatly more rewarding.

Like the work of Bach or Beethoven or Bartók, each generation must make him its own, experiencing Pike with new eyes and ears, relating him to life as they understand it.

It works; and that is the final proof of Pike's relevance and greatness.

Appendix
Albert Pike's Masonic Career

The Masonic Career Of Albert Pike

YEAR	SYMBOLIC LODGE	SCOTTISH RITE	YORK RITE	OTHER
1850	Initiated, Passed, and Raised at Western Star Lodge #2, Little Rock / Member of Committee to obtain a Charter for St. John's College		Received Mark Master, Past Master Most Excellent Master Degrees	
1851			Member of Convention which formed the Grand Chapter	
1852	Charter Member of Magnolia Lodge #60		High Priest / Chairman of Grand Chapter Committee on Masonic Law and Usage / Chairman of Grand Chapter Committee on Foreign Correspondence / Received Degree of Royal and Select Master	
1853	Chairman, Grand Lodge Committee on Masonic Law and Usage / Chairman, Grand Lodge Committee to Revise and Collate the Decisions of the Grand Lodge / Chairman, Grand Lodge Committee on Foreign Correspondence / Trustee and President of the Board of Trustees, St. John's College	Received 4th. through 32nd. Degrees at Charleston, SC / began work on revision of the Degrees / made Deputy Inspector General for Arkansas	Grand High Priest / Chairman, Grand Chapter Committee on Masonic Library / Assisted in the formation and was Thrice Illustrious Master of Occidental Council #1, Little Rock / Received Templar Degrees / First Eminent Commander of Hugh de Payene Commandery	
1854	Worshipful Master of Magnolia Lodge #60, Little Rock / Chairman, Grand Lodge Committee on Library / Chairman, Grand Lodge Committee to Prepare a system of laws and bylaws for the governance of subordinate Lodges	Appointed Deputy Inspector General for West Tennessee	Re-elected Grand High Priest / Member, Grand Chapter Committee on Masonic Library / Arkansas Council of High Priesthood / Eminent Commander of Hugh de Payene Commandery	
1856		Became Commander in Chief of the Grand Consistory of Louisiana	Chairman, Grand Chapter Committee on Masonic Law and Usage / Represented Grand Chapter of Louisiana at the General Grand Chapter of the U.S. at Hartford / Member of the Grand Chapter Committee to prepare a formula for the installation of Grand Chapter Officers / Member Grand Chapter Committee on Foreign Correspondence / First Eminent Commander of Hugh de Payene Commandery	
1857		Received 33rd Degree / S.G.I.G., special session, New Orleans / Made Special Deputy for Louisiana		

YEAR	SYMBOLIC LODGE	SCOTTISH RITE	YORK RITE	OTHER
1858	Affiliated with Marion Lodge #68, New Orleans	Elected Active Member of the Supreme Council		
1859	Representative of the Grand Lodge of Arkansas to the National Masonic Convention / Member, Board of Regents of the American Masonic Home for Widows & Orphans of Freemasons, Washington, DC	**Elected Sovereign Grand Commander** of the Supreme Council, 33rd Degree, Southern Jurisdiction, served until his death in 1891	Chairman, Grand Chapter Committee on Masonic Law and Usage / Represented Grand Chapter of Arkansas at the General Grand Chapter of the U.S. in Chicago / Chairman, General Grand Chapter Committee on Foreign Correspondence / Member General Grand Chapter Committee on Royal Arch Regalia	
1860	Representative of the Grand Lodge of Kansas near the Grand Lodge of Arkansas	Completed revision of 4th. through 32nd. Degrees	President of the Convention forming the Grand Council of Arkansas	
1861			Member, Grand Chapter Committee on Masonic Law and Usage	
1864	Grand Orator / Re-elected Trustee of St. John's College			
1865	Re-elected Trustee of St. John's College			
1866		Honorary Member, New Granada / Honorary Member, Supreme Council of Northern Jurisdiction / Honorary Member, Supreme Council of Peru		
1869	Honorary Member, Alpha Home Lodge #72, New Orleans / Honorary Member, Perfect Union Lodge #1, New Orleans / Honorary Member, San Andreas Lodge #9, Havana, Cuba			
1870	Representative of the Grand Lodge of Louisiana near the Grand Lodge of the District of Columbia	Honorary Member of the Supreme Council of England and Wales / Honorary Member of the Supreme Council of Ireland	Grand Representative of the Grand Chapter of Oregon near the Grand Chapter of the District of Columbia	
1871	Honorary Member of Kilwinning Lodge #341, Memphis			

YEAR	SYMBOLIC LODGE	SCOTTISH RITE	YORK RITE	OTHER
1873	Honorary Member, Star in the East Lodge #218, St. Thomas, West Indies	Honorary Member of Supreme Council of Brazil		
1874		Honorary Member of Supreme Council of Belgium / Honorary Grand Master Grand Commander of the Grand Orient and Supreme Council of Brazil / Honorary Member of Supreme Council of Canada / Honorary Member of Supreme Council of Egypt/ Honorary Member of Supreme Council of Scotland	Honorary Past Provincial Grand Prior of the Grand Priory of Canada	
1875		Honorary Member of Supreme Council of Italy		
1876	Elected Perpetual Master of Albert Pike Lodge #55, Mexico City (the Lodge elected a Pro-Tem Master each year to govern the Lodge)			
1877	Honorary Member, Kane Lodge #454, New York City / Honorary Member *Temple des Aims de l'Honneur Francaise Lodge* Paris	Honorary Sovereign Grand Commander of the Supreme Council of Italy	Chairman, Grand Chapter Committee on the District of Columbia / Grand Representative of the Grand Chapter of Mississippi near the Grand Chapter of the District of Columbia / Represented the Grand Chapter of the District of Columbia at the General Grand Chapter of the U.S. at Buffalo / Chairman, General Grand Chapter Committee on Royal Arch Cipher / Member General Grand Chapter Committee on Jurisprudence	Appointed as the first Provincial Grand Master of the Provincial Grand Lodge of the United States of the Royal Order of Scotland
1878		Honorary Member of Supreme Council of Hungary / Honorary Member of Supreme Council of Mexico		
1879		Honorary Member of Supreme Council of Spain	Grand Representative of the Grand Chapter of Nevada near the Grand Chapter of the District of Columbia	President of the Masonic Veteran Association of the District of Columbia from its organization until his death

YEAR	SYMBOLIC LODGE	SCOTTISH RITE	YORK RITE	OTHER
1880	Affiliated with Pentalpha Lodge #23, District of Columbia			Supreme Magus of the Rosecrucian Society
1881	Honorary Member *Columnas de Hidalgo Lodge,* Mexico, Venerable Master *ad vitam*	Honorary Member and Honorary Sovereign Grand Commander, Supreme Council of Romania		Honorary Past Supreme Magus of the Grand High Council of the Society of Rosecrucians in the United States / Grand Protector of the Rite of Adoption
1884	Honorary Member, Grand Lodge of Peru			
1885	Grand Representative of the Grand Lodge of Lower California (Mexico) near the Grand Lodge of the District of Columbia / Honorary Member of *Egalite-Humanitem* Lodge #20, Buenos Aires / Honorary Member Verdad Lodge #8, Seville, Spain			
1886	Honorary Member of the Grand Lodge of Caxaca, Mexico / Honorary Worshipful Master, *Losanna* Lodge, Naples, Italy / Honorary Member, *Perfecto Unione* Lodge, Naples / Honorary Member *Ruiz* Lodge #2, Leon, Mexico	Grand Representative of the Supreme Council of Colon (Cuba)		
1887		Honorary Member of Supreme Council of Switzerland / Honorary Member of the Supreme Council of Tunis / Honorary Grand Commander of the Supreme Council of Uruguay		Honorary Member of the Masonic Veteran Association of the Pacific Coast
1888	Honorary Member *Hijos del Trabejo* Lodge #83, Barcelona, Spain	Honorary Grand Commander of the Supreme Council of Santa Domingo		Honorary Member of the Masonic Veteran Association of Illinois
1889		Honorary Member of the Supreme Council of France		
1890			Honorary Member of the Grand Commandery of Arkansas	

Chapter Endnotes

Chapter I, On Albert Pike, The Man

1. Pike as honorary Chief, Duncan, *Reluctant General: The Life and Times of Albert Pike,* 152; as a practical joker, Brown, *Albert Pike, 1809–1891,* 19; as an explorer, Forman, quoted by David Weber, *Prose Sketches and Poems,* ix.
2. Introductory to Albert Pike's *The Meaning of Masonry,* vii.
3. Allsopp, *Albert Pike: A Biography,* 70.
4. Duncan, 11.
5. Nash, "Albert Pike, Lawyer," 16.
6. Allsopp, 95.
7. Hatch, *In Memorium: Albert Pike,* 17.
8. Hatch, 4.
9. Nash, 14.
10. Hatch, 5.
11. Allsopp, 111.
12. Moore, "Albert Pike, The Mason," 26.
13. McLeod, *The Grand Design,* 53.
14. Schley, "Albert Pike, Soldier and Explorer," 181.
15. Pike, quoted by Weber, *Preface to Prose Sketches and Poems,* xxxi.
16. Kleinknecht, "Albert Pike—A Freemason Forever," 2.
17. Allsopp, 173–74.
18. Roome, *General Albert Pike's Poems,* 10.
19. Pike, *Autobiography,* 70.
20. Pike, "Essay V—Of Wrecks and Waifs of Poetry," 291–92.
21. Pike, "Essay XIV—Of Shattered Idols," 125–26.

Chapter 2, On Pike's Sketches of Extraordinary People

1. Pike, *Prose Sketches and Poems Written in the Western Country,* 281–82.
2. Pike, "Essay XII—Of Law and Lawyers," 512–14.
3. Ibid., 557–58.
4. Pike, *Autobiography,* 79.
5. Pike, *Prose Sketches and Poems,* 34–35.
6. Pike, *Autobiography,* 77.
7. Pike, *Lyrics and Love Songs,* 222.
8. Pike, "The Fine Arkansas Gentleman," *Lyrics and Love Songs,* 223–27.
9. Allsopp, *Albert Pike: A Biography,* 80.
10. Brown, *Albert Pike, 1809–1891,* 144.
11. Ibid., 146.
12. Nash, "Albert Pike, Lawyer," 13.
13. Easterly, "Albert Pike and the Louisiana Civil Code: An Unfinished Epic," 39.
14. Pike, quoted in Duncan, *The Reluctant General,* 96.
15. Ibid., 98.
16. Pike, *Autobiography,* 31.
17. Ibid., 72–73.
18. Ibid., 71–72.
19. Ibid., 86.
20. Pike, "Essay XII—Of Law and Lawyers," 543–44.
21. Pike, "Essay II—Of Self-Education," 154.
22. Pike, *Autobiography,* 26–27.
23. Ibid., 27–28.

24. Pike, quoted in Duncan, *The Reluctant General*, 91.
25. Pike, "Essay X—Of Indian Nature and Wrongs," 196–99.
26. Ibid., 209.
27. Ibid., 310–13.
28. Pike, "Essay XVII—Of Poverty and Its Compensations," 383–88.

Chapter 3, On Education

1. Pike, *Morals and Dogma*, 40.
2. Ibid., 712.
3. Pike, *Autobiography*, 6.
4. Pike, "Letters from Arkansas No. II," quoted in Brown, *Albert Pike,* 9.
5. Ibid.
6. Pike, editorials in *The Arkansas Advocate*, May, 1834, cited in Gern, "Albert Pike and Education," 22–23.
7. Pike, *Morals and Dogma*, 153.
8. Ibid., 152-53.
9. Ibid., 173.
10. Pike, "Essay III—Of Self-Education," 164.
11. Ibid., 165.
12. Ibid., 168.
13. Ibid., 164.
14. Ibid., 180.
15. Pike, "Essay XI—Of My Books and Studies," 410–12.

Chapter 4, On Morality

1. Stewart, "Albert Pike, The Philosopher," 38.
2. Pike, *The Meaning of Masonry*, 27–28.
3. Pike, *Morals and Dogma*, 854.
4. Ibid., 151.
5. Ibid., 578.
6. Pike, "Essay XVII—Of the Policy of Forgiveness," 241–42.
7. Ibid., 215.
8. Pike, "Essay XXII—Of Values," 371.
9. Pike, *Morals and Dogma*, 139.
10. Ibid., 140.
11. Pike, *Ritual for the Reception of a Louveteau*, 34–36.
12. Pike, "Essay XXII—Of Values," 330–32
13. Ibid., 341–44.

Chapter 5, On Pike And His Pipes

1. Pike, "Essay VII—Of Habits and Their Slaves," 5–7.
2. Ibid., 5–11, *passim.*
3. Pike, *Autobiography*, 13–14, 21.
4. Pike, *Prose Sketches and Poems*, 71–72.
5. Ibid., 51.
6. Pike, "Essay XI—Of My Books and Studies," 425.
7. Pike, "The Philosophy of a Cigar," 254–57.

Chapter 6, On Masonry

1. Pike, *The Meaning of Masonry*, x.
2. Ibid., 2–3.
3. Pike, *Morals and Dogma*, 76.
4. Ibid., 32.
5. Pike, *Liturgy of the Blue Degrees...Scottish Rite of Freemasonry*, 138.
6. Pike, *Lectures on Masonic Symbolism*, 171.
7. Pike, *Ex Corde Locutiones: Words from the Heart*, 119.
8. Pike, *Morals and Dogma*, 221.
9. Ibid.
10. Pike, *Lectures on Masonic Symbolism*, 14.
11. Ibid., 14–15.
12. Ibid., 213.
13. Ibid.

14. Pike, *The Meaning of Masonry*, 49.
15. Pike, *Legenda XIX to XXX*, 1.
16. Pike, *Morals and Dogma*, 25–26.
17. Moore, "Albert Pike, The Mason," 30.
18. Pike, *Morals and Dogma*, 288.
19. Ibid., 116.
20. Ibid., 219.
21. Ibid., 325.
22. Ibid., 856–57.
23. Ibid., 162–63.
24. Pike, *Morals and Dogma*, 238.
25. Ibid., 726–27.

Chapter 7, On Brotherhood and Social Relations

1. Pike, *Morals and Dogma*, 43–44.
2. Ibid., 176.
3. Pike, *The Book of the Lodge*, 101
4. Pike, "Ritual of the Apprentice Degree," 34.
5. Pike, *Morals and Dogma*, 32.
6. Pike, quoted in Allsopp, *Albert Pike: A Biography*, 177
7. Pike, "Letters to the People of the Northern States," 181.
8. Pike, *Morals and Dogma*, 70.
9. Pike, quoted in Allsopp, 104.
10. Brown, *Albert Pike, 1809–1891*, 506.
11. Pike, "Essay X—Of Indian Nature and Wrongs," 183.
12. Pike, *Lectures of the Arya*, 25.
13. Pike, "Ritual of the Degree of Apprentice," 41.
14. Ibid., 42.
15. Ibid., 45.
16. Ibid., 43.
17. Pike, written pleading to the Arkansas Supreme Court for a law suit in the interest of the Creek Nation.
18. Pike, "Essay I—Of Content in Age," 23.
19. Brown, 561.
20. Pike, *Prose Sketches and Poems Written in the Western Country*, 71–72.
21. Allsopp, *Albert Pike: A Biography*, 176.
22. Pike, "Essay I—Of Content in Age," 34–35.
23. Pike, Liturgy of the 33°.

Chapter 8, On Toleration And Religious Freedom

1. Pike, "Ariel," in *General Albert Pike's Poems*, 97–98.
2. Moore, "Albert Pike, The Mason," 30–31.
3. Pike, *Morals and Dogma*, 164–65.
4. Pike, *The Meaning of Masonry*, 30–31.
5. Pike, *Morals and Dogma*, 160.
6. Ibid., 223.
7. Pike, "Essay IX—Of Symbols Decaying into Idols," 37.
8. Pike, *Morals and Dogma*, 712.
9. Ibid., 223.
10. Ibid,, 74–75.
11. Pike, *Legenda XIX to XXX*, 87.
12. Pike, "Essay VII—Of Habits and Their Slaves," 5.
13. Allsopp, *Albert Pike: A Biography*, 66.
14. Pike, *Objects and Principles of the Democratic American Party.*
15. Pike, *Morals and Dogma*, 12.
16. Pike, *The Book of the Lodge*, 224.
17. Pike, *Lectures of the Arya*, 102.
18. "Introductory" Albert Pike, *The Meaning of Masonry*, xii.
19. Pike, *Ritual for the Reception of a Louveteau*, 14.
20. Pike, *Morals and Dogma*, 238.

21. Ibid., 525.
22. Ibid., 25.
23. Pike, *The Book of the Lodge*, 87.
24. Pike, *Morals and Dogma*, 713.
25. Pike, *The Book of the Lodge*, 101.
26. Pike, Letter to Dr. Thurston, included in *Ex Corde Locutiones,* 248.
27. Pike, *Morals and Dogma*, 581.
28. Ibid., 709.
29. Ibid., 713.
30. Pike, *Ritual for the Reception of a Louveteau*, 42–43.
31. Ibid., 44.
32. Pike, *Morals and Dogma*, 134.
33. Ibid., 530.
34. Ibid., 308–10.

Chapter 9, On Nature

1. Pike, *Morals and Dogma*, 215–16.
2. Brown, *Albert Pike, 1809–1891*, 222.
3. Pike, "Essay I—Of Content in Age," 24–25.
4. Noland, editorial published in the Little Rock *State Gazette and Democrat*, May 23, 1857.
5. Pike, "Ode to the Mockingbird," 111.
6. Pike, *Morals and Dogma*, 714.
7. Ibid., 64.
8. Pike, *Morals and Dogma*, 647.
9. Ibid., 526–27.
10. Ibid, n.p.

Chapter 10, On Pike's Infamous Duel

1. Lilian Pike Roome, Introductory essay to *General Albert Pike's Poems*, 14–15.
2. Allsopp, *Albert Pike: A Biography*, 131.
3. Ibid., 132.
4. Ibid., 133–134.
5. Ibid., 130.
6. Pike, "Buena Vista Letter," *Arkansas Gazette*, April 24, 1847, 207–208.
7. Pike, "Buena Vista," *General Albert Pike's Poems*, 177–83.

Chapter 11, On Physical And Spiritual Joys

1. Pike, "Essay I—Of Content in Age," 38.
2. Pike, "Essay II—Of Burning the Dead," 144–46.
3. Pike, *Autobiography*, 18.
4. Ibid., 52.
5. Smithee, cited by Allsopp, 292–93.
6. Bunn, *Old England and New England,* 253.
7. Pike, "Essay IV—Of Man's Opinions of Woman," 249–50.
8. Pike, "Essay VII—Of Habits and Their Slaves," 320.
9. Pike, "Essay II—Of Burning the Dead," 85–87.
10. Pike, *Morals and Dogma*, 854.
11. Pike, *The Book of the Lodge*, 87–88.
12. Pike, *Ritual for the Reception of a Louveteau*," 30–31.
13. Pike, *Morals and Dogma*, 196.
14. Ibid., 197.
15. Ibid., 854–55.

Chapter 12, On Pike At Play

1. Evans, "Albert Pike, The Poet," 50.
2. Pike, *Prose Sketches and Poems, Written in the Western Country*, 45.
3. Pike, "Canyon Sketches and Journeyings. No. I. ," 69.
4. Pike, *Prose Sketches and Poems, Written in the Western Country*, 245–46.
5. Pike, "American Monthly Magazine," 53–54.
6. Pike, *Morals and Dogma*, 187.
7. Pike, "Essay III—On Self-Education," 185.

8. Pike, *The Advocate*, May 22, 1835.
9. Pike, "Essay XII—Of Law and Lawyers," 463.
10. Ibid., 493-95.
11. Pike, "Essay VII—Of Habits and Their Slaves," 50–53.
12. Pike, "Essay IV—Of Man's Opinions of Woman," 262.
13. Pike, "Essay XX—Of Values," 317–18.
14. Pike, editorial in the *Memphis Daily Appeal*, October 12, 1867.
15. Pike, "Essay VII—Of Habits and Their Slaves," 59.
16. Pike, "Essay XI—Of My Books and Studies," 435.
17. Ibid., 436–37.
18. Pike, "Essay XXII—Of Values," 322–23.
19. Pike, Letter to Johnny Coyle, Little Rock, Arkansas, April 20, 1885.
20. Pike, *Autobiography*, 71.
21. Pike, "A Dollar or Two," *Lyrics and Love Songs*, 228–31.
22. Pike, "Essay XII—Of Law and Lawyers," 490–93.
23. Pike, "The Philosophy of Bowling," 687–89.
24. Pike, "Essay IV—Of Man's Opinions of Woman," 271–72.

Chapter 13, On Love

1. Pike, "Essay IV—Of Man's Opinions of Woman," 214.
2. Pike, "Essay I—Of Content in Age," 4–7.
3. Pike, *Morals and Dogma*, 683.
4. Pike, "Essay II—Of Burning the Dead," 85–87.
5. Pike, "Song," in *Lyrics and Love Songs*, 156–57.
6. Pike, "Essay IV—Of Man's Opinions of Woman," 267–68.
7. Ibid., 260.
8. Ibid., 282–83.
9. Pike, "Essay III—Of Self-Education," 188.
10. Pike, "Essay VI—Of Self-Investing," 390–407.
11. Pike, "Essay VIII—On the Death of Love," 62–70.
12. Pike, "Love," in *Lyrics and Love Songs*, 102–04.

Chapter 14, On Social Reform

1. Brown, *Albert Pike, 1809–1891*, 326.
2. Pike, "Plain Talk, Starvation, Migration or Railroads," December 25, 1851.
3. Pike, *Morals and Dogma*, 197.
4. Ibid., 23–24.
5. Pike, *Ex Corde Locutiones: Words from the Heart*, 187.
6. Pike, *Morals and Dogma*, 134–35.
7. Ibid., 130–31.
8. Ibid., 178.
9. Ibid., 837.
10. Pike, *The Meaning of Masonry*, 13–14.
11. Pike, *Morals and Dogma*, 297.
12. Pike, *Ex Corde Locutiones*, 191.
13. Pike, "Essay IV—Of Man's Opinions of Woman," 216–17.
14. Pike, *Morals and Dogma*, 238.
15. Ibid., 187–88.
16. Pike, *The New Age*, April, 1986, frontispiece.

Chapter 15, On Pike Attending His Own Wake

1. *Des Arc Arkansas Citizen*, December 25, 1858.
2. McKenzie, quoted in *The Life–Wake of the Fine Arkansas Gentleman Who Died Before His Time*, 42–53.
3. Ibid.
4. Pike, quoted in *The Life–Wake*, 16–24.
5. "One Of The Mourners," quoted in *The Life–Wake*, 13–16.
6. Pike, "One Spree at Johnny Coyle's," quoted in *The Life–Wake*, 25–31.
7. Poore, quoted in *The Life–Wake*, 37–38.
8. McMahon, quoted in *The Life–Wake*, 35–36.

Chapter 16, On Painting With Words

1. Pike, *Prose Sketches and Poems Written in the Western Country*, 226.
2. Ibid., 65–66.
3. Pike, "Narrative of a Journey in the Prairie," 10–11.
4. Pike, *Prose Sketches and Poems Written in the Western Country*, 235–36.
5. Ibid., 77.
6. Pike, "Essay V—Of Wrecks and Waifs of Poetry," 383–84.
7. Pike, "Essay I—Of Content in Age," 46–51.
8. Pike, "Essay V—Of Wrecks and Waifs of Poetry," 291–292.
9. Pike, *Morals and Dogma*, 650.
10. Pike, "Fragments. From 'The Brigand.'" *Lyrics and Love Songs*, 110–11.
11. Pike, *The Meaning of Masonry*, 28–29.
12. Pike, "Essay XI—Of My Books and Studies," 421–25.
13. Pike, *Morals and Dogma*, 317–20.
14. Pike, Address on the Occasion of Laying the Corner Stone for the Masonic–Odd Fellows Hall at Little Rock, 1854.
15. Pike, *Morals and Dogma*, 297.
16. Pike, "Fragments of an Unfinished Poem," *Lyrics and Love Songs*, 167–68.
17. Pike, "Essay XXII—Of Values," 335–37.
18. Pike, "An Evening Conversation," 124.
19. Pike, "Fantasma," *Hymns to the Gods and Other Poems*, 167.
20. Pike, "From 'The Brigand,'" 125.
21. Pike, "The First Wild-Flower of Spring," *Hymns to the Gods*, 177.
22. Pike, "A Dirge," *Hymns to the Gods and Other Poems*, 180.
23. Pike, *Liturgy of the 33°*.
24. Pike, "Lines," *Lyrics and Love Songs*, 179.
25. Pike, "Night," *Hymns to the Gods and Other Poems*, 227.
26. Pike, *Morals and Dogma*, 152.
27. Pike, "Agapou Pneuma," *Lyrics and Love Songs*, 184.
28. Pike, "Every Year," in Roome's *General Albert Pike's Poems*, 31–34.
29. Pike, "A Fragment," *Lyrics and Love Songs*, 50.

Chapter 17, On War

1. Pike, *Morals and Dogma*, 297.
2. Ibid., 124–125.
3. Pike, quoted in Fred W. Allsopp, *Albert Pike: A Biography*, 128.
4. Brown, *Albert Pike, 1809–1891*, 175.
5. Richardson, "Introduction: The Centenary Idea," 16.
6. G.B.B., "To the Editor," Washington, Arkansas, July 7, 1846, in the *Gazette*, quoted in Brown, 265.
7. Pike, letter to R.W. Johnson, published in the Little Rock State *Gazette and Democrat*, quoted in Brown, 265.
8. Ibid., 263.
9. Williams, *An Evening With General Albert Pike*, 22–23.
10. Pike, "Letter to the People of the Northern States," 182–83.
11. Pike, quoted in Roberts, *House Undivided: The Story of Freemasonry and the Civil War*, 16.
12. Pike, Letter to President Johnson after the Civil War, quoted in Allsopp, 183.
13. Clifford, "The Indian Regiments of the Battle of Pea Ridge," 42.
14. Pike, "Essay XVI—Of Greatness"
15. Pike, *Lectures on Masonic Symbolism*, 14.
16. Roberts, 17.
17. Pike, "Re-Union," 187–88.
18. Ibid, 427–29.
19. Pike, "Last Will and Testament," cited in Allsopp, 320.

Chapter 19, On Pike's Last Years

1. Hatch, *In Memoriam, Albert Pike*, 17.
2. Pike, "Essay 1—Of Content in Age," 17–18.
3. Ibid., 14.

4. Ibid., 38–41.
5. Pike, *The Meaning of Masonry*, 18.
6. Moore, "Albert Pike, The Mason," 26.
7. Pike, "Essay I—Of Content in Age," 35–36.
8. Pike, "Essay XVI—Of Greatness," 328.
9. Hatch, *In Memoriam, Albert Pike*, 18.
10. Moore, "Albert Pike, The Mason," 32.
11. Brown, *Albert Pike, 1809–1891*," 865–66.
12. Pike, quoted in Allsopp, *Albert Pike: A Biography*, 158.
13. Pike, "Essay I—Of Content in Age," 158.
14. Pike, Memorial, preserved in the Transactions of The Supreme Council, 33°, A.&A.S.R., S.J., October 22, 1895.

Chapter 20, On Pike's Relevance Today

1. Pike, *Autobiography*, 3–4.
2. Pike, *Offices of Adoption*, 27–29.
3. Pike, *Ritual for the Reception of a Louveteau*, 36.
4. Pike, *Offices of Adoption*, 55–56.
5. Pike, *Morals and Dogma*, 44.
6. Pike, *Autobiography*, 12.
7. Pike, *Morals and Dogma*, 124–25.
8. Pike, *Lectures of the Arya*, 54.
9. Pike, *Morals and Dogma*, 515–16.
10. Pike, "Essay IX—Of Symbols Decaying into Idols," 130.
11. Pike, "Essay VI—Of Self-Investing," 414–15.
12. Pike, "Essay II—Of Burning the Dead," 85–87.
13. Pike, Speech delivered March, 1860, at a Masonic Ceremonial in Washington, D.C.

Bibliography

Writings By Albert Pike

BOOKS

Autobiography of General Albert Pike: From Stenographic Notes Furnished by Himself. (unpublished rough-typed transcription of shorthand notes preserved in the Archives of the House of the Temple, The Supreme Council, 33°, Southern Jurisdiction of the Scottish Rite, Washington, D.C.).

Book of the Words, The. (Privately printed). 1878.

Book of the Lodge, The. (Privately printed). 1872.

Essays to Vinnie (Vinnie, Pegni D'Affetto): Holograph manuscript of essays written to Vinnie Ream, preserved in the Archives of the House of the Temple, The Supreme Council, 33°, Southern Jurisdiction of the Scottish Rite, Washington, D.C.

Essay 1—Of Content in Age.
Essay 2—Of Burning the Dead.
Essay 3—Of Self-Education.
Essay 4—Of Man's Opinions of Woman.
Essay 5—Of Wrecks and Waifs of Poetry.
Essay 6—Of Self-Investing.
Essay 7—Of Habits and Their Slaves.
Essay 8—Of the Death of Love.
Essay 9—Of Symbols Decaying into Idolatry.
Essay 10—Of Indian Nature and Wrongs.
Essay 11—Of My Books and Studies.
Essay 12—Of Law and Lawyers.
Essay 13—Of Rowing Against the Stream.
Essay 14—Of Shattered Idols.
Essay 15—Of Coin and Currency.
Essay 16—Of Greatness.
Essay 17—Of Poverty and Its Compensations.
Essay 18—Of The Policy of Forgiveness.
Essay 19—Of Some Old Dramatists.
Essay 20—Of Pay and Rewards for Public Service.
Essay 21—Of Forces.
Essay 22—Of Values.
Essay 23—Of The Ability to Say "No."
Essay 24—Of Pleasant and Sad Remembrances.
Essay 25—Of Sympathy.
Essay 26—Of Chance and School-teaching.
Essay 27—Of Godlessness and Retribution.
Essay 28—Of Leaves and Their Falling.

Ex Corde Locutiones: Words from the Heart; Spoken of Dead Brethren by the Grand Commander of the Supreme Council of the 33° for the Southern Jurisdiction of the United States. Washington, D.C.: (Privately printed). 1897.

General Albert Pike's Poems: With Introductory Biographical Sketch by Mrs. Lilian Pike Roome, Daughter of the Author. Little Rock: Fred. W. Allsopp, Publisher. 1900.

Hymns to the Gods and Other Poems. Little Rock: Democrat P&L Co. 1916.

Indo–Aryan Deities and Worship: As Contained in the Rig–Veda. (Privately printed, n.d.).

Lecture on Masonic Symbolism. (Privately published, n.d.).

Lectures on Masonic Symbolism: The Omkara and Other Ineffable Words. (Privately printed, n.d.).

Lectures of the Arya. (Privately Printed. The Supreme Council). 1930.

Legenda: XIX to XXX. (Privately printed, n.d.). Reprinted 1984.

Liturgy of the Blue Degrees. (Privately printed). 1878.

Lyrics and Love Songs by Gen. Albert Pike: Edited by Mrs. Lilian Pike Roome, Daughter of the Author. Little Rock: Fred W. Allsopp. 1916.

Masonry of Adoption, The: Masonic Rituals for Women. (n.d.).

Meaning of Masonry, The. (n.d.).

Prose Sketches and Poems Written in the Western Country. edited by David J. Weber College Station. Texas: Texas A&M University Press. 1987.

Ritual for the Reception of a Louveteau. (n.d.).

ARTICLES

"Canyon Sketches and Journeyings, No. I." *The Boston Pearl and Literary Gazette.* (November 8, 1834).

"Letters from Arkansas, No. II." *American Monthly Magazine.* I, 25.

"Philosophy of Bowling, The." *American Monthly Magazine.* v. 2, # 10. January, 1831.

"Philosophy of a Cigar, The." *American Monthly Magazine.* v. 2, # 4. July, 1830.

"Philosophy of Walking, The." *American Monthly Magazine.* v. 2, # 5. August, 1830.

"Plain Talk, Starvation, Migration or Railroads, No.1" *Little Rock Whig.* December 25, 1851.

Writings By Other Authors

BOOKS

______, *The Life–Wake of The Fine Arkansas Gentleman Who Died Before His Time.* Washington, D.C.: Franklin Philp. 1859.

Allsopp, Fred W. *Albert Pike: A Biography.* Little Rock: Parke–Harper Company. 1928.

Boyden, William L. *Bibliography of the Writings of Albert Pike: Prose, Poetry, Manuscript.* Washington: Privately printed. 1921.

Brown, Walter Lee. *Albert Pike, 1809–1891: Dissertation Presented to the Faculty of the Graduate School of the University of Texas in Partial Fulfillment of the Requirements for the Degree of Doctor of Philosophy.* (unpublished). 1955.

Duncan, Robert Lipscomb. *Reluctant General: The Life and Times of Albert Pike.* New York: E. P. Dutton & Co., Inc. 1961.

[Hatch, Thomas E.] *In Memoriam: Albert Pike.* (Privately printed. The Supreme Council, n.d.).

Roberts, Allen E. *House Undivided: The Story of Freemasonry and The Civil War.* Richmond, Virginia: Macoy Publishing and Masonic Supply Co., Inc. 1990.

Williams, George. *An Evening With General Albert Pike.* An unpublished play based on the life of Albert Pike. Guthrie, Okla. 1991.

ARTICLES

Boyden, William L. "The Masonic Record of Albert Pike." *New Age Magazine.* XVIII. January, 1920.

Clifford, Roy A. "The Indian Regiments in the Battle of Pea Ridge." in *The Battle of Pea Ridge: 1862.* Rogers, Arkansas: Shofner's, (n.d.).

Easterly, Ernest III, Ph.D. "Albert Pike and the Louisiana Civil Code: An Unfinished Epic" in *Albert Pike.* Pub. by The Supreme Council, 33°, Southern Jurisdiction. April, 1986.

Evans, Henry R. "Albert Pike, The Poet" in *Albert Pike: Centenary Souvenir of His Birth 1809-1909.* Pub. by The Supreme Council, 33°, Southern Jurisdiction. 1909.

Gern, Jess W. "Albert Pike and Education" in *Albert Pike.* Pub. by The Supreme Council, 33°, Southern Jurisdiction. April, 1986.

Kleinknecht, C. Fred. "Albert Pike—A Freemason Forever" in *Albert Pike.* Pub. by The Supreme Council, 33°, Southern Jurisdiction. April, 1986.

Moore, George F. "Albert Pike, The Mason" in *Albert Pike: Centenary Souvenir of His Birth 1809–1909.* Pub. by The Supreme Council, 33°, Southern Jurisdiction. 1909.

Nash, William. "Albert Pike, Lawyer" in *Albert Pike.* Pub. by The Supreme Council, 33°, Southern Jurisdiction, 33°, Southern Jurisdiction. April, 1986.

Richardson, James D. "Introduction: The Centenary Idea" in *Albert Pike: Centenary Souvenir of His Birth 1809–1909.* Pub. by The Supreme Council, 33°, Southern Jurisdiction. 1909.

Rogers, James R. "Albert Pike—The Freemason," in *Albert Pike.* Pub. by The Supreme Council, 33°, Southern Jurisdiction. April 1986.

Steward, Alphonso C. "Albert Pike, The Philosopher" in *Albert Pike: Centenary Souvenir of His Birth 1809–1909.* Pub. by The Supreme Council, 33°, Southern Jurisdiction. 1909.

Schely, Admiral Winfield Scott. "Albert Pike, Soldier and Explorer" in *Albert Pike: Centenary Souvenir of His Birth 1809–1909.* Pub. by The Supreme Council, 33°, Southern Jurisdiction. 1909.

Index